WEALD OF KENT AND SUSSEX

WEALD OF KENT AND SUSSEX

SHEILA KAYE-SMITH

ROBERT HALE & COMPANY
63 Old Brompton Road London S.W.7

© *Sheila Kaye-Smith 1953*
First published (in the Regional Series) 1953
Reprinted 1963
Reprinted 1966
Reprinted 1973

ISBN 0 7091 2640 9

PRINTED IN GREAT BRITAIN BY
REDWOOD PRESS LIMITED
TROWBRIDGE, WILTSHIRE

CONTENTS

ILLUSTRATIONS

ACKNOWLEDGMENTS

All the illustrations, with the exception of the last three which were provided by Patricia Stevens, are reproduced from photographs specially taken for this book by Mr J. Allan Cash, F.I.B.P., F.R.P.S.

PROLOGUE

WHERE and what is the Weald?

The first part of this question is the more difficult to answer, because the exact Wealden boundaries have always been a matter of argument. Roughly speaking, the Weald is that part of England lying between the North and the South Downs, which includes a fair-sized part of Kent, the greater part of Sussex and also fragments of Surrey and Hampshire. But it is only very roughly speaking, for the South Downs come no further east than Beachy Head, some thirty miles short of the North Downs' coastal end.

The intervening gap has been variously charted. According to some authorities the southern boundary of the Weald is well inland, running through Penshurst, north of Battle, to Sandhurst and thence to Hurst and Lympne. But if we are to take, as I think we must, the word "Weald" to be derived from the Saxon *wald* or forest, it seems reasonable that the frontiers of the Weald should extend as far as the original forest land from which it gets its name. Early maps show the trees running down as close to the sea as the marshes of Horse Eye and Pevensey, while beyond what is now Hastings they must have struggled to the edge of the sandstone cliffs, between which their descendants can still be seen wind-shaven in the ridiculously termed "glens" of Ecclesbourne and Fairlight. Romney Marsh carries the southern frontier to its eastern limit at Hythe, for undoubtedly this marsh formed no part of the original forest, being in those days only partially submerged shingle banks. The subsoil throughout the area is largely the mixture of clay and gravel known as marl or more learnedly as the Hastings Beds, and is found as far north as Cranbrook and Goudhurst, indisputably villages of the Weald. So I do not think we shall go far wrong if we include within our measure all this countryside, which was densely wooded until comparatively

I   I

recent times and moreover one of the most productive regions in the days of iron-smelting, a characteristic Wealden industry.

Now what is the Weald?

To answer this we must go back to the beginning, or rather, near the beginning, for I do not propose to go right back to the beginning of the archæologists, with their ocean of Tethys and their continent of Gondwanaland, so pleasantly reminiscent of Edward Lear and the Great Grombolian Plain. In those days the Weald had its vicissitudes as a part of the sea's bed and as a tropical country of steaming, warm lagoons shaded by the columns and arches of gigantic ferns, and dwelt in by those lumbering Dragons of the Prime which have left their three-toed footprints in the Hastings Beds and even a clutch of fossilised eggs from which one might indeed expect to hatch a cockatrice.

At the beginning of the Cœnozoic age, when the whole of Southern England lay under the sea, the Weald was an island of chalk rising up out of the water. The basin we know now was upside-down, an inverted bowl of chalk, which in time rose above cracking point and broke. By then it was no longer an island, but joined to the rest of the country in the grip of the last Ice Age. The ice did not come as far south as the Weald, but it must have been a bleak and dismal waste, not unlike the Canadian tundras or the Russian steppes, a sub-arctic land where life was fugitive.

Slowly through the centuries the ice withdrew and the land grew warm again. From north to south and south to north the rivers flowed across the Weald, as they still flow from the water-parting of the Forest-Ridge—the Arun, the Ouse, the Cuckmere, the Stour, the Medway and all the smaller streams whose function it was to turn the hill into a valley by carrying the chalk away. In the course of the ages they washed it out of the whole district between the broken edges of the bowl, that is the North and the South Downs, leaving only the marl, the clay and in certain places the sand. Instead of the smooth dome was a valley of tilted levels, enclosed in a broken ring of chalk downs, which remained as it were as samples of what all once had been.

Then came the trees. They filled the valley which was thirty miles across and over a hundred miles long. What once was a chalky ridge and is now a richly-coloured, undulating floor of fields and copses, was then a dark, impenetrable forest, later to be known as Andredsleah or Andredsweald, "the wood where nobody dwells". Thus it remained for many hundreds of years, cutting off the South Downs and the Sussex coast from what civilisation the rest of Britain had to offer. The Romans when they came made very few attempts to penetrate it, and built only one road across it and that at its narrowest part. Their settlements were all to the north of it or along the coast or in the greensand country of the river valleys. Silva Anderida remained a forest undwelt in, with none to disturb the deer or the wild boar in its thickets. There is said to have been a British town where Newenden is now, on the western Rother. But at that time a great arm of the sea came up over the Rother marshes and the town would have been virtually a port and independent of the wilds behind it.

It was the Saxons who gave the Weald its present name, though there is an opinion that Andredsweald is only a corruption of the Roman Anderida and has nothing to do with the wildness and emptiness of the district. It is a fact, however, that in many records the Weald is referred to as the Wild.

The Saxon penetration, to which is due the civilisation of these parts, took at the beginning a very humble form. The forest had always been the home of the wild hog, and it was only natural that as settlements sprang up on its borders the swineherds should take their charges into it to feed on the acorns and oak-mast with which it abounded. Camden the historian, describing how a certain "poor hogherd" found and slew a wicked King Sigbert who had taken refuge in the forest, adds the following pleasant paragraph:

> "The history of this hogherd presenteth to my mind an opinion that some men maintain concerning this Weald, which is, that it was a great while together in manner nothing else than a desert and waste wilderness, not planted with towns or peopled with men, as the outsides of the shire were, but stored and stuffed with herds of deer and droves of hogs only. Which conceit, though happily it may seem a paradox, yet in mine own fantasy it wanteth not the feet of sound reason to stand upon."

The feet of sound reason soon took the pasturing herds into the far interior of this pigs' paradise. Hog-owners sent their hogs into the forest much as present-day sheep-owners on Romney Marsh send up their sheep into the hills behind it. The oaks which some hundreds of years later were to provide fuel for the furnaces of the Tudor and Caroline ironmasters, provided both the Saxons and the Normans with hog-meat, either eaten fresh as pork or salted down for winter stores. At first the hogs seem to have roamed at will and it was the task of their respective hogherds to keep track of them. But this soon led to confusion, and separate enclosures or "dens" were made for their pasturing.

The Saxon word "den" means an enclosed space and from it derive all the "dens" of the Weald—Tenterden, Rolvenden, Benenden, Bethersden, Witsunden, Harlakenden, Haffenden, Plurenden and countless others. These are mainly found on the Kentish side, for though hog-breeding flourished almost to an equal extent in Sussex the human settlements that followed the pigs into the forest seem, as they developed into towns and villages, to have shed the termination of their origin in favour of some other woodland word, such as "hurst" or "stede" or "ley". East and West Grinstead, Billingshurst, Midhurst, Hoathly, Chiddingly were all at one time clearings in the forest similar to the "dens" of Kent.

The Normans found the civilisation of the Weald developing and carried it on along the same lines. The swine pastures became settlements and the settlements became villages, but it was not till the Flemish weavers were brought over and established by King Edward III that any part of the district was ever populous or important. The cloth trade transformed the Kentish side of the Weald, and later came the iron industry, to fill the whole forest with furnaces and forges. It had always been known that there was iron in the Weald and the Romans had made some elementary attempts at smelting it, but it was not till the fifteenth century that the use of water-power transformed the district into the Black Country of the Middle Ages. The iron brought about a second denudation, for just as the rivers had in the course of millenniums washed away the chalk, so in a couple of centuries the furnaces devoured the trees.

When the last furnace, at Ashburnham in Sussex, shut down

in 1828, the Wealden forest had been nearly all eaten up and the Weald had become what it is now, a country of small mixed farms—a little arable, a little pasture, a little fruit, and in the neighbourhood of the Kentish border a few acres of hops. The towns that once were considered big and prosperous now appear as little more than villages in comparison with the resorts along the coast; while the woods, including the new chestnut plantations, are mere tatters of the woods that used to be. Only the heights of Ashdown Forest, at the old water-parting of the Weald, with the western forest lands of St Leonards and Tilgate, survive to tell us of the vanished forest of Andredsweald—the forest where nobody dwells.

2

The Weald is not a simple subject. In the first place it extends over parts of four counties, and even though we limit our survey to Kent and Sussex we do not profit much, for the Wealden acreage in Surrey is very small and that in Hampshire even smaller.

By far the greater part of the Weald is in Sussex, so perhaps it is strange that so often and for so many Sussex is represented only by the Downs. The South Downs are in fact no more than a coastal rampart only a few miles wide and stretching no further east than the Sussex marshes. They are entirely uncharacteristic of the general Sussex countryside. From their chalk arises not only a different plant and animal life but a different style of building, of road-making and of farming. The grey farms with their flint walls and rolling acres of pasture, the white, chalky lanes with their white hedge-tangles of old-man's-beard, the villages that crouch small and compact in the hollows instead of scattering over the ridges, the wide, unwooded fields, views that are green and clear instead of blue and hazy, and horizons that the hills carry up almost as high as noonday, are more unlike the country of the Weald than are the rural parts of the North and Midlands.

The fact is that all most people see of Sussex is the Downs. They form the background to all the well-known coastal resorts except Bexhill and Hastings, and all the westward roads, except to those two towns, run through them like the rivers that long ago washed the chalk into the sea. To the seekers of health and holiday the Downs *are* Sussex. Those who actually live among them of course know better, for the soil of the Weald—the marl, the sand and the clay—rolls up to the very foothills of the chalk, so that in April the primroses fade only a few yards from the cowslips on the hill.

For the people of the Weald—the "Weldishmen" as the old documents call them—Sussex will always be a country of small tilted fields, red farms and miry lanes where the hedges blossom with honeysuckle and wild roses and other lovers of the clay. The villages string along the roads, with their churches squatting in the fields, often at quite a distance from them. Here and there are outcrops of heathy, sandy, even rocky country—sometimes no larger than a field, sometimes spreading into a whole landscape; and everywhere are the little woods with their funny names—Yellowcoat, Wagmary, Fright, Towncreep, Eighteen-Pound-a-Year and other names that are the charred embers of local history.

This is the landscape of the Sussex Weald, and that of Kent is very much the same. Indeed the border between Kent and Sussex is purely artificial. The natural boundary-line lies many miles further west, and follows the valley of the Cuckmere instead of the valley of the Rother and the Kent Ditch. For many miles on each side of the legal frontier the countryside is Kent rather than Sussex. The watersprings are mainly on the high ground, hence the roads follow the ridges rather than the valleys, and the villages are in their straggled way hill villages—Northiam on the ridge between the marshes of the Rother and the Tillingham, Rolvenden and Benenden dividing the Hexden and the Newmill Channels, Goudhurst looking down on one side on the Teise and on the other on the springs of the Beult, and so on up to the great river that divides the Men of Kent from Kentish Men.

This is the country of the hop-gardens and the big fruit farms. In springtime the valleys and sheltered hillsides are bridal with blossoming orchards, and in autumn the air drifts with the smoky sweetness of drying hops. The wide, gentle curves of the western Sussex Weald are here broken into small hills and valleys checkered with many-coloured fields and spotted with farms among which the white cowls of the oasthouses are like doves perched among the roofs. The chestnut shaws, nearly as many and small

6

as the fields, are like shadows on the bright patchwork of the view.

The oaks of course are here as well as further west, in the woods and in the hedges, reminding us here as there of the forest that used to be. But here we have only a straggle of the beeches that make the beauty of woodlands beyond the Cuckmere. The beech tree does not like the clay, nor is he really happy in the marl. A light soil is required, either chalky or sandy, so we find beeches in the neighbourhood of Balcombe, Cowdray and Midhurst as well as in the crown of the Chanctonbury Ring. They flourish, too, near and on the North Downs, but there are few in south-west Kent and almost none between the Sussex border and the sea.

3

The difference between Kent and Sussex may not appear striking to us to-day, but in earlier times the contrast was real enough. Except for a strip of land along the coast Sussex was no more than the Undwelt-in-Wood, and even that strip suffered from being cut off by that same wood from the rest of the country. The small trading stations on the coast were able to maintain communications only by sea; as far as inland travel was concerned Kent might have been five hundred miles away. Because of their isolation, the Sussex Britons, or Welsh as the Saxons called them, were in civilisation far behind those in more accessible regions and their Saxon supplanters did not find themselves much better off. Indeed the benighted heathen of Sussex were for many years a challenge to the Christian shires, and it is worth noting that when their evangelisation finally came it did not come from the neighbour across the Weald but from the far-distant North.

Kent was very differently situated. Not only was it accessible from other parts of Britain but when the Romans came it had been for some time in regular communication with Gaul. We may doubt if at any time in recorded history there existed the land-bridge which once almost certainly joined our island to the Continent, but the men of Cantium had ships which, though built only of osiers covered with leather, were quite capable of crossing the Channel and could even engage in warfare. On at least one occasion a fleet of Kentish ships helped the Gauls against Cæsar.

The close connection between Kent and Gaul was not a mere trade relationship, for every communication had led to immigration and intermarriage, and by the time the Romans landed the inhabitants were mostly of Gallic rather than of Celtic extraction. Cæsar found them taller than the Gauls, though not so strong. As was to be expected in a densely wooded country their houses were built of logs and thatched with reeds, but their settlements were large enough to be considered towns and they used horses and chariots for civilian as well as for military purposes. The woad which is inseparable from our ideas of an ancient Briton had in Kent been developed from mere warpaint into an artistic bodily decoration of animals and flowers.

For many centuries Kent maintained its advantage over its neighbour Sussex. The great civilising influence of the age was Christianity, for its establishment in a region meant the building of monasteries with the consequent introduction of the arts and sciences and the reclaiming of wild lands for agriculture. In Kent the monks arrived long before they came to Sussex, and as owners of many forest "dens" did much to colonise the Kentish side of the Weald by the homely method of keeping hogs. Kent, too, some centuries later, was to benefit from the arrival of the Flemish weavers, who made no settlements in the western Weald. It was not till the iron industry began really to boom in the sixteenth century that Sussex had anything like equal opportunities. Then before long it had gained the advantage, for not only was the Weald of Sussex larger than the Weald of Kent, but as settlements in it were fewer and more recent a greater part of the primeval forest had been left standing for the ironmaster's fuel. Many Sussex furnaces were still alive and working when those in Kent had ceased to blow.

By that time the Weald which for so long had kept the two counties apart had closely welded them with joint commercial interests and easy ways of communication. No longer a trackless forest divided them, for thanks to the furnaces old Andredsweald had been torn to rags. Nor could a man of Kent standing on the high ground beyond Linton and Boughton Monchelsea in those days be compared to the pioneer settlers in Ohio, as they gazed

Bodiam Castle from Ewhurst

from their last height on a shoreless ocean of trees. For he would have looked down on much the same sort of countryside as is there to-day—a landscape of farms and fields and copses, netted over with the lanes that had linked up the forge and the bloomery with the homes of those who worked in them.

After this period it is difficult to separate the histories of Kent and Sussex. No longer an industrial area, they both developed simultaneously as a playground. Sussex had the start with Brighton, but Kent soon followed with Ramsgate, and now all round their coasts, from Whitstable to Bognor, the resorts crowd up the beaches. They do not belong to this survey, but no part of the Weald is far enough from the coast to be un-affected by them. The needs of the big coast towns have not only encouraged farming by providing a steady and easily accessible market, but have also stimulated the woodcrafts that have sprung up with the chestnut plantations on the site of the old forests.

Apart from certain legendary regions in the West, the Weald may claim to be the oldest part of England. Here English history was born, and its earliest traces linger still in old buildings, old trees, old names, old stories. Even the fields are old—small roughly shaped enclosures with obstinate hedges that persistently renew themselves when grubbed up in the interests of modern agriculture, while some of the fieldnames take us back nearly as far as the first Saxon clearings in the Undwelt-in-Wood. In no other district of England could it more truly be said:

"The present sings itself against the past,
A slight tune pondered to deep harmonies."

Brickwall Manor, Northiam

Part One
Conducted Tours

CHAPTER I

FROM SALEHURST TO HEADCORN

I

To enter a district at one end and drive on till you come out at the other is surely an unimaginative and unenterprising way of exploring it, so I propose that we should learn the geography of the Weald by some other method. It is true that if we were to drive through it from Lenham in the foothills of the North Downs to Rogate on the Hampshire border we should meet with a greater variety of scenery than between New York and New Orleans, but we could hardly avoid the monotony of succession, the flatness of a horizontal approach. Let us rather examine our subject *sub specie æternitas* and see it as much as we can as a shape, as a pattern, as a whole.

Therefore I propose to make our first, purely topographical, survey of the Weald not by road but by rail. This may seem an inadequate as well as a reactionary method of showing it. I can remember being rebuked as a schoolgirl for saying that I enjoyed travelling by train because I could see so much of the country from the window. I was told that no part of the country worth seeing could be seen from a train. The passing of the years has only added strength to the conviction that I held privately at the time that I was right and my instructors were wrong. Some of the finest scenery in Britain is offered to the traveller by rail. Unlike the roads, the railways have not attached to themselves a mass of heterogeneous and unsightly building. Once the wayside station is left behind—and a wayside station has charms that no wayside garage possesses—you are alone in the fields or in the mountains. Even the roads are only sections, crossed and forgotten. There may be occasional blinkers of cuttings or blindness of tunnels, but apart from these the earth spreads as freely as the sky. You have, besides, the pleasures of a changing angle of vision, of gazing down on roofs or into farmyards or up into the tents of shadowing and foreshortened trees; while the close foreground, being the line's private property, is often gay with flowers that have long been stripped by spoilers from the roadside.

The railways of the Weald are particularly well suited to our purpose of showing it. For one thing, they remove even the possibility of an end-to-end trip. There is a railway along the coast, linking the coast towns from Margate to Portsmouth, and of course there are the main lines from the coast to London. But I am not suggesting that we should travel on any of these. The railway lines we shall follow are all single tracks, running the same way as the Weald rivers, from south to north or from north to south, and dating from the time some years later than the great national railway boom, when the various companies already in occupation of the coast decided to "open up" the neglected districts behind it. Never, never, thought the directors of the South Eastern, the London, Brighton & South Coast, and the London, Chatham & Dover Railways, never, never, would the roads be used again for transport or travel. So they built lines between towns scarcely thirty miles apart, between Lewes and East Grinstead, between Eastbourne and Tunbridge Wells, between Brighton and Horsham, and latest of all—and in its setting loveliest—between two villages, Robertsbridge and Headcorn. The total distances covered by many of these lines would to-day be more quickly travelled by car—indeed I have beaten the train from Crowborough to East Grinstead on a bicycle—but they certainly did "open up" the hidden country of the Weald, and many of my young memories are set in friendly, talkative railway carriages, crowded with market people, cottagers and farmers, all the company one meets to-day in a country bus.

We will take our first trip on the Kent & East Sussex Railway, as it used to be called in the days before it lost its individuality to the State. Even before then its independence had been compromised by Southern influences and infiltrations, but a Kent & Sussex railway takes a lot of nationalising, "and I assure you," said the station-master cum porter cum signalman at our nearest station, "they get no co-operation from us." Known to its intimates as the Rother Valley Railway it follows the Rother very faithfully from Robertsbridge to Methersham, where the river swings south, making for the sea at Rye, while the railway follows the marshes of the Newmill Channel past Freezingham and Morghew Farm to Tenterden. After that it breaks off all connection with the Rother, as it ignores even its upper levels during the rest of its journey over the high, flat lands between Tenterden and Headcorn. It links what used to be two main lines of the old South Eastern Railway, and at one time the economically minded could travel by it to Dover from Hastings for fivepence less than the cost of the direct route, via Rye and Ashford, the only drawback being that the trip took four hours instead of one and a half.

Now the line is threatened with extinction, at least as far as its passenger traffic is concerned. Motor transport has certainly robbed it of much usefulness, since even the slowest car or bus could cover its twenty-odd miles more quickly than the train. Nevertheless its closing would be a loss, for it is the only means we have of exploring one of the loveliest and most perfectly rural valleys in England. There is no road along the Rother Valley, only roads cross it, and the Rother itself is not the shipping highway that it used to be. Perhaps with the disappearance of the railway its traffic may revive, at least as far as it existed in my youth, when the crowning delight of summer was a trip up the Rother from the Star Lock to Newenden.

2

The memory of those days is fixed for me in heat and sunshine, and indeed I cannot suppose that my elders could have endured the expedition in any different sort of weather. At an early hour we would set out from Hastings for Rye and then walk the mile or more between the station and the Lock. Here a little inn looks out across the marsh at the low roofs of the cottages which were once the officers' quarters when our troops waited on the South Coast to repel invading Buonaparte. All along our way the Military Canal, engineering triumph of its day, now little more than a reedy channel, lay upon the right, while beyond it seawards spread the first flat wonder of Romney Marsh. On our left the wooded bank that once had been the coast of England rose steeply up to Playden, with one enticing gap to show Reighton Farm and Sluice House and the road up to Mock-beggar—a whole country to explore if only we were not bound for one yet more wonderful.

At the Star Lock the little motor-boat would be waiting, just big enough to hold our family, and off we would glide over a broad spread of water, for at the Lock the canal and the river are one and still further widened by the various channels that drain the marsh between Sussex and the Isle of Oxney—the Union Channel, the White Kemp Sewer, the Highknock, the Five-watering. Over this (as it seemed to me) waste of waters we moved to the slow stroke of our little engine till just before Willow Farm the canal left us, to take its way to Appledore and Hythe under the seaward fall of Oxney, while we slid round the elbow of Sussex with the Island on our right, and on our left the coast of an earlier England, green and shady against the blind blue dazzle of the south. The river now had become a mere stream, the ghost of the old Limene that the Romans knew, but in those days it still had its traffic, the lighters with the red sails that tacked along it, carrying coal to the inland villages from Rye.

Iden—"Yew-tree swine-pasture" and one of the few "dens" between the Rother and the coast—is almost unseen from the river, except for an occasional roof, whereas on the Kent side the gentler slope of Oxney is visibly crowned with the houses and church of Wittersham. The Isle of Oxney must be considered a part of the Weald, even though for centuries it was an island in the great estuary which let the Rother into Appledore Bay. Though there is now no need for the ferry which used until fairly recently to ply between Oxney and the "mainland", it can still be made an island in the winter by floodwater, when the Rother is filled to overflowing with tides and storms. It has two parish churches, Wittersham and Stone-cum-Ebony, and one curiously romantic Nonconformist graveyard.

This rarity crowns the eminence known as Chapel Bank, which you pass on your left on the way to Tenterden from Appledore. Here a chapel stood once but stands no longer, leaving only its old graveyard to notch the sunset with a few tombstones. It has the shape of an ancient barrow, a prehistoric burying place, but in fact its formation is entirely natural, the work of many years and many waters, and those who sleep on it were awake among us not so very long ago.

I could not see Chapel Bank from my boat on the Rother. Indeed I could see very little except water-meadows and grazing sheep and cattle, and sometimes not even those if the reeds grew very high. The scenery of the Rother Valley might by some be considered unbearably tame—a river little wider or less sluggish than a ditch, flat marshland spreading into gentle slopes that could barely be called hills, a few distant villages, some scattered farms and scarcely a human creature, for only two roads crossed the river in the whole course of our journey. Yet I would sit there hour after hour, still and enchanted, watching for my landmarks—the oasts of Baron's Grange, the redness of Corkwood in the trees, the tiny watersmeet when the Rother became one with the Kent Ditch and a boundary between Kent and Sussex. I do not suppose that many young people to-day would enjoy or even put up with such an expedition, which brought no entertainment beyond the contemplation of an un-spoilt but at the same time almost featureless countryside.

At Black Wall Bridge the boat would stop, for there were various bill-posting duties attached to the trip and the bridge commanded all the publicity of the road from Wittersham to Peasmarsh. The notices were mainly of farm auctions, but there would often be a circus among them, for it is only since the last war that the little family circuses have ceased to visit us— father, mother, sons and daughters, aunts and uncles, with their couple of trained horses or troupe of performing dogs, or even an old amiable lion, the outfit complete with a shooting-gallery and a merry-go-round.

Our trip usually ended at Newenden Bridge, so that we could take the train home from Northiam, for though the river was navigable as far as Bodiam, the reeds grew so high that we could see nothing over them. I personally would have been glad to make the return journey by water, but it was already afternoon and I expect that my elders had borne all they could endure in the way of sloth and sunshine.

I doubt if in these days it would "pay" to run a motor-boat trip up the Rother, and there are other more expeditious ways of pasting notices on Black Wall Bridge. That bridge carries in its name the wall that was built in the early part of 1600 across the estuary, to force the sea to take a course up the Appledore Channel by Ebony and Smallhythe. It shut off the newly inned lands that now form Wet Level and kept at bay the tides that used to surge round Oxney as far west as Newenden or even Bodiam. If you want to know exactly the extent of the great estuary which used to be here, come and stand one summer morning before sunrise in a field below Great Knelle or some other part of the ridge between the Rother and Tillingham, and see the mists filling both valleys, having at night crept up just as far as the sea used to creep up in years gone by. The ghost sea of the mist fills the Rother Valley up to Bodiam and the Tillingham as far as Conster, and if you are in the mood you may see the pennoned masts of navies riding at anchor off the port of Tenterden, while merchant-men discharge their cargoes at wharfs that have long been pastures. The sun rises and the water becomes fog and the riding ships are tree-tops rising out of it, but for a moment you have seen what our fathers saw long ago before the mixed acts of God and man changed the water into land.

3

The Rother Valley Railway is not unknown to fame. It has been pictured by Emmett, and the late Will Hay borrowed one of its engines for his film *Oh, Mr. Porter*. I do not propose that we should make our excursion down the valley behind this film-star, with its dog-toothed funnel and eruptive boiler, nor will we commit ourselves to the Bumper, a Janus-like vehicle made up of two motor-buses fixed back to back and living most shatteringly up to its name. The two friends of my youth, Juno and Rolvenden, are scrap by now, so a small, comparatively new, saddle-tank engine, with the initials K.E.S.R. still ghostly beneath the palimpsest of British Railways, shall convey our single coach with a tail of four or five goods wagons out of Roberts-bridge station.

Robertsbridge bears out my contention that some of the best views of rural England can be had from the railway. Seen from its own street the village presents the too common amalgam of the shoddy (new), the shabby (old) and the meretricious (Ye Olde), high-lighted by what is surely the most hideous war memorial in Sussex. But walk the half-mile to the station, and there look back at the old red-roofs, sloping and tumbling towards the water-meadows in a scramble of cat-slides and hipped gables, and you have a village street that time has only weathered instead of changing with soft earthy colours and lines so free and natural that they seem to grow.

As we go on our journey, the traffic duly warned by a porter with a red flag at the gateless level crossing, the beauty remains, for we come to Salehurst, with its noble monastic church and attendant farm. This group, familiar throughout the country, and with some particularly rich examples in the Weald, is surely one of the most satisfying in architecture. Apart from the homogeneous beauty which they seem to acquire by growing up together, there is a special rightness in this juxtaposition of heaven and earth, the heavenly and the homely needs of men. In this case the union is emphasised by the fact that the farm was once a part of the Cistercian abbey to which the church belonged. Some fragments of the original building still remain, and if the groined double crypt of the abbey was to be robbed of its ecclesiastical character, what better or more suitable fate could it have than to become a dairy?

The church is very old, for parts remain of the building that stood here before the Norman Conquest. But when faith is alive the churches seem to be alive too, and to grow and change with the centuries. Salehurst Church presents the familiar jumble of Early English, Norman, Decorated and Perpendicular, ending, alas! in the equally familiar catastrophe of a Victorian restoration. But this at least has rescued from underfoot the original altar stone of Robertsbridge Abbey and set it up as a pedestal for the credence table, which is doing for it very much what was done for the crypt when it was made a dairy.

Robertsbridge has no church of its own, though it is at least a mile away across the Rother. According to some, its name was originally Rotherbridge, but there is strong evidence of the existence of an original Pons Roberti, and the common history of place-names suggests a personal rather than a local origin.

Our railway follows the river closely, though it has left the road

at Salehurst, or rather the road has left the railway, to climb up
through the woods to High Wigsell, where it meets another
road which, after meandering as a lane as far as Silver Hill (a
large stretch of unspoilt agricultural country, offered to the
National Trust, but declined because of difficulties of tenure),
becomes a part of the great westward road that would sweep us
through Haywards Heath, Cowfold, Billingshurst, Petworth
and Rogate, right out of the county and down to Land's End.

We must resist the temptation of roads, even when, as at
Junction Road, they are considered important enough to be
given a station. Our railway line will take us out of Salehurst
between the church and the Abbey Farm, across Junction Road
(built in coaching days to connect Hastings with Hawkhurst by
a more direct route than a net of wandering lanes), and on into
Guinness Land. Here all around us are the hop-gardens, and
the train jogs through them so slowly that we can snuff the scented
shadows of their aisles, or watch the gaily coloured groups of
pickers at their bins among the stripped poles, or admire the careful skill of the hop-tiers on their stilts, according to the season our
imagination chooses for this journey. There were always hop-
gardens in the Rother Valley, but in later years of agricultural
difficulty they became a burden to their owners, and might have
been grubbed up had not the big corporation from another
country stepped in to save them and increase them, making beauty
with one hand and spoiling it with the other as it built hideous
factory-like variations of the old-fashioned oasthouse. Bodiam
is the capital of Guinness Land as well as the third station after
Salehurst, but we shall ignore for the present the two great
hop farms of Ockham and Udiam, and spend the time while our
little train is shunting in a visit to the castle.

Bodiam Castle is one of the loveliest in the Weald, and the
most disappointing. It is lovely because the setting is perfect.
Girdled by its moat and groups of noble trees, it faces the Rother
Marshes with towers that still stand their full height and show
their crisp battlements. The full, sudden sight of it, as you come
to it from the village over the old jousting ground, catches your
breath with beauty and surprise. But it is disappointing because
it has no history. It was built too late for history, at a time when
the fortified manor-house had already begun to supplant the

embattled keep. Designed to protect the upper reaches of the Rother, it stands where the marsh's width shows the spread of the waters that used to be there in the days when the image of Ewhurst Church across the valley floated in them with the sky. But no invaders came and the castle lived on as little more than a vastly inconvenient private house. It was built in the fourteenth century by a knight with the richly sounding name of Sir Edward Dalyngruge, and is now the property of the National Trust, who have so energetically restored it that at a first exterior glance it might have been built last year.

I have known it in days when its walls were snubbed by weather and draped with huge swatches of ivy, the home of numberless jackdaws, while its moat, now gay with white and yellow water-lilies, was almost choked by them. I have climbed its towers by unwalled stairs twisting on a void the mere thought of which now makes my head swim. In the eighteenth century it was noted for its romantic decay. "This venerable structure," writes Grose in his *Antiquities*, "whose mouldering towers and rugged walls, beautifully mantled with ivy, afford at once a most picturesque subject for the pencil and a solemn and pleasing theme to the pensive philosopher . . ." How Jane Austen's Marianne Dashwood, Catherine Morland and Fanny Price would all have lamented its present state of restoration—"I am disappointed. There is nothing awful here, nothing melancholy, nothing grand." Fanny's strictures on the chapel at Sotherton might well have been passed on Bodiam Castle as it stands to-day. But the rest of us who were not trained in the æsthetic standards of the Romantic Revival may be thankful for the preservation of an ancient and lovely building which otherwise might well have perished of its own picturesqueness.

4

The hop gardens come to an end a few miles before Northiam, which is the next halt on our line. The station is really much closer to Newenden, so let us go there first, crossing the Rother only a few yards from the train and finding ourselves in Kent. Newenden is a very old place, one of the oldest in England— that is, if it is really (and all the evidence points that way) the

British city which the Romans called Andredes Cæster. This ancient city—a city of logs and reeds—occupied an important strategic position at the mouth of the Rother or Limene; for in those days the sea was here, rolling up the estuary and linking the sea-going citizens with the outer world which was shut off from them on every other side by the denseness of the forest.

After the British were driven out by the Saxons, Andredes Cæster did not lose its importance. A castle is said to have stood on the little hill now known as Castle Toll above the Hexden Channel, and at one time this castle was taken by the Danes, who however did not triumph sufficiently to make any prolonged settlement in these parts. Later, in less warlike times, Newenden became the market town for that end of the Kingdom of Kent, and the swine pastures from which it derives its name were presented by King Edward the Confessor to the Archbishop of Canterbury. Another King Edward is connected with this ancient place, for Edward the First built his summer palace at Newenden and visited it regularly for hunting.

Few villages can have had their history more completely wiped out. The castle, the palace, the Carmelite priory which was established here by the Auger family of Lossenham—all have vanished. To-day Newenden is little more than a straggle of houses, an inn and a church. Most of the building (which includes two sets of council houses, one for each world war, and the second lot unfortunately not yet absorbed into the landscape) is off the main road and along the lane that runs at right angles to it between the marsh and the sloping fields of Frogs Farm. The church is very small, for the chancel and steeple of the original building were demolished more than a century ago for reasons of safety; but it is well worth a visit because it contains a very fine Saxon font, one of the most remarkable pieces of antiquity in the county.

Northiam, on the Sussex side of the Rother, is to-day a much bigger and more important village than its Kentish neighbour. But to reach it we have to walk a mile up Station Road, through a muddle of uncontrolled building. The railway was intended to "open up" the Rother Valley, and to its construction may be attributed the large mill and small hotel that stand close to the station. The mill is plain and functional (as that word was understood in the eighteen-eighties), therefore not unsightly, and creepers have mercifully covered the worst of the hotel, but the road all the way up to the village is lined with the chaotic efforts of private enterprise (most of them, however, redeeming themselves with their gardens), until just as we are about to enter the Main Street at Clench Green we are confronted with what the District Council and the State can do, which is no better.

Once, however, we have turned the corner and find ourselves in Northiam's mile-long-street, we can forget the sorriness of our approach. From the Crown & Thistle at one end to the Six Bells at the other it is a pleasing jumble of homes and gardens, with a particularly lovely group around the church. At each end of the village stands an ancient house—Brickwall to the east and Dixter to the west. Great Dixter is a carefully restored old farmhouse to which has been added a complete house of similar type that used to stand at Benenden and was removed and set up in its present position by the late Nathaniel Lloyd. The great hall at Dixter is a beautiful example of its period, and the entire house with its appropriate hangings and furnishings gives us a modern impression of the beauty, as well as the darkness and the chills, amidst which our ancestors lived their daily lives.

Brickwall, at the other end of the village, is a very different sort of house with a very different story. It presents to the Rye road a high frontage of three timbered gables, which seems at a first glance too good to be true. But it is true, and Brickwall is in fact what it appears, a genuine Elizabethan house, to which succeeding reigns have made their characteristic additions. It was built in the sixteenth century as the country house of a Rye shipbuilding family named White. The Whites, however, soon gave place to the Frewens, a clerical family rising on the tide of the Reformation. Accepted Frewen (who afterwards became Archbishop of York) and his brother Thankful were the sons of John Frewen, Rector of Northiam, and must often have gazed at the roofs and pleasaunces of Brickwall from the old Rectory which is now Carriers Farm. The Frewens, when they took possession in the seventeenth century, made the more striking additions to the house, including a fine staircase with a baroque "lantern", while very much later they added the more practical parts in the shape of Victorian kitchens and pantries.

For Brickwall—unlike its opposite at Dixter—has belonged to a single family for nearly three hundred years. The Frewen mausoleum is an important part of Northiam Church (otherwise uninteresting), to which they supplied a succession of their younger sons as pastors. Except for one short interval, the living has been held by a Frewen or a Lord from the days of John Frewen till the selling of the living with most of the family estate after the first world war. The Lord family still occupy the attractive Georgian-looking house behind the church. This house is a good example of eighteenth-century fashions in building, for its Georgian front is imposed on a huddle of low-pitched roofs and walls dating from a much earlier period, with the result that while the front view of the house is most impressive, its profile can be described only as picturesque.

The oldest house in Northiam, however, is neither Dixter nor Brickwall, but a much transformed and enlarged house called Hayes, now an hotel. This stands close to the church, above the village green with its sweet, bee-murmuring limes and the bald and battered tree known as Queen Elizabeth's Oak. In its leafy days this tree gave shade and shelter to Great Bess as she breakfasted on her way from Rye. The meal was cooked and sent out to her by the owner of Hayes, Master Bishopp, so it was surprising to see in the Battle Abbey Pageant of a few years ago this incident transferred to "Mistress Frewen of Brickwall". Actually the Queen was never at Brickwall, which was in those days occupied by the Whites; but her shoe has been preserved there, though no one has ever told us by what experiment with time Queen Elizabeth was able to wear a Queen Anne shoe.

5

After Northiam station our train leaves Sussex and the Rother Valley, turning into Kent under the Castle Toll and running between the Isle of Oxney and the meadow hills of Rolvenden and Tenterden. The first stop is at Wittersham Road, and the fact that the name of the village is qualified by its approach suggests after our experience at Northiam that Wittersham is not very near. Indeed it is several miles away, but the road to it is so lovely that we shall not wish it any nearer. There are as

The Weald from Swailes Green

it happens two roads to Wittersham and it is hard to know which to choose. The road by Moon's Green is on the whole the more beautiful if you are coming from the village towards the marsh, especially when the floods are out and a lake of floodwater shines among the hills to which its spread and pallor give both height and darkness. But going the other way, we should choose the road by Palster Court, if only to gaze at the quaint beauty of this old house, with the head and shoulders of an oast rising out of the middle of its roof.

Palster as a place, not as a house, must be nearly as old as Newenden, for its name is one of the few Wealden place-names (though there may be more than is commonly supposed) which are of Latin origin. The inhabitants of the Isle of Oxney were called by the Romans *viri palustres* or men of the Marsh, and the land on which Palster Court now stands was their place of habitation. In the reign of Canute it was bestowed among other lands at Wihtriceshamme by "King Cnut and Ælgiva the lady" on a monk by the name of Eadsige, "as foster land for his soul"— that is, land on which he could depend for sustenance. Palster, according to the Domesday survey, was one of the only four places in the Weald of Kent possessing a church, the other three being Benenden, Hadlow and Tudely. The church has totally disappeared and the parish has long been absorbed into that of Wittersham. Only the Manor Farm with its hump of oast is there to carry in its name the vanished importance of the *viri palustres*.

Wittersham itself, though old enough, belongs to a much later age. The church is twelfth-century, with a Perpendicular tower, visible for miles around and in a beacon line with Fairlight on the coast and Tenterden some sixteen miles inland. In the village there are some lovely old houses and some rather terrible new ones, and we shall be tempted to make our way out of it by one of two enticing roads. Just as it was hard to decide between Palster and Moon's Green, so it is hard to decide between Smallhythe and Reading Street. Both roads, though they cross the marsh in different directions, would take us ultimately to Tenterden, but as we are shortly to visit that town from the railway, we shall resist the temptation that they offer, allowing ourselves only to stand for a moment on the northward slope of the Isle,

Old Houses at Smarden

to gaze across the marshes of the Reading Channel towards the group of small timbered houses which, with a red-brick church (one of the last churches built in England before the Reformation), is all that is left of a once flourishing seaport. One of these old houses was for many years the home of Ellen Terry and is now open to the public as a museum of her treasures and associations. In the garden is a fine old Kentish barn, transformed into a theatre, where every year, on or about the anniversary of her death, Shakespeare comes alive in surroundings more akin than many to those in which his plays were originally performed.

Turning from our view of Smallhythe, we make our way back to the station, and choose this time the road by Moon's Green and the month of February, so that the spreading sheets of flood-water may take us back to the days when Oxney really was an island and the ferry plied regularly between Stone and Appledore. At the station we shall ignore the waiting train and go to visit Rolvenden, which perversely is nearer Wittersham Road than its own station. Moreover, approaching it from here, we walk up the hill through the beauty of Rolvenden Layne, a scatter of old houses, some with history in their names, such as Wesley's House, where he stayed when he brought the Good News to Rolvenden, and some which have kept the secret of their past, such as seventeenth-century Gate House Farm, on the slope above Freezingham, which for me is full of memories of loveliness and loneliness, bound up with moist earth and primroses, and sharp with the piercing cold of April in an old damp house.

Rolvenden was not yet in existence as a village at the time of the Norman Conquest, for it is mentioned in Domesday only as a Hundred, one of the seven Hundreds of the Kent Weald. Not much later, however, it became a vill or settlement, after the manner of other "dens", and by the thirteenth century it certainly had a church, for in the Plea Rolls of King Henry III it is recorded that "Ralph La Weyte struck Adam de Croucheshorne with a certain club on the head, so that on the eighth day afterwards he died thereof. And Ralph fled, and put himself into the church of Rulvendene, and abjured the realm before the coroner." Having thus taken sanctuary, Ralph was safe, but his brothers William and Eustace were not so fortunate, for they were arrested and imprisoned at Rochester. But "the twelve jurors of the Hundreds of Selfbrytesden and Tentwardene and the four nearest vills say upon their oath that they are not guilty". So all ended well, not only for the escapist brother but for those who had to face the music.

Rolvenden has an attractive main street of crumpled red houses, which unlike many early instances of ribbon development have huddled close together along the ridge with barely a gap between them. Halfway up the street there is a road to Benenden, and we suffer our familiar temptation to go down it. But Benenden properly belongs to Cranbrook and should be visited from there, so we will walk no further than the ancient Mill House and admire the taste and skill with which it has been restored, trying not to think that we liked it better in the days when it seemed in imminent danger of falling down.

6

Rolvenden station is down by the Mill, in the valley between Rolvenden and Tenterden and very much nearer the latter. But any surprise at its naming is removed when we find that Tenterden station, uniquely on this system, is in the town itself. Proudly it proclaims itself as Tenterden Town, and, though the single-track line continues from it uninterruptedly on its course to Headcorn, it has always been treated as a junction. No train ever goes through Tenterden, and as the delay there amounts to an hour or more most people have discovered that the stations further up the line can be reached more expeditiously by almost any other means of transport.

Tenterden, however, may well occupy us for an hour, even though we do not have to walk far from the station. It is one of the few places in the Weald that really is a town, complete with mayor and jurats, and not merely an enlarged village. It rose into prosperity on Kentish broadcloth and little is known of it before the fourteenth century. Like the other "dens", it no doubt started its existence as a swine-pasture, then became a vill and finally a township. We might know more of its earlier history if the Town Hall, with all its records, had not been destroyed by fire in 1660.

As things are, we know that King Henry VIII visited Tenterden

on his way to France and that James II passed through it
or near it in his flight in the same direction. It is also famous as
the birthplace of William Caxton, a man who was great and
diverse enough in spirit to combine the activities of a merchant
adventurer with the invention of printing. In 1449 it was made a
"limb" of the Cinque Ports, being annexed to Rye, which was
then in financial difficulties. At that date it was only a mile or two
from the coast at Smallhythe, but its tall Perpendicular church
tower of Bethersden marble is still, though nearly sixteen miles
inland, a landmark for ships at sea.

In the days of my youth that tower contained besides its peal
of bells a musical box or carillon that played old-fashioned tunes
at the times when Continental churches ring the Angelus. It
was pleasant to walk in the sunshine up that wide tree-planted
High Street to the tune of "The Blue Bells of Scotland" or "My
Lodging is on the Cold, Cold Ground."

> "And still I cry, O turn, my love
> And O my love, turn unto me. . . ."

This homely minstrelsy could still be heard (though with a few
notes missing) up till the last war, but I have never heard it since.

It was installed too late for Cobbett to have heard it when he
visited Tenterden one Sunday morning as the people were coming
out of church: "I saw drawn out before me the dress and beauty
of the town; and a great many very, very pretty girls I saw;
and saw them too in their best attire." No wonder that he found
Tenterden a "singularly bright spot".

He had his strictures to make, however:

> "Let it be observed that when these churches were built
> people had not yet thought of cramming into them *pews* as a
> stable is filled with stalls. Those who built these churches
> had no idea that worshipping God meant going to *sit* to hear a
> man talk out what he called preaching. By *worship* they meant
> very different things, when they had made a fine noble building
> they did not dream of disfiguring the inside of it by filling
> its floor with large and deep boxes made of deal boards. In
> short, the floor was the place for the worshippers to stand
> or kneel; and there was *no distinction*; no *high* and no *low* place;

all were level *before God* at any rate. Some were not stuck into pews lined with green or red cloth, while the others were crammed into corners to stand erect, or sit on the floor."

I cannot refrain from quoting this lively picture of an early nineteenth-century church, even though I do not share Cobbett's dislike of old-fashioned box-pews and wish that they had not been so drastically uprooted from so many churches. There are still some left on Romney Marsh (always the last corner of England to yield to civilisation), but almost everywhere else they have disappeared and a characteristic period of Anglicanism with them. The box-pew and the three-decker pulpit and the blazon of the Royal Arms with the Creed and Ten Commandments over the altar are the only form of church furniture and decoration that can be called distinctively Anglican; and as their removal has not meant any return to the open spaces of the builder's intention, only another and often inferior kind of seating and ornament, even those of us who do not belong to the National Church must deplore the change.

I do not, however, as Cobbett does, attribute pews entirely to the Reformation. They did not come into common use even in England until the eighteenth century, and nowadays some form of private seating for the more illustrious members of their congregations is to be found in the churches of almost every country. I recall with pleasure a church in Dubrovnik which had been made to look like a theatre with *loges* and balconies, greatly enhanced by ingenious *trompe-l'œil* effects.

The gallery which usually accompanied the pews was a practical attempt to cram into the building a much larger congregation than that for which it had been built. Most towns and villages had between the twelfth and the eighteenth centuries greatly increased their populations, and the introduction of pews had at the same time reduced the space available for worship. There is still a gallery in the Unitarian Chapel in Tenterden, with a pulpit not unlike the Anglican three-deckers of the past. This plain yet dignified building is in refreshing contrast with the more blatant Victorian type of chapel. It was built nearly two hundred years ago at a time when Nonconformity was still more or less proscribed, and its externals have the formal discretion of a private house. There are still a few left of these "private house" chapels in the Weald, built either to disguise their purpose or, as at Ewhurst, in the days when the Methodists, like the early Christians, forgathered in private houses.

Tenterden abounds in beautiful old buildings and in its street we shall find examples of almost every type and period. There is more than one row of ancient cottages huddling together under one roof like chickens under a hen, and at the cross-roads beyond the eighteenth-century Town Hall stands a terrace of tall, tile-hung houses, too lovely and unusual in its style to have been marred by the shop-front that has appeared on one of them. The modern shop-front is the most likely form of blight on the beauty of an old street, and the trouble is not only for our day, for as far back as King Edward the First's reign it is recorded that "Seven shops have been built lately upon the High Street in the Hundred of Tenwardenn, and are rented at 3ˢ & 5ᵈ per annum."

Tenterden rose to prosperity as a weaving town, so we are not surprised to find many houses dating at least in their origins from the days of the Flemish weavers, and there are some fine specimens of early timber and plaster work in the High Street, though this type of house is perhaps better represented at Biddenden. Still more impressive is the number of large, dignified houses belonging to later periods—Jacobean, William & Mary, Queen Anne, and Georgian. For having attained prosperity, Tenterden maintained it, and when the weavers passed they were succeeded by the ironmasters, so that throughout the town the building is good and has survived, to delight us and reproach us—for recent efforts in this line have fallen far short of past achievements.

7

There is little difference whether we continue our way to Headcorn by road or by rail, for though there was no road up the Rother Valley, so that the railway or the river were our only alternatives, we are now on a first-class road to which the railway runs roughly parallel. Perhaps we had better use it for the first stage of our journey, as by doing so we shall not have so close a view of the "development" which has been allowed to spoil the northern end of this lovely old town.

For Tenterden straggles nearly all the way to St Michael's—
the parochial name that has supplanted the older, more attractive
name of Boar's Isle. Though place-names are seldom so simply
derived, we may in this case take it to have been originally a boar
enclosure adjoining the swine pastures of old Tenwardenne.
The District Council suggests a much more deadly kind of animal
by labelling its row of council houses Boresisle, but spelling was
always conveniently fluid till it set in the nineteenth century, and
Boresisle undoubtedly goes back with Boreham and Borehill
and Borzell to the days when this part of the country was still
the forest where no one dwelt but swine.

After Boar's Isle the road shakes off the town, and when we
leave the railway at London Beach we are once more in the open
country. London Beach is the name of the farm at the corner
where the road forks east and west for High Halden and Biddenden respectively, but the railway station is ominously named High
Halden Road and we have another long walk in front of us.
Nevertheless High Halden is worth a visit, if only for the sake of
the church, which is of a most unusual construction and must
contain more timber than any other church in the Weald. There
is said to be no less than fifty tons of oak in the tower, spire and
west entrance alone, while the interior is a forest of rough, un-
trimmed trunks of oak, almost as they were cut down in the wild
woods that surrounded it when it was built. High Halden is one
of the very oldest of the "dens", and its name has been variously
interpreted as "the healthful valley", "the den containing an inn
or place of entertainment", or (more likely) "the high unculti-
vated den". Another "den" equally old is Tiffenden in the same
parish, so here we stand on very ancient ground.

To arrive at Biddenden we can either return to the railway at
High Halden Road station, or we can make our way less directly
but more agreeably cross-country by Middle Quarter or Stede
Quarter (names that recall the "quartiers" of the French Huguenot
occupation) till we find ourselves rather suddenly at the fork of
the Headcorn road with Biddenden main street. That is, if we
do not lose our way, which we are likely to do, for these small,
interweaving lanes are scantily signposted. The country here is
very different from that in the more southerly parts of the Kentish
Weald. It is flat and rather featureless, and some would call it

uninteresting. But I would never do so, because we have here in these unfrequented parts a perfect treasury of old houses—not necessarily the type that antiquarians love or tourists long to live in, but homely, honest dwellings that were planted long ago and ever since have continued to grow and change, as their successive owners have altered or added to them—a window here, a gable there, a porch, a room, a roof, a wing. There are houses with humps and tumescences, with slicings and stubbings, houses that pile two or three stories as high as a mill, or crawl low against the comfort of the earth, houses that humbly share a roof with their own barns or stand apart wearing the garland of their orchards. No one has ever meddled with them by peeling off their tiled or tarry fronts to find the timber and plaster work which some owner of two hundred years ago covered up because even then they let in the draughts.

On the rare occasions we meet a signpost we shall be tempted to go to Smarden, and it is a temptation to which I think we had better yield, for at Smarden, in the valley of the Beult, the old houses have concentrated their quaintness and their charm. It is one of the loveliest villages in Kent, though not everyone has always been of this opinion, for it has been described as being in a "flat, low situation, very unpleasant and watery" (Hasted), and also as "obscurely and disagreeably situated" (Dearn). But those words were written before the apples were ripe—that is, before the buildings in its street had reached their full maturity. Enter the village by any one of three roads and you pass a string of them, some large, some small, some retired in gardens, some leaning towards the lane, till in the street they close in on all sides, with a particularly happy cottage group beside the church. The name of Smarden means "fat den"—probably in reference to the pastures by the river. It is not a very pretty name, nor is it the worst of Smarden, for on our way out of the village we shall pass a row of council houses that are utterly unworthy of it. We may, however, perhaps forget those when we come to Smarden Bell, where a friendly-looking inn makes picturesque contrast with an old Nonconformist burying-ground. From Smarden Bell a wandering lane will bring us at last to the main road at Heartsap Hill, and we shall enter Biddenden from the north, having made almost a complete circle in the country east of it.

32

8

On our way into the village we pass one of its most interesting and attractive houses. The Old Cloth Hall stands just outside Biddenden, and is a noble survival from the days of the Flemish weavers. It was actually a hall or factory where the cloth was made, as distinct from the homes of the master weavers, which have sometimes been confused with the cloth halls themselves. For this reason the interior is not so ancient as the exterior, having been made over to domestic use at a latter period when the looms were no longer worked. But the outside atones for any disappointment within, for it offers a wonderful array of gables, weathered tiles and black-and-white timber work. During the last war it was used as a storehouse and showed signs of decrepitude, but it has recently been repaired and put in order and looks as if it would stand another two or three hundred years.

There are several more beautiful old houses in Biddenden Street. Indeed I know no lovelier village view than this same street as seen from the Headcorn road, with the parish church at the end of it, and a row of leaning, black-and-white old houses at the corner—unless it is the view of those old houses from the fields at the back, with a huge brown hillside of tiled roofs sweeping almost to the ground.

The village's two most notable inhabitants are featured on a sign at the entrance to the street. The Biddenden Maids, Eliza and Mary Chulkhurst, were born in the year 1100 and were what are to-day called Siamese twins, for they were joined together at the hip and shoulder. Their condition as far as we can judge inspired pride and respect rather than vulgar curiosity. They were women of substance and position and lived thus united for thirty-four years. When they died within a few hours of each other they had bequeathed a sum for the distribution to the poor at Easter of cakes stamped with their image. Like many medieval charities dependent on land values, this sum has greatly increased and distributors are not inclined to inquire too closely into the means of those who receive their bounty. I certainly obtained one of these cakes without difficulty some years ago. It is an anatomically realistic portrait of the two

33

benefactors, and better, I think, considered as a portrait than a cake, as which I should call it a failure.

Next to Biddenden on the railway comes Frittenden Road, and I doubt if this village is worth the long walk from the station, for it consists of little more than a scatter of houses and a church that has been virtually rebuilt. Dearn, the Weald historian, proclaims that "it possesses little to repay the stranger for a visit", while Hasted in his *History of Kent* (1799) states that "the roads, from the soil, except in the driest seasons, are so deep and miry as to be almost impossible, though it is so obscure that there is but little traffic through it". Strange as it would have seemed to him, it is those very roads that will tempt us to visit Frittenden, for they will take us wandering in a landscape very like that on the other side of Biddenden, and in their twentieth-century condition will expose us to no worse dangers than losing our way.

Here we find ourselves once more among scattered farms and muddled old houses. These few square miles on both sides of the Headcorn road contain moreover, some of the most fascinating and suggestive (though not perhaps the most beautiful) place-names in the county—Witsunden, Ibornden, Lashenden, Dashnanden, Omenden (one of the very oldest of the dens), Hareplain, Honeyfield Wood, Potkiln Farm, Dogkennel, Wagstaff and many others stammering and mumbling forgotten tales. We are of course in the very midst of the dens. Nowhere else are they crowded so thickly. Furley in his *History of the Weald of Kent*, that mine in which all later writers must dig for information, declares that there are 470 dens or parts of dens in Kent alone. Those in Sussex are fewer and more scattered, but Sussex, as we know, was always behind Kent in civilisation, even in those early days when hogs rather than men made up the population of the Undwelt-in-Wood.

Both Biddenden and Frittenden belong to the iron as well as the broadcloth period of the Weald. When their looms ceased to chatter and sigh their furnaces thumped and roared, and the Hammer Stream that flows between them supported both industries. For in those days water was the only power that men had harnessed, and a dammed-up stream drove the hammers both of the forges and the fulling-mills.

Once we have left Frittenden we shall be tempted to make

our way cross-country to Headcorn rather than return to Frittenden Road station. We should certainly arrive there just as
quickly, for we are only a couple of miles or so away. But it
we yielded to this temptation we should be entering the place
from the wrong direction and that is very important. Headcorn
should be entered from the east, as that way you look up all
the length of its wide and pleasant street towards the church, a
view nearly as attractive, though not so sensationally "Ye Olde",
as the view of Biddenden. The entry from Maidstone would spoil
our first impression of the town, for right opposite the turning is
a hideous red-brick chapel which with its pretentious Victorian
Gothic seems to poison all the street. The church then is on the
right and might be missed by our hastily averted gaze, which
would be a pity, not only for its own sake, but for the sake
of the old, old oak that stands beside it and is said to be one ot
the few remaining trees of Andredsweald.

At Headcorn—once a cloth town and famous for "the brood
and poultry of fat, big and commended capons"—we are at the
terminus of the former Kent & East Sussex Railway and on the
platform which the great Continental expresses thunder past on
their way to the coast. We have finished our journey through
a very old country—some might call it dead, for it seems to have
left all its life and importance behind it. In the past are forts and
castles, ports and naval shipyards, mills and forges, times ot
industry and prosperity. In the present we have only a rural
area, not particularly prosperous, and with no industry save
farming, unless the provision of "teas" (oh hideous plural!)
can be counted as an industry. The towns which used to be industrial could now be described only as "residential", with the
great houses of their ironmasters, weavers and fullers taken over
by those who have made their money in other trades or by these
same trades in other parts of the country. Even the railway has
most of its life behind it, for probably by the time these lines
appear the section from Robertsbridge to Tenterden will be open
for goods traffic only, while the section from Tenterden to Headcorn will be closed altogether.

A dead country seen from a dying railway . . . what an
excursion! And I fear that most of our excursions in the Weald
will be of the same nature; that is, if you consider a country to be

dead because it is no longer industrially and commercially prosperous. But these small single-track railways are becoming an anachronism in an era of cars and cement road-surfaces, and as for the countryside, its industrial activity and importance may be gone, but its beauty remains, just as the beauty of Andredsweald remained when the leaves were fallen.

CHAPTER II

FROM PADDOCK WOOD TO HAWKHURST

I

THE next railway on which we shall travel is equally threatened with its end, and perhaps even more justly, for it serves a country-side already well provided with good roads which would take us from Tonbridge to Hawkhurst more quickly than the train. This line is no small venture like the Rother Valley Railway, but the attempt of a big company, the old South Eastern, to "open up" the country between their two main lines to Dover and Hastings. It is an even shorter line than the one we have just forsaken and there are only four stations on its entire length. The reason it goes no further than Hawkhurst lies doubtless in the nature of the landscape, which here confronts it with a ridge. It does not even go as far as Hawkhurst itself but provides it with a station at Gill's Green in the valley below the town.

I have never travelled on this line and indeed have only once seen a train upon it. But if we choose it for our next conducted tour it will show us the valleys, while the roads cling chiefly to the heights, swooping only occasionally to cross the river and the railway together. For the first few miles we shall follow the main Dover line to Paddock Wood. Here in the far-off days of An-dredsweald was held the swinemote at which all matters of pan-nage and enclosure were discussed. It is not to-day of any special interest, though its neighbour Brenchley is a picturesque and well-sited village with some attractive old houses. The country we now are in is not unlike that round Biddenden and Headcorn, except that it is more fertile and the farms instead of being "mixed" go in for fruit and hops in a big way. All round us are the apple and cherry orchards, filling the valley for miles, so that to look down on it in April from the heights is like looking down on a snowfield tinted with sunset. The hop gardens are broken up with oast-houses, some with only a few kilns, others with rows of them standing like soldiers on guard down the sides of the oast barn.

Apart from the oasts and the orchards this is not such a pleasing landscape as that round Biddenden. The fields are just as flat, while the lanes are less adventurous and the buildings more conventional—though I have always been sensitive to the corny charms of the ridiculous house at Hadlow which Cobbett describes as "stuck all over with a parcel of chimneys . . . like carnation sticks with caps on top to catch the earwigs". Beside it stands a fabulous tower modelled on the tower at Fonthill Abbey, and I am glad that this is to be spared, though the house as I write these lines is, perhaps deservedly, being pulled down. At the top of the tower is a lantern which the owner built in 1830 to spy on his wife who had run away but apparently not very far.

I am writing as if we had abandoned our railway and had taken the road across the valley to Kippings Cross. It is a pleasant drive in spring through all the beauty of the orchards and in early autumn through the sweetness of the hops. But the railway will take us through country in which we shall not have to depend for our enjoyment on two short seasons, for we are returning now to the broken landscape of the Kent and Sussex borders, to the meadow hills and the chestnut shaws and the small mixed farms. Our line winds through the valleys, but we shall see the villages of the Weald, Horsmonden, Goudhurst, Cranbrook and Hawkhurst, perched on the heights above us like Mediterranean hill-towns.

Our first stop is at Horsmonden, "the Vale of the horseman", and the main part of the village is indeed in the Vale, but the church stands high above it on the hill. We shall find it well worth while to climb this hill if only for the view. From the churchyard we can look down steep wooded slopes into the Teise valley and over miles of rolling country to a sea of golden mist in which swim the South Downs. The church itself has no remarkable features but a great deal of charm, due mainly to its grouping in true traditional style with a farm and a mansion house, the latter standing in its park and a fine example of Strawberry Hill Gothic. So here we may imagine ourselves back in the eighteenth century, with the church, the farm and the Great House offering their triad of religious respectability, agricultural prosperity and patrician culture. Church-going at so long a distance from the village must have been an arduous matter for all save the parson, the farmer and the Squire, but I should not be surprised if there were not then more villagers in church than there are to-day, though possibly their motives for coming were not much better than those of their descendants for staying away. In front of the main church door stands an enormous tree, which is unique among churchyard trees in being neither an oak nor a yew but a walnut tree. It is an exceptionally huge specimen; indeed with its propped and spreading branches that cover almost all the space in front of the church it might well be a survivor of Andredsweald, instead of, as I suspect, an early planting from the Squire's garden.

From Horsmonden the line goes on to Goudhurst, following for some way the valley of the Teise. This is one of the smaller Kentish rivers and a tributary of the Beult. It has triple springs in the woods of Glassenbury, Bedgebury and Furnace Farm, and one or other of these brooks will be with us most of the way to Hawkhurst. But at Goudhurst—or rather at the foot of the hill on which Goudhurst stands—the Teise is still a single stream wide enough to turn a water-mill, which whether in use or not— and it has had an interlude as a tea-garden—makes a pleasant contrast with the station buildings.

Goudhurst itself is a mile away and at the top of one of the steepest hills in the district. The whole village is up here, so we must make the ascent and be rewarded near the top with a climbing street of old and picturesque houses and a village pond which may or may not have a swan floating upon it. Goudhurst is a large village sprinkled in all directions from the top of the hill. Dearn in his *History of the Weald* states that "its appearance is picturesque rather than *respectable*" (italics his). What can he possibly mean by that? Furley suggests that he was referring to the accommodation provided by the inns, "which after a lapse of sixty years certainly cannot be called 'respectable' ", and advises travellers in need of sustenance to proceed to Kilndown, an uninteresting village two miles away, where "all their reasonable wants will be satisfied, as a better conducted roadside inn is not to be met with in this locality". But after the lapse of another eighty years I can confidently assert that anyone who wants a good inn cannot do better than stay where he is.

Goudhurst belongs to Kent's industrial past and is surrounded by noble houses and large estates, which though dating in many cases from earlier times than the era of cloth and iron, doubtless owe their enlargement and continued survival to its prosperity. Perhaps the most beautiful as well as the most ancient of these is Glassenbury, named after the hill on which it stood before it was pulled down and rebuilt on its present moated site in the valley below. It properly belongs to the parish of Cranbrook, of which it is a manor, but as it is only just across the border we shall find it easier to visit from Goudhurst. It has the distinction of having belonged to the same family since the reign of Richard II.

Indeed we may go back further still, for in that reign Stephen Rookehurst married the daughter of William Tilley whose family had lived at Glassenbury since the days of Edward I. The name was changed from Rookehurst to Roberts when the present house was built in 1473. Walter Rookehurst or Roberts obtained a grant to "impark" six hundred acres of land and one thousand acres of forest in the parishes of Cranbrook, Goudhurst and Ticehurst, so that his estates spread right across the border into Sussex. Not long afterwards they were confiscated by Richard III, who accused him of hiding his enemy Sir John Guilford, but they were restored to the family by Henry VII, and when baronetcies were created by James I, Sir Thomas Roberts of Glassenbury became one of the earliest baronets.

Since that date the house has been enlarged and refronted but has not lost its beauty, which it owes in part to its surrounding moat. In the park is a chalybeate spring, similar to that which made the fortune of Tunbridge Wells, and also the grave of Jaffa, the favourite charger of Napoleon. We do not know how Jaffa came to be at Glassenbury, but it is good to think of him, after all the danger and the turmoil, ending his days in peace in this lovely spot. Evidently those last years were happy and healthy as well as peaceful, for he lived to the age of thirty-seven, a great age for a horse. Perhaps he had drunk from the chalybeate spring and like many an eighteenth-century dowager owed his prolonged life to "the Tunbridge Waters".

Cranbrook Church

Another great estate is Bedgebury, where there used to be a furnace and where there is still an enormous wooded park. Unlike Glassenbury, Bedgebury has changed hands more than once. It originally belonged to a family of the same name, but in 1528 became the property of the Culpepers, whose tombs are a feature of Goudhurst church. Not long afterwards it was the scene of a remarkable plot to kidnap Cardinal Wolsey, who was then the guest of Sir Alexander Culpeper. The plot was hatched by a number of disaffected clothworkers and farmers, who planned to "take him by force, with his harness, armour and weapons". They did not however intend to kill him, as that might have meant an Interdict, but to do what would come to the same thing, though without—or so they imagined—such a dire ecclesiastical reaction. They would put him in a boat bored with large temporarily stopped holes, tow him out to sea and sink him. They counted on the support of fifty men in Cranbrook and no fewer than a hundred in Frittenden, which must have been a very different place then from what it is now, with fifty more from Goudhurst to "take the ordnance at the block-house at Rye". The plot was discovered and came to nothing, but unfortunately the records have been badly mutilated, so we do not know how, when or why, or who reaped the whirlwind.

Nearly a hundred years later Queen Elizabeth visited Bedgebury and was presented by the Culpeper then in occupation with a handsome silver-gilt cup. She was making a progress through the Weald of Kent, and evidently did not find it to her liking, for Lord Burleigh who accompanied her wrote to the Earl of Shrewsbury: "The Queen has had a hard beginning of her progress in the Wild of Kent, and in some part of Sussex, where surely were more dangerous rocks and valleys, as she said, and much worse ground than was in the Peak."

Bedgebury is no longer in private hands. The house has become a school and most of the park belongs to the Forestry Commissioners. In a sheltered corner of it is a nursery of rare trees for Kew. During the war the whole place was nearly destroyed by fire, not owing to enemy action but to our native predilection for boiling kettles out of doors. Fire brigades from all over Kent and Sussex were sent to extinguish the blaze, which roared terrifyingly through the tops of the trees as well

Sissinghurst Castle

as crackling through the pine-needles underfoot. The only time I have ever been in Bedgebury Park was the Sunday after this catastrophe, so I cannot claim to have seen it at its best. Fire hoses were coiling everywhere like snakes, through the undergrowth and over the clearing roads, while above everything hung the smell of fire and a drifting fog of smoke. But it was a beautiful day, and the wives and families of the firemen had decided severally, yet with one accord, that their men had been away too long and that the time had come for a visit combined with a picnic in the woods. But this time no one attempted to boil a kettle for tea.

2

I feel sure that the nineteenth-century promoters of the Tonbridge to Hawkhurst line never dreamed that anyone—except perhaps a few carriage folk—would ever again make the journey by road. The days of the coaches, the chaises and the curricles which made the eighteenth-century roads so bustling were no more, and though sometimes people who had carriages would adventurously set out in them on a journey of twenty miles—my own parents once drove from Hastings to Crowborough, which is thirty—the farm wagons and family dog-carts seldom attempted more than seven or eight. If we go by car from Goudhurst to Cranbrook we shall be there in a few minutes. We shall have the further advantage of arriving in the town itself instead of in the valley below it. But even though we follow the heights I do not think we shall look upon a fairer country than if we take the train, which in forsaking the road has also forsaken the outcrops of unsightly building that have accompanied its restoration. Down in the valley we are in an old, forgotten land, where only an unfrequented lane meanders from Bedgebury Forge to Bedgebury Furnace, and then like the river breaks into tributaries that link up farms with provocative names like Whitelime, Mopesden, Frights, and Little Pix Hall.

Cranbrook stands high on the hill, and Cranbrook is not a village but a town. It is the capital of the Weald of Kent, and its magnificent parish church has been called the Cathedral of the Weald. It is dedicated to St Dunstan and owes its size and beauty to the generosity of succeeding generations of weavers, who enlarged and enriched it with their wealth. The date of the first church building is uncertain, except for the fact that it was not very early, probably much later than Norman times. For Cranbrook as a town is not very old—not as we count age in the Weald. It is not mentioned in Domesday, and the Hundred of Cranbrook did not take its name from any vill or ham but from the Crane brook that has its source in this neighbourhood. Here, in this part of the forest, there were several of the oldest "dens"—Lashenden, Swetlynden, Rodelinden, Swatterden, Plushingden and many others—and the usual course of history followed: human settlements were made among the swine-pastures, then the settlers banded together for protection in a village, which finally grew into a town. But Cranbrook did not reach full stature till the reign of Edward III and the coming of the Flemish weavers.

The oldest parts of the church are the south porch and some of the north wall. But to the weavers it owes its later improvements and enlargements, its great height and space and the tall windows that fill it with light. The cloth industry continued to flourish in Cranbrook until the end of the eighteenth century, but after the Reformation it stopped its benefactions to the church, with the result that the structure was neglected to the point of imperilling its safety, and in 1725 a great part of it fell down. The necessary repairs took six years, and then about fifty years later the tower was struck by lightning and a great deal more damage was done. This fate had already befallen the church tower of Goudhurst, and we can realise the danger run by these high towers on high places in the days when lightning conductors were unknown. The tower at Cranbrook is adorned with a huge and handsome clock, surmounted by an effigy of Father Time. People will tell you there is a quaint old legend that at the stroke of midnight Father Time descends with his scythe and mows the churchyard. But indeed there is nothing legendary in the story. For generations the children of Cranbrook have been told that when Father Time hears the clock strike twelve at midnight he comes down to mow the churchyard, which is as absolutely and literally true as the fact that if you pick a guinea-pig up by its tail its eyes will drop out.

Inside the church there is a feature which I believe is unique

43

in English parish churches—a font for adult baptism by total immersion. It was constructed by the Rev. John Johnson, a rather eccentric Vicar of Cranbrook in the early eighteenth century. Unlike the font for infant baptism it makes no concessions to art, consisting of little more than a pit into which a flight of steps descends. When filled with water it must have looked quite dangerous and we cannot be surprised that it was used no more than once. In 1732 a certain John Munn was baptised at the age of twenty-three, but not by the font's originator, who died some years earlier without ever having made practical use of his invention.

Next in importance to the church as a feature of the town is the Union Windmill. It is seventy feet high, and the tallest and largest in the Weald if not in the country. Another distinction is that it is still working and driven by wind-power when the winds are favourable. There is a gas-engine for the days when they are not. It is a smock mill—that is, the octagonal tower is constructed of boarding and supposed to resemble a smock-frock—and was built in 1814 by James Humphrey, a local wheelwright. For over a hundred years it has been in the hands of the Russell family and to them and their knowledge as mechanics and millwrights its present working efficiency is due. At its feet cluster some of the oldest houses in Cranbrook, making an almost perfect group of beauty and antiquity. It is sad to think that there are so few like it left in the Weald. When I was a child there was a windmill in almost every village, but one by one these ceased to be economic and fell into disuse. From the disuse of a windmill it is only a short step to its disappearance, and though lovers of the countryside have tried to keep certain windmills in repair, the undertaking has proved too expensive and difficult to maintain, and in any case involves the removal of the sails, without which a windmill looks as tragic as a butterfly without its wings.

Cranbrook is famous for its school, which is one of England's public schools and housed in buildings worthy of its position and of the town. It was founded by John Blubery, a clerk to the King's Armoury at Greenwich, who made the curious provision in his will that if his daughter Jone's first child was a boy it was to be his heir, but if a girl his property was to be used to establish

a school for the poor children of the town. At that time Jone
was not even married but betrothed to one of the citizens, who
must have loved her for herself alone, since though she was the
daughter of a rich man her inheritance was a gamble. We hope
that neither of them minded too much when the game was lost.

Their first child was a girl, and at the death of Blubery's widow
(who had the use of it for her lifetime) his house became a school,
with William Lynch as its first headmaster. This was another
provision of the will, and he seems to have regarded himself
not only as master but also as proprietor, for when he died his son
Simon claimed the school as his own. For some time there was
litigation between Simon Lynch and the parishioners of Cranbrook, who finally won their case and made the school the town's
property. When Queen Elizabeth visited Cranbrook she granted
it a charter and it then became "Queen Elizabeth's Grammar
School".

It was on this occasion that the great Queen trod all of a mile
on a lane made of broadcloth from the town to the house known
as Coursehorne. Our mind's eye is entertained with the picture
of Elizabeth and her ladies and courtiers stepping high and carefully along this road, whose surface smoothness doubtless concealed and made all the more dangerous those "rocks and valleys"
of which she had so bitterly complained elsewhere on this progress. However, we hear of no catastrophe, and the company
duly arrive at Coursehorne, where it was suitably entertained.

Coursehorne is one of the oldest of the weavers' houses that
surround Cranbrook. The men who made their fortunes in the
cloth trade naturally built large, comfortable houses for themselves and their families, and many of these remain until this day.
Perhaps the most beautiful is Old Wilsley, dating from the end
of the fifteenth century. Sunk deep in its hollow it seems in very
truth the abode of peace and sheltered sunshine. The old timbered
house has seen many changes, both in construction and occupation, but its beauty has never been lost. When I last saw it there
was an air of dereliction about it, because, perhaps for the first
time in its long life, it was standing empty and forsaken. But
I shall not forget the scent of a daphne in the garden, and how
the sunshine seemed to drink it up and fill every corner with its
sweetness.

Not far from Old Wilsley is the cross-roads known as Wilsley Pound on account of the enclosure which still stands there and in which straying animals used to be impounded until released by payment from their owners. The remains of this custom still exist in farming lore to-day, for I have known a farmer take possession of beasts that had strayed into his fields and refuse to release them until he had been paid for the damage they had done. I doubt if he had any legal right to do this, but in the Weald lore and law are often very much the same, and certainly the matter was settled much more quickly and satisfactorily than if it had been taken into court.

Wilsley Pound is nearer Sissinghurst than Cranbrook, and before returning to the railway we shall yield to the temptation to visit Milkhouse Street, as this village was always called until the nineteenth century. It is a pretty village, though the church is modern, succeeding after a long interval a chapel built in the reign of Henry VI to allow the parishioners to attend church in winter, when the badness of the roads made it quite impossible for them to reach their parish church at Cranbrook. This chapel was suppressed at the time of the Reformation, though the ruins remained until 1844. It is said to have been re-established for a short time under Queen Mary, when its plate and ornaments, unlike those of many churches in the Weald, were discovered to be intact. Doubtless at the place's second suppression under Elizabeth, they found their way with the rest to the Master of the Queen's Jewel House.

Close to the village is Sissinghurst Castle, an unusual and beautiful building that has had a varied history. It was built in the reign of Henry VIII, but nothing could be more unlike that other castle dating from the same period, Camber Castle, near Rye. Camber is squat and low, shaped like a clover leaf, while Sissinghurst dominates two squares, with far fewer curves than angles in its construction, while the fairest and most striking part of it is the immensely tall gatehouse with its two crowned turrets. Unlike Camber, but like Herstmonceux, it is a brick building, and again unlike Camber but like Herstmonceux,* its ruined state is due

* Not as it is now in its restored immaculacy, but as it was when I knew it best—a lovely, lonely red-brick ruin, its moat choked up and the sheep grazing under its walls.

not so much to age as to the neighbourhood's need for building materials.

In actual fact it was never called a castle till it was beginning to fall down in the middle of the eighteenth century, but was known less elegantly as Bloody Baker's House after its original builder Sir John Baker, who for some time was ambassador to Denmark in the reign of Henry VIII. He was also Speaker of the House of Commons, Attorney-General, Recorder of London and a Privy Councillor, but he owes his adjective to his later activities during the reign of that similarly ensanguined queen whose champion and favourite he was. We shall meet him again when we come to deal with the religion of the Weald. At present we need no more than note that he must have been a most unpleasant character, and was rightly abominated by the inhabitants of Cranbrook and Milkhouse Street.

Queen Elizabeth stayed at Bloody Baker's House as the guest of his son, Sir Richard, during that progress through the Wild of Kent on which we have already met her more than once. That was the time when she walked that mile on broadcloth from Cranbrook to Coursehorne, and she must have felt she had fully earned the reward of a handsome silver-gilt cup with which her host presented her—the second she had collected within a very few miles.

Another famous visitor was Horace Walpole, who arrived "after twenty mishaps" to find "a park in ruins and house in ten times greater ruins". By this time the Baker family were no longer at Sissinghurst, for the last direct male heir had left it to the husbands of his four daughters. After that it passed into the hands of Sir Galfridus Mann, and then for forty years stood neglected and empty, except for some French prisoners who were interned there during the Seven Years' War. When they were repatriated the place was uninhabited till in 1794 it was leased by the Cranbrook Poor Law authorities, and the fine castle where once a queen had been entertained became the parish Poor House.

From this ignominy—or rather from the dereliction that succeeded it—it was rescued by its present owners and is at the moment not only as lovely but, I will wager, lovelier than it has ever been. The two courtyards are now a garden, transformed by the gardening poet Miss V. Sackville-West. The remains of the Castle itself, with the two old houses, built out of the ruins, that huddle against its walls, have been made into a romantically unusual home, where the entrance is carpeted with flower-beds and the rooms are reached by sheltered garden paths. There are many old buildings in the Weald that might inspire a poet, but few which like Sissinghurst have had the good fortune to become a poet's home, especially of one whose poems are written not only in ink.

4

Before we reach the Castle a road turns south to Benenden, which we must certainly visit, because it is one of the oldest villages in the Weald. It was a "den" in Saxon times, and granted with others by King Ethelred to his mother Elfthryth for "as long as she shall retain her vital spirit unextinguished in her mortal flesh". It is mentioned in the Domesday Book, and by that time must have become a vill, for it is distinguished as possessing a church. The name is said to spring from a Saxon root meaning "twofold", as it contained within itself at least one other "den"—Hempsted, which existed as a "den" in the tenth century and much later became the home of the Earls of Cranbrook. After the Conquest Benenden, together with many others of the better properties in the Weald, was handed over to the Bishop of Bayeux as tenant in chief.

After this early start it does not seem to have had a particularly eventful history. In 1673 its church was struck by lightning, but this has happened to so many other churches in these parts that it might not be thought a distinction. However, the account of it in a contemporary pamphlet is sufficiently bloodcurdling:

"On the 29th of December last, being Sabbath day about eleven of the clock at night in the parish of Benenden, a pretty considerable town in the Wild of Kent, appeared on the east side of the town a very great light, to the amazement of all the inhabitants. It being the winter they little dreamed of lightning, but after a little observation of the elements they were convinced that it was little else but lightning, but that so terrible, the flashes so long, that the beholders were afraid not only their houses but themselves should be consumed by it. . . .

"Others feared that Almighty God was rending the heavens and coming down amongst them for judgment. Such formidable thunder-claps, say the old inhabitants, have not been heard in the age of man.

"These messengers of the Lord's anger had not been long executing his will and pleasure; not many volleys of the great ordnance of Heaven had been discharged but the poor inhabitants might see their parish church (that place where on the same day they had been taking counsel at God's Oracle) in a flame, and all the town in a danger also to be burnt with flames or overthrown with thunder. . . . The devouring flames and impetuous thunder found no great resistance from this stoney pile. The steeple, which was one of the highest in that part of Kent, what with the fiery flashes and mighty thunder-claps, was quickly forced to resign itself to that earth it was first fixed; so that the fabric and the frame began to incorporate with its own foundations."

As a piece of descriptive writing, our modern journalism would find this seventeenth-century example hard to beat.

The church was rebuilt in 1678, but again it was to share the not unusual fate of churches of the Weald, and by the middle of the nineteenth century had suffered such neglect that it was almost a ruin. Then in 1862 it was restored at the expense of the first Earl of Cranbrook and is now one of the most beautiful parish churches in this part of Kent. Perhaps I should say one of the most beautifully situated churches, for the structure itself has nothing very remarkable about it. The beauty lies mainly in its position at the southern boundary of the village green, with which, and the old houses nearby, it makes an almost perfect group, especially, I think, when cricket is being played on a Saturday afternoon.

Benenden Green, formerly known as the Playstool, has long been famous for its cricket, and in the early days of the nineteenth century two Benenden men, Richard Mills and Edward Wenman, were giants of the Kent eleven, which at that time could be trusted to beat any team produced by the rest of England. On

Mills' tombstone in Benenden churchyard are a sculptured bat, ball and wicket. His family lived at Pympe Manor, one of the most ancient of Benenden's many timbered houses. The village is particularly rich in these, for in its industrial days both cloth and iron made fortunes for its inhabitants, and wealth, then as now, found substance in a home. Another fine old house is the Old Manor, which at one time was moated and still retains a fragment of its moat—enough to float a swan.

There are many more of these timbered houses in the country between Benenden and Hawkhurst, and they have some quaint and lovely names—Crit Hall, Scullsgate, Great Nineveh, Little Nineveh, Dinglesden, Pookwell, Ellenden. To Crit Hall belong my very earliest memories of the Weald, for I was no more than two when I stayed there one summer long ago. My mind carries many clear pictures of it, but they are all pictures of a child's world —hens large as Newfoundland dogs, a hop garden that might be Andredsweald itself, and a great brick house soaring into the sky. They are all rather terrifying, for the hens might eat me, I might be lost in the hop garden and the house might fall. But the sun that shines on them is brighter than any sun that has shone since.

5

We are now almost as far south as Hawkhurst, so we shall do well if we forget the train waiting for us at Cranbrook, especially as we now approach the headquarters of the Hawkhurst Gang, whose track we should have followed all the way from Goudhurst had we travelled by road.

This notorious gang of smugglers trafficked between Goudhurst and Romney Marsh. The contraband—mainly tea, coffee, brandy and silk—would be set ashore at some desolate spot and brought inland by "carriers" using a succession of "hides". Hawhurst was one of the first stopping places, though the best "hides" were to be found in the neighbourhood of Cranbrook— at Angley, at Hartley and at Sissinghurst. The head of the gang, Tom Kingsmill, was a native of Goudhurst and his followers were recruited from all over the countryside.

Smuggling to-day is a small and furtive business, with risks out of all proportion to the rewards. In the eighteenth century it was an industry, openly carried on, and so profitable to those concerned in it that the only opposition came from those others who for some reason were excluded from its benefits. Farmers were its chief opponents, as they could not offer wages that competed with those paid to the "carriers", and the land was drained of its workers. But there was nothing much that could be done about it, except send petitions to Parliament, which ignored them. Law-abiding citizens were kept in their place either by favour or by fear. Free gifts of tea—then an expensive luxury, much dearer than wine—would buy the silence or even the connivance of some, while the fate of those who betrayed a smuggler—or gave evidence against him when he was brought to trial—was so hideous that it required either a very brave or a very stupid man to take the risk.

The countryside was indeed completely terrorised by these people, who combined highway robbery with their other delinquencies and openly spent their ill-gotten wealth in building large houses equipped with still larger barns for the storing of contraband. Farmers dared not protest when their horses were "borrowed" overnight and returned sweating and exhausted, as if in fact the legendary hag had ridden them, and magistrates if a smuggler were brought to trial before them would, when forced by the evidence to convict, send the prisoner by cart to Maidstone gaol without a guard, so that his friends had plenty of opportunity to rescue him on the way.

In 1747 the inhabitants of Goudhurst assembled enough courage and resolution to form a "Band of Militia" for the express purpose of combating the Hawkhurst Gang. News of their activities reached Kingsmill, who forthwith announced that he would attack and burn the village, cynically giving to his enemy the actual date and the hour of his attack. The "Militia" had been trained after a fashion by a man called Sturt who had once been in the army, and they put up a much more formidable defence than Kingsmill had expected. They had dug trenches across the road on which the smugglers marched and had covered the rooftops with snipers. The battle that ensued was quite "professional" and would not have discredited the Home Guard had the Germans landed. The smugglers were driven off, leaving many casualties, including four dead, while others were taken alive and afterwards hanged. Unfortunately all the leaders escaped and in consequence the life of the Hawkhurst Gang went on very much as before. It was not till two years later that Kingsmill was caught with two of his associates, Perrin and Fairall, while robbing a coach, sufficiently far from their usual haunts to ensure them a hanging at Tyburn. Kingsmill's body was, however, afterwards sent back to Kent and hanged in chains outside Goudhurst, while that of Fairall endured the same fate on Horsendown Green.

A strange light is cast on the minds of these desperadoes by the openly acknowledged fact that the hanging in chains was the part of their sentence which they feared most. On the night before their execution Perrin, who for some reason had been spared this fate, was almost apologetic in his condolences with the others, much as a murderer who has been reprieved might show embarrassment in the company of those who were still to hang. But young Fairall, who was evidently the toughest of the three, retorted: "Why fret? When you are rotting in your grave, we shall be hanging in the sweet air." Later on when the gaoler ordered him away into his own cell he exclaimed: "Can't you let me stay a little longer with my friends? I shall not be able to drink with them to-morrow night." Fairall was only twenty-five, while Kingsmill was twenty-eight, but the amount of crime they had contrived to stuff into their short lives would not have disgraced the oldest lag.

Hawkhurst has other claims to interest besides smuggling. At the time of the Spanish Armada it was one of the five beacon towns of the Kentish Weald, the others being Goudhurst, Cranbrook, Rolvenden and Tenterden. In those days a beacon was no longer the simple bonfire that it used to be or as we have since revived it on national occasions, but an affair like a huge kettle or cauldron hanging from a beam on some high place, such as the church tower. When alight the beacon was taken charge of by a watchman or "hobiler", who was provided with a horse "of no great proportions but light and fitted for all manner of service". Hawkhurst had four "watch houses", all situated at cross-roads, and as the Armada sailed up the Channel the hobiler must have had a busy time galloping from Philpots to Badcocks, from High Gate to Scales Crouch, and up to Four Throws, to make sure that his kettle of pitch and resin kept well alight.

As a village, Hawkhurst sprawls more widely than almost any other I know. There are indeed three distinct hamlets making up its total area—Gill's Green down in the valley, Highgate up on the hill and Hawkhurst Moor, which in Cornwall would be called the church town, for there stands the parish church, at least a mile beyond the rest. Arriving from Cranbrook, either by road or rail, we come first to Gill's Green, where the station is and the sort of "development" one associates with a station. Then at the top of a long hill we come to the cross-roads known as Highgate and find at once a charming colonnade of shops and two excellent inns. Houses that are mainly old and pleasant—some were built by the Hawkhurst Gang—follow the road westward almost as far as Flimwell, while on the eastern road to Rye there are more old houses at Pipsden and Four Throws. If, however, we plunge on straight ahead and go down the hill we shall come at last to the Moor and the large and handsome parish church—badly damaged by a fly-bomb in 1944, but now in process of recovery. The Moor is actually the village green, and the grouping of it with the church and some ancient houses makes a definitely rural scene in contrast with the miniature urbanity of Highgate on the hill.

Round Hawkhurst is some of the most beautiful country in the Weald, whether we look north from Pipsden (where the best views are) and see all the little red farms with their coloured oasts among the fields at the back of Benenden, or gaze southward to Sussex and the woods. It is here that the poet of the Weald, Miss V. Sackville-West, might have stood when she wrote of "the glaucous country like a hilly sea", though her vision is greener than any before us now when ploughing-up orders and an agricultural revival have broken the "paler and darker green of Kentish miles" with the rich brown of newly ploughed earth or the changing gold of corn. But certainly when we look south to Sussex

" . . . the horizon's sweep
Deepens to blue in woods, with the pointed spire
Pricking the foreground by the village tiles."

And as we continue our way southward from the Moor, before very long we find ourselves in Sussex, into which the parish of Hawkhurst overflows. For hère the boundary line between the two counties is not the Rother but the Kent Ditch, and at the cross-roads by Brickhurst Wood, Kent but not Hawkhurst comes to an end.

Chapter III

FROM POLEGATE TO GROOMBRIDGE

I

OUR next tour is carried out entirely in Sussex, though I shall be surprised if we notice any difference. We are still in that "glaucous country like a hilly sea", and the fact that our county is divided into rapes instead of lathes is not likely to affect us. The division of Kent into lathes goes back to the days of King Alfred, of whom Lambarde records: "These shires [East and West Kent, which were once two separate kingdoms] he also breke into smaller parts. whereof some were called lathes, of the word *gelathean*, which is to assemble together." The rapes of Sussex are of a later date, but why two adjoining and similar systems of dividing up the land should be given different names I cannot say. The word rape in this connection is said to derive from the Icelandic *hrippr*, meaning a division, which is another puzzle, for though Sussex has very few Norse associations the system of rapes is peculiar to Sussex alone.

The county is divided into six nearly equal strips from north to south, each strip taking its name from the most important township at the time of its creation. Thus we have, from east to west, the Rape of Hastings, the Rape of Pevensey, the Rape of Lewes, the Rape of Bramber, the Rape of Arundel, and the Rape of Chichester. Each rape, as each lathe in Kent, includes several hundreds.

Our excursion starts in the Rape of Pevensey. Polegate is a junction some six miles inland from Eastbourne, on what used to be once the London, Brighton & South Coast Railway. When the directors decided to "open up" the country between the coast and Tunbridge Wells, they made Polegate the starting point of their new venture. Otherwise it has little claim to distinction. A large, shapeless village, it dates almost entirely from the time of its importance on the railway, before which it was not even a parish, but a part of the parish of Hailsham.

This fine old market town has a handsome Perpendicular church, and a peal of bells which are indeed the singing voice of Hailsham, for they were cast at Bell Bank, only a short way from the tower in which they ring. About two miles out of the town is Michelham Priory, founded early in the thirteenth century by the Augustinian Friars. At the Dissolution it became a private house, and the lovely old Elizabethan building blends its colours with the grey of the few remaining arches of the priory. Also remaining are the old fish-stews and the priory mill. For the beauty both of itself and of its setting Michelham is well worth a visit, even if we do no more than gaze at it from the lane.

Polegate need not detain us, except to wonder if its name really is derived from the figure outlined on the hill beyond it. The Long Man of Wilmington has been variously accounted for. Some say that he represents no more than a monkish pastime —the monks of Michelham Priory spending their recreation in carving a gigantic figure out of the chalk, much as centuries later British and Canadian troops amused themselves by carving giant replicas of their regimental badges on the Wiltshire Downs. But he is almost certainly of earlier origin than that. One theory is that he represents the god Baldur standing at the gate of Midsummer. On Midsummer Day the rising sun, appearing over the eastern rim of Andredsweald, would send a patch of light across the waves of trees to enter, as it were, the hillside beyond them. In that hillside the ancients saw a gate, the gate of midsummer and morning, and they saw a god opening the gate to the triumphantly entering sun. So where he stood they carved his likeness, a hand on each pillar of the gate. To us now he looks as if, instead of this, he were holding an upright pole in either hand. But even so, it is difficult to believe that Polegate is named after him, for he cannot be seen from the village itself. It is not till we are some miles along the Lewes road that we see him clearly, and then the village at his feet is Wilmington.

Nor shall we see him from our railway, though there is a good view of him from the main line. The single-line track from

Udimore Church

Polegate to Tunbridge Wells turns right away from the Downs, and after passing through Hailsham reaches Hellingly. In one respect it is a very different railway from either of the two on which we have already fared, for it has a frequent service of trains. From the high ground above Horse Eye Level you may watch them bustling by, one after the other, and by this route it is possible to reach London without too great inconvenience or delay.

It does not, however, take us through very interesting country until we have travelled some way. Not until we come to Heath-field and Mayfield shall we find our journey really worth while. Polegate and Hailsham are clotted together with recent building and the clot spreads through the two Horsebridges, Upper and Lower, as far as Hellingly. It is all no doubt an infection from Eastbourne, which seems to reach inland almost as far as does Brighton, possibly because its lateral development is prevented eastward by the marsh and westward by Beachy Head. We have barely shaken it off at Hellingly (pronounced Helling*lye*, I beg you), where there are, however, some agreeable old houses to counteract the rest. Close to Hellingly, too, stands the Horse-lunges, an immensely old house which restoration has made to look even older than it is. It has no history to match its appearance, and its name, like that of the Horsebridges, is probably of woodland derivation, "horse" being in both cases a corruption of "hurst".

For here in Sussex the "hursts" have taken the place of the "dens". Civilisation came later to Sussex than to Kent, and the woodland termination or prefix (for it can be either) "hurst" denotes a later clearing of the forest than a "den". In other words, the Sussex end of Andresweald was still a matted jungle when the Kentish side was being civilised by hogs. Not that there are no "dens" in Sussex—the most beautifully named of them all, Witherenden, is near Burwash—but they are few, and mostly near the Kentish border. "Hurst" equally with "den"—as with "stead" and "field" in these parts—represents a clearing in the forest, and it is certain that Andresweald came as far south as Hellingly and the River Cuckmere. So as we leave the valley of that lovely but eccentric river and make our way inland we shall be surrounded by the "hursts"—Ramshurst, Winkenhurst,

57

Dumbwoman's Lane, Udimore

Beech Hurst, Wellshurst, Chilthurst, Tilehurst, Hackhurst and many others, all telling us where very long ago Sussex men found pasture for their swine.

So far we have not lingered on our journey. There has been little to detain us at Polegate, Hailsham or Hellingly, and at the next station, Horam, it would profit us less to leave the train than to consider for a moment the sad intrusions of prudery into place-names.

Until quite recently this grotesquely named village was Horeham Road, which is its original name without the first letter. The home of some notorious harlot must have stood here long ago, but that fact does not seem to have distressed the inhabitants until shortly before the last war. Then it was agreed by the majority that the name should be changed to Horam, an etymological monstrosity which spares them only their disgrace in print, since unless they find a new way of pronouncing it, speech restores it to its full meaning. Mr Richard Church in his County Book on Kent laments a similar change at Curtisden Green, which used to be Courtesan Green. But his case is not as bad as mine, for Curtisden is one of the original "dens" in the parish of Goudhurst, so it is only a question of a still older name being restored. Nor can I feel quite sure that "its charming name was doubtless due to the fact that on this spot, where the Lords of Glassenbury were first settled before they went to the next hill, one of these lords must have set up an auxiliary *ménage* for his leman". These charming names have a way of arriving through mispronunciation by a people that dislikes consonants; and though Ladiesden Rokehurst appears as an alternative to Curtisden in some of the records, I find it hard to believe that if a lord's leman had lived here the name chosen for her would have been as foreign and flowery as courtesan. It is a sad fact, however, that in the nineteenth century Courtesan Green was discovered to be improper, and our surprise is that Horeham Road should have survived unquestioned throughout this period before disappearing in times that, so we have been told, were of almost Restoration licence.

I hope the reformers will not purify many more names of this type, especially the name of an old farmhouse between Brede and Ewhurst. Ellenwhorne tells us even more about its origins than Horeham Road. No anonymous harlot here, but Wicked Ellen. Long may she remain.

2

When I said that Hawkhurst was the most widely scattered village that I know, I must have forgotten Heathfield. Heathfield is scattered over a vast area and along innumerable roads, and the scatter is more wanton than at Hawkhurst, where it is mostly confined to the roads between three centres, all of which have good historic reasons for being where and what they are. But Heathfield is like a burst string of beads. The string has snapped and the houses have rolled in all directions. Most of them cluster about the station or along the road that runs from Woods Corner to Cross-in-Hand, but there is no shape or pattern anywhere.

Unlike Hawkhurst, too, only one part of Heathfield is really old, and that is hidden well out of sight behind the trees of Heathfield Park. The parish church is partly pre-Norman, but has been much restored. The tower, built of chalk and faced with local stone, bears the date 1445 in Arabic numerals, which is said to be the earliest use of these figures in England. Close to the church are some old cottages, and when we stand here the rest of the village is three hundred years away.

Heathfield Park was built—on the site of a much older house—towards the end of the seventeenth century, and later became the home of George Augustus Elliott, hero of Gibraltar and afterwards Lord Heathfield, who bought it with the prize-money he won during the French wars. The Gibraltar Tower in the grounds, however, was not built by him but by his successor, Francis Newbery, whose fortune had been made by the very different adventure of selling books. The tower stands in the highest part of the park and commands from the summit a truly wonderful view over the surrounding country. But it is not necessary for us to climb it in order to obtain a view. There are magnificent views from Heathfield in all directions, and indeed as long as we look away from the village we shall see nothing but what is beautiful.

The soil here is different from that we have trodden hitherto, for the Hastings Beds of marl and clay have given place to the

Tunbridge Wells Sand, and we are now on light peaty soil that favours the growth of pines and heather. In fact there is evidence that Heathfield derives its name directly from the ground on which it stands. Mawer and Stenton's *Place Names of Sussex* gives it as a compound of *hæp* and *feld*, "signifying a stretch of open land in the Weald", a blasted heath in fact. In Andredsweald the trees were not continuous, and there were open spaces, sometimes marshy, sometimes heathy. These would not make suitable pannage, and Heathfield had probably a later start than those villages which grew out of swine pastures. Certainly until it was "opened up" by the railway it was a very small and obscure place.

To-day it cannot be called either. It straggles along almost five miles of road on the crest of a ridge from which it scatters towards other villages north and south. If we travel eastward there are buildings nearly all the way to Cross-in-Hand, if westward it has linked up Cade Street, Punnett's Town and Three Cups Corner, none of which in the past consisted of more than one or two cottages and an inn. Its growth has been in three stages, and I give them as typical of many other places—first the old village, created by human needs in two worlds, then the ugly red-brick streets created by the railway, and all the red-brick villas attracted by the new civilisation, and finally the third civilisation of the motor-car, removing from the countryside the last reproach of dullness and stagnation and attracting herds of the urban-minded to live among the ruins of agriculture.

It is mainly this last which had changed the face of Heathfield. After the first world war the district, on account of its light soil, was seen to be especially favourable to poultry-keeping, and those servicemen who did not invest their gratuities in garages put them hopefully into chicken farms. The many high hopes that have been lost in that heady arithmetic, as well as the full disaster of the agricultural slump, may be seen in the good land that became building plots and has lined the country lanes with rows of shoddy houses. Those who have seen farm after farm brought to ruin by the premature removal of controls are thankful that for once the hard lessons of experience seem to have been learned, and the land is protected at least in some degree from those who would exploit it to urban advantage.

Heathfield is the seat of two flourishing legends. The first is that the cuckoo is not heard in Sussex until after Cuckoo Fair. At this fair he is said to be released by an old woman who carries him in her basket, but if so he has been her captive a long time, for Cuckoo Fair is held in the second week of April and generally the cuckoo has been heard in Sussex long before that. In the spring of 1951, which was particularly bleak, he called in Wagmary Wood near Beckley Furnace on the nineteenth of March. This of course is unusually early, for as a rule he is not heard until right at the end of the month or at the beginning of April, but he is seldom as late as Cuckoo Fair.

Others beside myself have noticed that there are fewer cuckoos now than there used to be. When first I came to live in my present home they made a veritable nuisance of their calling, which went on all day and sometimes also at night. Heard in the distance and among the voices of other birds, there is nothing lovelier than a cuckoo's call, and a duet between a cuckoo and a nightingale to which I once listened on a moonlight night will always remain a seductive memory. I would rather have too many cuckoos than too few; but every year we seem to hear them less, and I believe that this is so in other parts of the country. Is it that their numbers have been reduced or that another country has attracted their summer migration? France, perhaps . . . in which case their chance of survival is slender indeed, as they could come under the spreading doom of *la chasse*. I hope that there is no real justification for alarm at this decline, for it will be a sad spring indeed when the cuckoo no longer calls in Wagmary Wood.

Another Heathfield legend, and one which will be more difficult to dispose of, if indeed it is disposable, is that here Jack Cade was killed by a yeoman named Iden. There is eastward of the village a small hamlet known as Cade Street, where a monument proclaims that "near this spot was slain the notorious rebel Jack Cade, by Alexander Iden Esq.". Shakespeare, however, places the scene in Kent, in which case the setting becomes Hothfield, on the borders of the Weald—a name very like Heathfield, so the confusion is easy to explain.

The Idens were undoubtedly a Kentish family, and though part of their estate was in Sussex, at Iden, it was nowhere near Heathfield. Philipott, the topographer and historian, writing in 1659, states: "Of this family was Alexander Iden, Esq. who slew

61

Jack Cade . . . who shrouded himself in some of these grounds
which belong to Ripley Court, and lay not far distant from Hothfield." And then later—"In a field not far removed from Ripley,
a manor belonging to Alexander Iden Esq., was Jack Cade, that
counterfeit Mortimer, slain by Iden, who was invested with the
honour of knighthood. The age wherein he lived admired him;
nor shall there be any history for the future which shall not record him"—a prophecy which has certainly been fulfilled. Most
of the early historians write to the same purpose, and it was on
them evidently that Shakespeare based his scene in *King Henry VI*.

The supporters of Heathfield in Sussex write at a later date,
and write more cautiously of a "supposition". Indeed it is hard
to guess why Cade should have travelled over thirty miles into
Sussex at the collapse of his rebellion, which certainly took place
in Kent. Mark Anthony Lower in his *Worthies of Sussex* quotes
an old Heathfield tradition that Cade hid at a moated farm then
known as Newick but afterwards called Cade's Castle. The
tradition says further that Cade was playing at bowls in the
garden of an alehouse "when he was pierced by an arrow from
Mr Iden's well-strung bow".

As there were only five days between the proclamation putting
a price on his head (which was his reason for "shrouding himself")
and the arrival of that head in London, it is hard to see how he
found time to travel so far over bad roads, lie hidden for several
days in a farmhouse, and be slain in another part of the parish.
But Furley, who particularly dwells on this difficulty, declares
himself a convert from the Kent to Sussex theory, and writes
that "though Kent may claim the *Captor*, Sussex, I am now willing to admit, is entitled to the *Capture*". He attributes his conversion to the evidence of general historians as opposed to local ones.
The evidence of place-names he discounts, for Cade is not an
uncommon name either in Kent or Sussex, and in any case Cade
Street is no more than a corruption of the much older Cat Street,
which, though Mawer and Stenton dismiss it as "vulgo", may
be found in documents as early as 1288.

3

We are now some two miles east of Heathfield, but before we
go further on the road that narrows like a river as it approaches

its source at Woods Corner, I should like to comment on the almost universal tendency among Sussex topographers to refer to the village we have left as Heffull. Such no doubt it has been called in the past by the less articulate of its inhabitants, but if we are to take our pronunciation from these, rather than from others better mentally and dentally provided, we should at least be consistent and speak of Mumfull instead of Mountfield, Bursh instead of Burwash, or even Ystinks instead of Hastings.

The right pronunciation of the names of Sussex villages is a controversial subject. Even those who are not rural purists shudder when the Three-Lies-and-All-True (Ardingly, Hellingly and Hoathly) are jingled out of their proper stresses by ignorant strangers, and certainly Berwick near Lewes should not be pronounced in the same way as Berwick-on-Tweed. But there are other cases like Heathfield, where it would seem that the purists cling to names that were never thus written or indeed pronounced by the educated, and sound artificial and slightly ridiculous on the tongues of this generation. The village of Selmeston, for instance, they insist should be called Simpson. One day, doubting this, I sat by the wayside just outside the village and asked every likely inhabitant that came out, "What is the name of this place?" I obtained some astonishingly varied replies—enough to confirm my sympathy with the Domesday surveyors, who, we are told, were baffled by the native pronunciation of proper names— Selmeston (the favourite), Selmston, Semston, but never Simpson. No doubt it may have been called this in the past, for it is a characteristic of the local dialect to substitute *i* for *e*, but to insist on Simpson as if it were a parallel with Toaster for Towcester or Bister for Bicester seems as mannered and unreal as when a hitherto meticulously Oxford accent suddenly rolls into a broad *a* for Dallington, the village we come to next.

Dallington or Darlington or Dolington (correct in 1232) is visible for some miles before we reach it. Soon after leaving Three Cups Corner, the road, which has lost its tributaries from Burwash, Warbleton and Rushlake Green, and has narrowed almost to a lane, dips into the valley of Dallington Forest, where a little stream runs through the trees to join the River Dudwell. If we look across the valley we see Dallington on the hill beyond it, a lovely, homely sight with its old roofs and sturdy yet graceful

spire. The best time to see it is at sunset, when church and trees
and houses are blocked against the coloured light, which lingering also on the eastern meadow-slopes makes the tree-tops in
the valley to bud with fire.

To reach the village, we can either go up a precipitous little
lane on our right, or follow the main road to Woods Corner.
The latter should be our choice, for from Woods Corner we may
stand and gaze north and south and east and west over nearly
the whole of East Sussex. It is the country we have known all
the way, for we are not yet beyond the natural frontiers of Kent,
and it looks very like "a hilly sea", as it heaves and spreads towards
the coast, more broken with woods than we have hitherto found
it, for here we are in a lingering of Andredsweald—Dallington
Forest, Hazelden Wood and the immensely ancient and legended
Towncreep Wood were all here more or less from the beginning.

The spilt red bricks of Heathfield are far away, and when
we look in that direction we see nothing of it but a rare windmill. At Woods Corner we are on one of the highest hills in the
Sussex Weald—a hill on which only Brightling Needle and North
Seat (by Hastings) can claim to look down—and from our feet
flow miles of meadow and woodland with farms weathered
to their colours. The only lack that some might find is an oast-
house, for hops have long ceased to be grown in these parts,
and the oasts have fallen to other uses, which always end if they
do not begin with the removal of their white cowls, these being
far too much the wind's playthings to be preserved if they
are no longer working.

The abandonment of the hops is doubtless due to "those vile
sea-breezes", which are as inimical to them as they were once
thought to be to the female complexion. There are oast-houses
as close to the sea as Crowhurst, only a few miles north of Bexhill,
but these probably meant little more than the farmhouse's
private brewing for its own people, and did not involve chancy
matters of trade and profit. At Woods Corner we are still some
miles from the sea, but we can see it clearly and even smell it
when the wind blows from the south-west. A less clear but to
my mind a more enchanting view belongs to a day when the air
is still and a haze dances between the Swan Inn and the blue lake
which has Beachy Head for its western shore.

We can look out to sea all the way from the cross-roads here
to Dallington, a walk of under a mile along a road which has
no other destination on the signpost, though the adventurous
—preferably without their cars—may follow the little lane that
twists down the hill until it becomes knotted up with a veritable
mat of lanes. These wander like the cattle that first made them
from farm to farm, from Thornden to Lattenden, from Egypt
to Summertree, from Bucksteep to Redpale, and in and out
and on and on until in the end—if we have not completely lost
our way—we come to the comparative civilisation of Bodlestreet
Green.

Dallington village itself is small and refreshingly unmodern-
ised, though the church, on the contrary, has been entirely rebuilt
except for the tower. This tower is one of the four old church
towers in Sussex possessing a stone steeple, which accounts for
the combination of solidity and grace of its shape against the
evening sky.

On our return to Woods Corner, if we take the Netherfield
road we shall encounter a curious manifestation of that same
church spire. A rather battered version of it appears to rise
suddenly out of a field just above Christmas Farm, and is the
creation of Squire Jack Fuller, that eccentric patron of Turner,
who lived at Rose Hill nearby, and whose doings both in London
and in Sussex have become a legend. The story is that one day
when drinking with some friends he asserted that Dallington
church spire was visible from his house. His company denied it,
he continued to assert, and in the end a bet—a sound, substantial
eighteenth-century bet—was made. On his return to Rose Hill
he found to his consternation that his friends were right and the
steeple was out of sight beyond Woods Corner. Rather than lose
his money he took the cheaper course of having an imitation
steeple erected on his land, just where, as seen from the house,
it would look like a church spire rising above the hill. It may
have convinced his friends for a moment, and perhaps that
moment of their discomfiture was enough to console him for
the loss of his money.

Another explanation of the mock steeple which I have heard
locally is that the parish, both parson and people, objected to his
open consort with ladies of easy virtue, whom he admitted to

his house without dissembling. Infuriated by such prudery, he built a tower on the most conspicuous site he could find—a high field, close to the main road—for the sole purpose of entertaining his lady friends. If this story is true, which perhaps we may doubt, the ladies must have been exceptionally accommodating, for the tower offers no amenities beyond a floor and a door.

Fuller was twice a Member of Parliament and on one occasion was forcibly removed from the House by the Sergeant-at-Arms, for refusing to give way in a debate and insulting the Speaker. Being a Member of Parliament in those days was an expensive matter. Fuller's election cost £50,000, of which he paid £20,000 out of his own pocket, while the county provided the rest. Pitt offered him a peerage, but he declined it for the reason that "I was born Jack Fuller and Jack Fuller I'll die". He died in 1834 and is buried at Brightling, where there is a bust of him in the church and in the churchyard an odd sinister-looking mausoleum, shaped like a pyramid. I shall never lose my first impression of it many years ago, when I knew nothing of its history, but saw only its weird pagan shape among the crosses of a Christian churchyard, with two ghostly white peacocks moving in the shadows round it.

Brightling and Dallington are linked together, much in the same way as Newick and Chailey, Chalvington and Ripe and other village doubles peculiar, I think, to Sussex. Yet they are two distinct parishes and several miles apart. To reach Brightling we must continue the Netherfield road down the hill, past the mock-steeple and a charming little old white Nonconformist chapel, and then on and down and down again till we come to a crossroads rightly named Darwell Hole. Straight ahead the road climbs once more, to Netherfield and Battle, while Brightling is on the left, beyond and above the woods. But we shall be rewarded if we turn right for a mile or two and visit Penhurst, for here is beauty and here is peace.

Deep in the sheltered valley, reached only by a narrow lane, Penhurst Church and Churchhouse Farm have kept their joint watch through the centuries. They are one of the most perfect examples of a partnership I have already praised. Their kinship is proclaimed by the Caen stone in their walls—that stone which barges used to bring over from Normandy to Rye. There are no other buildings, just the two. The church is well worth a visit, for though it has been restored it has not been spoilt. The Ashburnham Chapel is there, with the tombs of certain members of that family who have lived a mile or two away at Ashburnham Place for many hundred years, and to whom the unspoilt, unchanging condition of this countryside is due.

The lane, so narrow that in places it will take single traffic only, rambles on to Brownbread Street, a small hamlet more easily reached directly from Woods Corner. The same can be said of Brightling. To both these places the cross-roads on the hill will take us more quickly than the cross-roads in the valley, and from the high road we shall have a splendid view which the low road would have denied us. Brightling Needle, erected by Squire Fuller, is one of those competing "highest points" in Sussex, and much of this country is actually higher than the Downs, which are deceptive because of their sudden rise out of a country almost at sea-level. I will not, however, determine whether Brightling Needle, North Seat, Chanctonbury Ring or Ditchling Beacon really is the highest.

Brightling, like Dallington, is small and unspoilt, but more scattered. In fact we may miss it altogether, for the little lanes that wind in and out of each other round the village are confusing, even to those who know them well. It is true that we could take the main road to Burwash, passing close to Rudyard Kipling's house, Bateman's, in the valley of the River Dudwell; but the byways are more exciting and enchanting, as they rush up and down many small hills and hollows, for unless you travel along the ridges it is impossible to go anywhere in these parts on a level road. We shall also pass farms and houses with names like Grandturzel, Squibs, Oldhole, Socknersh, while on the other side of Burwash ridge, in the valley of the Rother, a river we have met before nearer its mouth, we shall find Borzell, Churchsettle, Mountpumps and Shoyswell.

The country round here is rich in ancient houses, but most of them are very different from those we met in the flat countryside round Biddenden. For they are altogether more sophisticated, being in the hands of those who have spent time and taste and money on their restoration. They are set in pleasant gardens and have an air of trimness and prosperity. I will not say that this detracts from their beauty, and I acknowledge that it is a mere sentimental nostalgia that makes me think lovingly of the old Shoyswell that was in process of being dragged down by the weight of the ivy swags on its chimney into the waters of its own bowels. It certainly would not have stood long in that condition. But sometimes the restoration of these old houses has made them altogether too neat.

Socknersh is of special interest because of the four carved images that stand in pairs over its two doors. These are known as the Baby Eaters, and the first pair looks very fat and prosperous, evidently sated with childflesh, while the other pair, on the contrary, has a lean and hungry look, with chains about them to show they have been brought to justice. I have no idea, nor I think has anyone, whom they represent, but this legend of child-eating is very common in Sussex. The habit is attributed to the blameless Sir Goddard Oxenbridge of Brede Place, also to Colonel Thomas Lunsford of East Hoathly, who was a friend of Charles the First and equally irreproachable. In the case of Sir Goddard it probably has some symbolic origin and remained as a legend, but the Cavalier Colonel's peculiar habit was extensively adver-tised in print. It is mentioned in Butler's *Hudibras*, and recorded in sundry ballads, one of which tells how he was found when at the point of death to have a child's arm in his pocket. In those days political opponents stopped at nothing.

Burwash itself has a fine street of old houses, most notable among them the Rampyndene House, with its beautiful shell-like porch and delicately carved ceilings. This house represents a period and style of building rarer in Sussex than the heavier, darker, sturdier kind that is generally but erroneously called Tudor. There are, however, some good examples of the more familiar type in this same village street—old houses and cottages, many huddling together under a single roof, all mingling shades and depths of colour between red and brown. A row of clipped limes casts a grateful shadow on the sidewalk, and across the way, close to Rampyndene House, is the old pre-Norman church, containing an iron tomb which is said to be the oldest specimen of Sussex ironwork in existence—"orate p. annema Jhone Coline".

The names of two Burwash clergymen, the Rev. James Hurdis and the Rev. John Coker Egerton, have attained a modest fame outside their parish, or perhaps we should say have spread the fame of their parish in regions where it might otherwise be quite unknown, for they are valuable local chroniclers in prose and verse. Mr Hurdis is the poet; indeed for a time he was Professor of Poetry at Oxford, though at Burwash he was no more than curate for a non-resident rector. Those were the days towards the end of the eighteenth century when such arrangements were common. Being doubly of the same profession as Crabbe, he wrote *The Village Curate*, a long narrative poem in the same style as Crabbe's *Tales*. His style is lighter than his metre. Here are a few lines of blank verse which describe Burwash's annual donkey-race for the prize of a "lac'd hat".

> "Then comes the ass-race. Let not wisdom frown,
> If the grave clerk look on, and now and then
> Bestow a smile; for we may see, Alcanor,
> In this untoward race the ways of life.
> Are we not asses all? What ranting politician,
> What prating lawyer, what ambitious clerk,
> Is but an ass that gallops for a hat?
> For what do Princes strive, but golden hats?
> For diadems, whose bare and scanty brims
> Will hardly keep the sunbeam from their eyes.
> For what do poets strive? A leafy hat,
> Without or crown or brim, which hardly screens
> The empty noddle from the fist of scorn,
> Much less repels the critic's thund'ring arm."

That other clerical chronicler, the Rev. John Coker Egerton shows us the Burwash of a hundred years later. For nearly all the mid-Victorian era he was either curate or rector of the parish, and his true understanding of his parishioners and deep sympathy with them find expression in his book *Sussex Folk and Sussex Ways*, which if it is not a classic, ought to be. He is a student of social conditions as well as of human nature, and gives a very mixed account of those "good old days" which every Sussex

farm labourer says he wants back again, though one may wonder
how much he could enjoy

> "Pork and cabbage all the year,
> Mouldy bread and sour beer,
> Rusty bacon, stinking cheese,
> A chaff bed full of fleas."

As for his wife—

"When I was sixteen years old I was had out like a cow to
the market, and any farmer who wanted a servant come and
choosed one. I went first as nurse-girl and I got 1/3 a week.
Then I went to Early Farm in Wadhurst parish, and there
I was to have 1/6 a week—but then I'd more work to do.
I'd churning twice a week, and cheesing twice a week, and
brewing twice a week, besides washing and baking; and six
cows to milk every night and morning, and sometimes a
dozen pigs to feed. There were four men lived in the house,
and I'd all the biling to do—the cabbage and the peas and
pork for their dinners—besides all the beds to make; and
sometimes I did make'em in a fashion, that's sartin! One
morning, I mind, I got up at four and worked till twelve at
night, and then missus wanted me to pick a couple of ducks.

" 'No, Missus,' I says, 'I really can't; I be quite tired.'

" 'Tired?' says she; 'if I was a young woman like you I
should be ashamed of myself.' "

I wish we could stay longer with Mr Coker Egerton and hear
more of what he has to tell us about Sussex folk and their ways.
But it is time that we left Burwash and returned to the railway.
We are already well on our way back, for we have made a big
loop in the countryside—Heathfield, Woods Corner, Dallington,
Penhurst, Brightling and Burwash—and are now only about
five miles from where we started.

4

The next station to Heathfield is Mayfield, of which we may
already have caught a glimpse on our way back from Burwash.
Seen from the road between Burwash Weald and Broad Oak, it

appears a hill village, not unlike Rye, for the slope of red, ancient roofs is crowned by a church, which like the church at Rye has a square tower and a short, broad spire, more like a hat than a steeple. It is dedicated to St Dunstan, and stands on the site of a much older church which was destroyed by fire in 1389. This was the church beside which the Saint is said to have had his little cell, where he made beautiful and useful things of Sussex iron and played on his harp.

St Dunstan, whom we have met before as patron of Cranbrook, is of course the great man of Mayfield, and has, like the Cornish saints, become a part of folklore as well as hagiography. Just as a native of St Ruan will tell you that his saint was a giant and that those great stones you see were what he threw at St Kevin, so a native of old-time Mayfield would have told you that St Dunstan thrust the church from a leaning to an upright position with a heave of his great shoulder. It was while he was busy at his forge that the devil came to tempt him, disguised as a beauteous maiden. Unfortunately he did not know how to manage his unaccustomed skirts and the sight of his cloven hoof betrayed him to the saint, who immediately seized his nose in a pair of red-hot tongs. With a yell the devil rushed away and plunged his nose in the spring at Tunbridge Wells, giving it the peculiar flavour it has had ever since and also, it would seem, its medicinal properties. Surely it is a strange reversal of right order that cures should be wrought by the devil's nose.

The tongs with which St Dunstan did this deed are preserved in the convent adjoining the church, and it seems worse than frivolous of the Catholic Encyclopædia to dismiss the episode as a legend and, as a crowning insult, to transfer the scene of it from Mayfield to Glastonbury. It is true that St Dunstan was for a time an anchorite at Glastonbury, and that there is no evidence of his having set foot in Mayfield until he became Archbishop of Canterbury. But Archbishops, we know, can be tempted of the devil, and why should not one of them catch his nose in a pair of tongs? Besides, what about those tongs themselves? There they are for all to see—not at Glastonbury but at Mayfield.

The Convent of the Holy Child stands on the site of the former Summer Palace of the Archbishops of Canterbury, and what was once their dining-hall is now the convent chapel. The place became a ruin at the Reformation, and remained so until towards the end of the nineteenth century, when that holy and valiant woman Cornelia Connelly, founder of the Society of the Holy Child and one of the pioneers of what was in her time called "female education", discovered it while on a school picnic. After much struggle and the determined opposition not only of her foes but of her friends, she acquired the land and built the present school, which was for a time the mother house of her Order. The chapel and some other parts of the building are shown to visitors on certain days—and do not forget to look at the tongs.

Those tongs symbolise the fact that St Dunstan, like so many of the saints, was a citizen of two worlds and taught his people the arts of both. Besides being a great saint, who brought peace and order into the Church and Kingdom, he was also a great smith, who worked not only in iron but in gold. Some say that when the devil approached him he was making a golden ornament for the altar of Mayfield Church.

It is notable that in this story the devil has a much more homely appearance than in Milton's *Paradise Lost*, and so it is we find him in most of the Sussex legends. When he attempted one night to drown all the churches of the Weald by digging a dyke from Saddlescombe across the Downs and letting in the sea, he was frustrated by an old woman who lit a candle in her cottage near by. The silly devil thought it was the dawn, and fled in terror, leaving his work unfinished, and apparently did not dare return to it. Truly a very simple Satan, easily frightened and easily outwitted. He can be friendly too. There is a certain wood—I am sorry to say that I have forgotten its exact situation, but it is somewhere in the Downs—which he is said to haunt, but far from wishing to attack or scare you, if you walk round it three times he will bring you out a bowl of soup. The devil of Sussex legend may well be a pook or nature spirit lurking in his old haunts and eager for a restoration of past friendliness.

The old-time Sussex rustic was reputed never to speak the devil's name—he invariably referred to him as "he". In Parish's *Dictionary of the Sussex Dialect* occurs the following dialogue: " 'In the Down there's a golden calf buried; people know very well where it is—I could show you the place any day.' 'Then

72

why don't you dig it up?' 'Oh, it's not allowed: *he* wouldn't let them.' 'Has anyone ever tried?' 'Oh yes, but it's never there when you look; *he* moves it away.' "

But we seem to have fled from Mayfield with the devil, and should return at least for a look at its pleasant street and fine old timbered houses, notably the Middle House, which is now an inn and stands opposite the church. An inn is nearly as good a companion for a church as a farm, and from the garden of this one we may gaze across the Weald for as long a view as we had at Woods Corner; and though we cannot see the sea, we can see the Downs massing to the south-west in the blue distance that is so characteristic of the Weald. For we are here in the highlands of Sussex, and the soil is the Tunbridge Wells Sand that we found at Heathfield. Indeed there is very little else between us and the town from which it takes its name.

If we should decide to go there, though Tunbridge Wells itself does not properly belong to the Weald, we had better take the northward road through Mark Cross and Frant, for the railway begins to show a certain indifference as to its destination, and wanders off in the direction of Rotherfield, the station of which, however, is perversely on another line. It joins this line at Hodgate Hill, but the junction is some miles further north at Eridge. Here we may take our choice of Tunbridge Wells, East Grinstead or London, and I propose to go one station further towards the first of these, so that we may look at Groombridge, which is as lovely a village as any in Kent, where after this long ramble we find ourselves again.

5

Groombridge is in Kent, but there is in the village one house that shall be for ever Sussex. That is Court Lodge, which used some years ago to stand beside the church at Udimore. If there had ever been an award for the most perfect union of church and farm it would have been won by this pair, which maintained their lovely marriage until shortly before the first world war. It was in those days hard to tell which had most to offer of beauty and antiquity, the farm or the church. The charms of the former were perhaps the more obvious—an old timbered house of eight

73

The Causeway, Horsham

bays and many moulded shafts and corbels, it had a history going back far into Udimore's manorial times. King Edward the First, ridden over from his Summer Palace of Newenden, is said to have stood here and watched a battle between the French and English fleets in the great estuary which is now the marsh between Winchelsea and Rye. The church is more humble, with a homely, stunted air due to the fact that the walls of its tower are actually lower than the roof of the nave. More than almost any Sussex church it has the look of a sitting hen,   Indeed, in this alliance, unlike most similar ones elsewhere, the church appears to be the junior partner. But to the separate beauties of the house of man and the house of God must be added their united reflection in the farmyard pond beside them, and the comeliness of their position on this ridge which at one time used to be the coast of England, then running out in a spit between the mouths of the Tillingham and Brede rivers, now sinking into soft green marshes, with Winchelsea and Rye on their hills beyond.

The wicked divorce of this couple took place in 1912, and like many divorces followed long years of misery and degradation for one of the partners. From the death in 1690 of the last owner of the Manor of Udimore to occupy Court Lodge, the house was neglected and allowed to deteriorate. Formerly it stood on four sides of a court, but during two centuries three sides of it fell victim partly to natural causes—its situation exposed it fully to the Channel storms—partly to that human need for building materials which has been the destruction of so many old houses. For the last part of its life at Udimore it was broken up into farm-labourers' cottages, which in no wise detracted from its beauty but did not help its preservation; and when reasons of health and sanitation compelled the owner to choose between its demolition and spending a large sum of money on its repair, he decided, amid the groans of half a county, to pull it down. It was saved by the public-spirited action of Mr Lawson Wood, the artist, who bought the actual building, but as the owner refused to part with the site, there was nothing to do but engage a firm of experts to do what so often has been done before, but generally with a view to a transatlantic destination. Court Lodge was carefully and reverently take to pieces and carefully and reverently re-erected at Groombridge, where it stands to-day. In its place at Udimore is a row of hideous cottages, which time is just beginning to strip of some of its horrors, but which will never be worthy of its reflection with the church in the farmyard pond.

Groombridge did not give asylum to Court Lodge because of any local deficiency. There are some very fine old houses in the village, including an apple-red inn, and Groombridge Place itself has seen quite as much history as Court Lodge. It is a moated house and was once the prison of the Duke of Angoulême, where he was interned as a hostage before the Battle of Agincourt. It also belonged for a time to a Mr Packer, who was a friend of John Evelyn, the diarist. Evelyn often visited there and is said to have designed the garden.

In Groombridge we are in a country quite unlike that in which we have travelled hitherto, though it is geologically akin to the soil of Heathfield and Mayfield, indeed to the whole of Ashdown Forest further west. But here all round us are trees—trees of every growth and kind, no longer mainly oaks and ashes. Among them are those naturally associated with the bracken and heath which cover large tracts of Eridge Park, the seat of the Marquis of Abergavenny—the dark, austere pines and the delicate silver birches that follow the heather wherever it grows from Bournemouth to John o' Groats. We are quite remote from the typical scenery of the Weald, but we are still definitely of it, for we are on the ridge that separates north and south, from which the rivers flow, and where is said to linger some of the ancient character of Silva Anderida. It is of course a highly civilised, almost artificial survival, and it is typical only of certain aspects of the vanished wilderness. This we know contained among its thickets comparatively open spaces, sometimes heathy, sometimes marshy, sometimes filled with the lagoons of an excessive rainfall; and Eridge—like Broadwater, like Ashdown—no doubt carries a memory of the first of these.

The woods we know now in England are tame, domestic woods, bearing the same relation to the primitive forest as a dog bears to a wolf or a cow to a wild buffalo. A clearer picture of lost Anderida is given by any American forest on land that has no owner but the State. There are the thickets matted with creepers and savage thorns, the tall trees toppling and leaning together, too closely packed for the dead to fall, so that they die upright as it were in each other's arms, or else tear their neighbours to pieces as they crash to the ground; while in every hollow the swamp spreads round their roots, the black water thickened with broken, rotting wood. We have nothing over here, not even in Scotland, to suggest the full wilderness, denseness and struggle of old Andredsweald.

CHAPTER IV

A LOOP FROM LEWES

I

WE now enter Sussex—the true Sussex that has no part or lot in
Kent. The country of the Kentish Weald which overflowed
so far the Kentish border has disappeared, and in its place is a
landscape less sharply broken into different levels, more elegantly
wooded and parked. The building, too, has changed, though only
in a measure. We do not see the flint walls and lichen-yellowed
roofs that make us feel we are in another country when we have
moved, say, from Dallington to Firle; but most of the houses
have lost the apple faces they wore in Kent. At present the changes
are not striking, but if we look for them we shall find them everywhere.

Our journey begins in a Sussex that even a stranger would
recognise, because Lewes is surrounded by the Downs. Firle
Beacon and Mount Caburn are the pillars of its eastern gate.
Southward the Ouse flows between Bullock Down and Blackcap
Hill. To the west we go to Brighton between Newmarket Hill
and Stanmer Down with Ditchling Beacon beyond it; while to
the north the gate is watched by Malling Hill and Mount Harry.

Our railway escapes northward up the valley of the Ouse,
and our first stop is at Barcombe Mills. This is not the Weald
but peaceful river country, so we will travel on to Isfield before we
alight. Here we are still with the river—with two rivers, for the
Ouse's tributary, the Iron River, has joined us now. But Isfield
belongs to the Weald and to the road that climbs to Maresfield
and Ashdown Forest through a country of which the waves do
not break, but roll gently like a sea-swell.

It is a pretty village, made interesting by the remains of Isfield
Place, where the Shurley family once lived. The Shurley Chapel

in the parish church contains some beautiful and unusual tombs. On a canopied altar tomb Sir John Shurley, who died in 1631, lies with his two wives, and their nine children kneel in a row at their feet. An inscription states that some of these children were "called to heaven" and others into "several marriages of good quality", while of Sir John's second wife, Dorothy, it is charmingly said that "all her minutes were but steppes to heaven". Earlier, sixteenth-century Shurleys and their wives are commemorated in two fine brasses, while there are also some good examples of linenfold panelling and a leper's squint of more generous vision than we find as a rule. In the church itself was discovered in 1775 the tombstone of Gundrada, a daughter of William the Conqueror. Very little about her is known for certain, but she must have had strong local attachments, for her tomb had been in Lewes Priory until the dissolution of the monasteries, and its removal to Isfield was no doubt to save it from desecration. It has now been returned as near as possible to its first home, for it is at Southover, where a chapel has been built over it. Many more illustrious victims of the Reformation have had fewer amends made them.

The next station to Isfield on the line is Uckfield, a very different place. Here is no village but a fair-sized town. Perhaps it should be called a long town rather than a large, for apart from two delightfully named diversions on the side—to Puddingcake and Bird-in-Eye—it follows a long street down a hill, up another and then along the main road almost as far as Maresfield. It contains very little of interest. The church is not ancient, having been entirely rebuilt in 1839, though two seventeenth-century brasses survive from its earlier state. It is also the scene of a ghost-story, which I fear is typical of its kind. Some years ago a London newspaper described a ghostly manifestation in Uckfield churchyard to one of the town's inhabitants whose name and address it meticulously supplied. According to the newspaper the ghost had appeared through the churchyard railings. This naturally stirred the local Sussex paper, which with its credit for hot news at stake despatched a reporter to the scene. He found that no one of the name lived or had ever lived in Uckfield, nor was there anywhere in the parish such an address; and the churchyard had no railings. Otherwise, no doubt, the story was true.

Though lacking on the church side, Uckfield possesses a most admirable inn, to which I once fled from a pretentious hotel run on workhouse lines, to be welcomed with courtesy, hospitality, good food and good ale. Incidentally I was told by a delightful gipsy woman whose acquaintance I made during the war that Uckfield Workhouse (still real enough in those days) was one of the best in the kindgom for winter residence.

Outside Uckfield we are in the country of Ashdown Forest, almost on the borders of the forest itself, and we find what is rare in the Weald—a number of large rocks. Some of these are very large indeed, cliffs more than twenty feet high and able to hold their own with the famous High Rocks of Tunbridge Wells. Many are on the private property named after them The Rocks, but others are on open ground and some form the sides of the road from Uckfield to Piltdown via Puddingcake.

Piltdown, an open heathy space watched by cottages of which an alarming number receive "guests" or provide "teas", is now a golf course, but some millions of years ago it was the home or at least the grave of one of the very earliest of our race. It is now nearly fifty years since the Piltdown skull* was found and after examination was made the base of one of those reconstructions which are such a mystery to the lay mind. A model of the reconstructed head can be seen in the Barbican Museum at Lewes, and makes one wonder why it is that our pictures of prehistoric man all so uniformly represent him as of *horribile visu*. We know the shape of his skull, but can we guess how he looked inside it? A great many animals with hideous skulls (including ourselves) have pleasant countenances. Also the aboriginals of Australia, who are said to resemble primitive man more closely than any other living human beings, are far from bestial in their ways and looks. Those who have lived among them have found them not merely harmless, intelligent and artistically gifted, with all the human virtues of kindness, generosity, hospitality, but also capable of true affection and noble self-sacrifice. Of course the "black fella" is a very much more recent manifestation of humanity than Eoanthropus, our Piltdown Man. There is even now some doubt as to whether the Piltdown skull is a human skull at all and not one that

*The author died before the Piltdown skull was shown to be a fake.

79

belonged to some ancestor who had not yet received the Breath that made him a Living Soul. But one would like to know whether the scientific reconstruction of prehistoric man as a modified gorilla is inevitable or whether he might not just as probably resemble the *hrossas* or animal-men in one of Mr C. S. Lewis's delightful romances, with all the attributes of human personality in an animal body.

At Piltdown we find ourselves on that great western road the start of which tempted us at Silver Hill, but once more we turn away from it or rather follow it eastward towards Maresfield. On our way we pass two woods, one on the right and the other on the left. The one on the right is a freak, nothing more or less than a coppice of monkey-puzzles. It is not very large, but any group of these hideous trees larger than half a dozen has a startling appearance. On the left is something very different, a wood where, every spring, grows—or used to grow, for it is some years since I visited it in April—a carpet of wild daffodils. There is nothing lovelier than the sight of these delicate golden strewings, and soon there will be nothing rarer, for human rapacity is more fatal here even than in woods of bluebells and primroses. Daffodils, even the stouter garden variety, dislike being moved, and most of those hacked up by the trowel know no second spring.

On the way to Maresfield also is a military camp. The proximity of two large parks, to say nothing of Ashdown Forest itself, makes this part of Sussex an ideal military training ground. There were temporary camps here during both the first and the second world wars, but this camp looks as if it had come to stay. The Ashdown of early memories, when the only sound one heard as one lay in the heather was the tinkling of sheep bells, has been succeeded by an Ashdown from which rise bangs and cracks that can be naturalised with their surroundings only if one pretends that four centuries have rolled back and here is Master Huggett and his man John testing out the cannon they have made.

> "Master Huggett and his man John
> They did make the first can*non*."

Hogge's Place (Hogge or Huggett, he answered to either,

for in his day names were as fluid as their spelling) is not in Maresfield but in Buxted Park a mile or so away. Maresfield itself is a
small, attractive village, spoilt by its position at the junction of
two noisy roads—the road to the West and the road from London
to Eastbourne. All day long in summer the traffic tears down its
street, and on its outskirts have appeared all the camp-followers
of the car battalions—garages, snack-bars, tea-rooms. So, though
the old church is worth visiting for its two Norman windows and
the beautiful fourteenth-century barge-board over the north
porch, and though the birds sing sweetly in the tall trees
of what was once the Rectory garden, we will not linger
here but walk on to Buxted, not by the road but through
Buxted Park.

This park, like Maresfield Park behind us, has fallen a prey
to changed conditions and the builders. But there is a very
pleasant way through it to the next village, and in the midst of
it stands Buxted parish church, hidden from the majority of its
parishioners in the grounds of the Great House. This church
contains many interesting objects, including an Early English
font, the remains of a sedilia and a curiously placed aumbry,
also a fine old muniment chest. But to me the most beautiful
thing in it is the light, or rather the shadows of the trees which
the sun and wind send moving through the light until that too
seems to move and become a living thing.

2

Both Buxted and Maresfield are on the verges of Ashdown
Forest, which archæologists tell us preserves even more closely
than the forest land round Groombridge the character of ancient
Andredsweald. It is a wild, heathy expanse, broken with woods,
some of them very large and dark, and it stretches north from
Maresfield as far as Forest Row, while its eastern and western
boundaries are almost as wide apart as Rotherfield and West
Hoathly. From it flow three rivers, the Rother, the Ouse and
the Medway, all three setting out for three different points of
the compass from their springs under the heather.

But the heights of Ashdown are higher and sharper than elsewhere on this water-parting of the Weald, giving it under its

heathery cloak a Scottish shape, especially when seen from afar off. The best view of it is from the back of the High Street at East Grinstead, where you can stand in the garden of the Dorset Arms and look across the woods towards its lonely crouch against the sky. Seen from there, especially at twilight, it has a savage, feral look, totally unlike anything else in Sussex and a mocking contrast to the gentle Downs. These heights, hilly and bare, must look to-day very much as they looked five thousand years ago, when they rose above impenetrable miles of matted woodland, before the eastern Green Place had been cleared for men to dwell in.

Ashdown Forest does not, however, spring direct from Silva Anderida. In between comes Silva Regalis, the royal hunting ground. Indeed to that fact it owes its preservation—now secured by the Ashdown Forest Commissioners—and certain of its natural features. The clumps of trees, for instance, that crown its high places, mark where the king stood to watch the hunt being driven up towards him, much as the privileged hunters stand on an Indian *safari*. One of these clumps bears the name of King's Standing. The king was Edward III, and the game he hunted was wild boar and wild deer. Eventually he made over the hunting rights to John of Gaunt, who was succeeded by various hunting lords. Forest Row is where they built their hunting lodges and kept their huntsmen.

Cobbett did not think much of Ashdown Forest when he visited it in 1822. He calls it Ashurst Forest, and there is a mile or two from East Grinstead a village called Ashurstwood, but he means Ashdown, for he places it beyond Forest Row on the road to Uckfield. It probably looked in those days very much as it looks now, but Cobbett was no admirer of wild scenery. A man who loved to oppose his times, he jeered at the "picturesque" in much the same mood as he favoured Catholic Emancipation. He does not hesitate to call our Forest "the most villainously ugly spot I ever saw in England". We known that he liked to find comfort and prosperity on his rural rides, and like Jane Austen's Edward Ferrars had "more pleasure in a troop of tidy, happy villagers than the finest banditti in the world". But I doubt if the modern traveller on the road from Forest Row to Uckfield would agree that the scenery gets "if possible, uglier and uglier all the way, till at last, as if barren soil, nasty spewy gravel, heath and even that stunted, were not enough, you see some rising spots, which instead of trees, present you with black, ragged hideous rocks". These must be the rocks we admired in the neighbourhood of Uckfield, and thus he reflects on our taste: "There may be Englishmen who wish to see the coast of Nova Scotia. They need not go to sea; for here it is to the life." Truly the days seem far ahead when house-agents shall choose to advertise building sites on the margins of Ashdown Forest as "Scotland in Sussex".

Thirty years later Ashdown was still the subject of criticism, but this time on grounds of morality and respectability rather than of scenery. Indeed the writer's opinion of the latter seems exaggeratedly high, since though it is easy to see how the heathery expanses could suggest Scotland, or even Nova Scotia, I cannot really believe that anyone who had seen both could compare them to the Alps. But the local poet, Thomas Pentecost, calls them:

> "These Alpine hills of wide expanse
> (That fill the heart with wild romance)."

He then goes on to deplore the godless state of the denizens of the Forest, which seems in those days to have been infested with tramps and gipsies:

> "A heathy waste of huts and dens,
> Where human nature seldom mends;
> No polished schools, but turfy fires,
> Afar away from village spires. . . .
> Idly, (far from example's sway),
> In groups among the ferns they lay."

How trusting was our forefathers' belief in the strength of example. I am old enough to remember its constant use as an incitement to good behaviour, and how we hated the Good Examples themselves and rejoiced in their falls from grace, thus transforming the mere naughtiness of childhood into the malevolence of friends.

Through lack of Good Example the wretched inhabitants of Ashdown sank ever lower and

" . . . in some hidden nook, where reigns
Confusion, to distract their brains,
At some sly ginshop, sickening sight,
Profane the day, meet, drink, and fight. . . .
Then, O my harp! wail with the winds,
Nor cease till Ashdown yet amends."

The poet who, as we may gather from this example of his genius, was also a preacher, would doubtless consider Ashdown Forest much amended now, though to Cobbett it would appear as villainous as ever. The Commissioners have preserved what are called "amenities", whether scenic or human, and the gipsies make only a furtive and transitional appearance, while it is the sly tea-shop rather than the ginshop that we have to fear at the hamlet's edge.

Walking, cycling or motoring where Cobbett rode, we may view with a very different eye those tawny hills of brake and heather that sweep up from the road. The heather which he calls stunted must have sprung into a fresh growth since his day—unless his prejudices had affected his observation—for like most south country heather it grows almost arboreally, and some of the clumps have the appearance of small shrubs. Ashdown Forest is particularly well served with roads, and we may travel across it not only by the central line from Forest Row to Uckfield, but diverge at Wych Cross to its western borders and its western (Chelwood) Gate; or on the east we may go south past Fisher's Gate and Friar's Gate and the shady verges of Five Hundred Acre Wood into the bareness of Crowborough Warren, and then past King's Standing down the hill, past Duddleswell in its shady withdrawal, to Fairwarp and thence by Barn Gate to the fields again. There is also the less open road from Crowborough to Uckfield, by way of Heron's Gyll, with its pretty little Roman Catholic church, and Five Ash down with its large and hideous public house. But the loveliest road of all, and the loneliest, runs east from the Wych Cross road near Vetchery and cuts right across the wild heart of the forest to King's Standing. Here on its narrow open stretch we are so close to the heather that we can smell the honey and hear the bees, and unafflicted by the dust of passing cars we can stand and gaze southward to where the royal gold and purple of the Forest melt into the soft blue of a normal Sussex horizon, while over us flows the fresh yet gentle wind which is Ashdown Forest's especial gift and grace on a summer's day.

3

We have wandered far from the railway that brought us to Uckfield, though by another route we have visited Buxted, which is the next station. Difficulties of construction keep the line in the valley—a valley of little nameless streams, for we have not yet reached the springs of the Rother. These break under Rother-field, which shares with Crowborough the next station. It used to be called Rotherfield Station, but the superior claims of a rising Crowborough made the officials hesitate, and finally compromise with the name of Jervis Brook, which is the inconsiderable hamlet next the line. Both Crowborough and Rother-field are about a mile above the valley, standing east and west of the railway on their separate hills. Rotherfield is slightly the nearer of the two—in its heart and centre, that is to say, for Crowborough merges with Jervis Brook almost at the station, and the houses line the road in various degrees of density all the way up to the Beacon.

Rotherfield does not actually belong to Ashdown Forest, though the parish forms a part of that sandy watershed where the rivers are born. In appearance it is not unlike its neighbour Mayfield (which is now only a few miles away on the other line), being a cottaged hillside tapering to a church. But in Rotherfield the houses are more scattered, and the church instead of a shingle cap wears a tall, graceful spire. This is a landmark for many miles around, and mercifully takes the eye from other parts of the village, which, as if it had caught the infection of its neighbour, has allowed too much indiscriminate building of the villa type.

The church itself is Early English, but is on the site of a much older one, built by a Saxon chief in thanksgiving for his cure at the shrine of St Denys, to whom it was, as it still is, dedicated. The present church contains some interesting vestiges of mural paintings—the Annunciation on the splay of the east window, the Incredulity of St Thomas on the west arch, Domesday over the chancel arch, while on the wall of the south aisle is the painting of a fish.

These are all that survive of paintings which at one time no doubt covered the whole interior, as part of the normal decoration of a church. In days when the Scriptures could not be read because printing had not yet been invented, and the method of hand-copying and illuminating was far too slow and costly for the average purse, the events of the Old and New Testaments were kept in the people's minds by pictures and by plays. The plays we know through those that have come down to us, such as the York Cycle, which every year at Corpus Christi was performed by the city's various trade guilds, and which was revived and performed in the Cathedral for the Festival of Britain in 1951. But there were also many others, humbler performances in humbler places, of which traces remain in the West Wittering Tipteers' play, in folklore, and even in children's games. As for the pictures, the parish church was a Bible picture-book, of varying comprehensiveness and doubtless still more varying talent. At the Reformation and later during the Commonwealth the pictures were blotted out with whitewash, to which no doubt many of them owe their preservation and later re-emergence, as at Rotherfield. In their day they must have made the church a gay and coloured place, in which every picture indeed told a story. The windows told stories, too, in the jewels of their stained glass, and if in consequence the church was dark, what of it? For it was a gay, rich, merry darkness, and anyway nobody but the priest could read.

By way of contrast, on the outside many churches were white, being covered for their preservation with a wash of lime and tallow, which modern architects have recently discovered as the cheapest and most effective way of keeping out the weather. In the past this wash was used to cover not only churches but abbeys and cathedrals, and we may step for a moment out of our time and place to contemplate a snow-white Westminster Abbey, adorned with innumerable coloured saints, rising like a huge decorated wedding cake above the gables of a smokeless London. In those days Rotherfield church no doubt was also white and glistening; and the country round it would have shown just as strange a picture of itself, with a few sandy roads linking scattered pastures, beyond which lay the Forest untamed and nothing but the heather on Crowborough Beacon.

To-day the Beacon is the site of a large hotel, and round it cluster other hotels and guest-houses, while a plenitude of villas and *cottages ornées* swarm about the golf course. What a transformation the railway has brought just to this one place! To Rotherfield, Mayfield, Heathfield and Uckfield no doubt it brought changes and additions, but Crowborough was made by it entirely—its own creation. It is true that among all the welter of new buildings remains a small stone house where Richard Jefferies lived for a few years, but among so much that is new the old wants seeking out and is hard to find. Certainly before the railway came there was no building at all on wild and lovely Beacon Hill, but the late E. V. Lucas records in his *Highways and Byways in Sussex* that when he visited it in 1903

"the walls and fences of Crowborough were covered with the placards of a firm of estate agents describing the neighbourhood as 'Scotland in Sussex'. . . . Never was a fine, remote hill so be-villa'd. The east slope is all scaffold-poles and heaps of bricks, new churches and chapels are sprouting, and the many hoardings announce that Follies, Pierrots or Conjurers are continually imminent."

Things are not quite as bad as that now, for "development" (that abused word) has reached its end, and its ugly preliminaries no longer scar the earth. Houses that appeared soon after the railway have lost their raw looks, and everywhere trees and gardens are softening the view and helping us to forget all that has been done to spoil one of the loveliest places in Sussex.

Also it would be ungenerous to leave Crowborough without giving it the credit (and its despoilers the excuse) of one of the best climates in Britain. Here we are still within the sunshine belt of the South Coast, but bracingly high above sea-level, while the sea-winds have been tempered and sweetened by many miles of heather. From Crowborough the whole of Sussex seems to fall away in blue and violet ridges, and all about us on the heights are the pine-trees and the heather, aromats of health.

Withyham adjoins Crowborough, indeed the parish of St John's, Withyham, is almost part of it and provides a pretty little church-in-the-wood for those whose doctrinal views are opposed to those of the other parish church on the hill. The ancient church of Withyham itself and the main village are some miles away, beyond picturesque Ley Green, from which they are most pleasantly reached by a walk through Buckhurst Park, the ancestral home of the Sackvilles. In the church are many interesting memorials of the family, one of which is the work of Flaxman, while another is by Chantry. Nothing dates from earlier than the seventeenth century, for in 1663 Withyham Church shared the fate of other Wealden churches we have noted, and was totally destroyed by lightning.

4

If we had not forsaken the railway at Jervis Brook we should soon have found ourselves once more on the line which we followed some time ago from Polegate and purposefully bound for Tunbridge Wells. In order to reach Withyham it would have been necessary to change at Eridge, so in walking from Crowborough across Buckhurst Park we have certainly chosen the quickest as well as the pleasantest way. The railway now has abandoned its course from south to north and is running from east and west along a wide shallow valley which is strangely enough the valley of the Medway. That river is a Sussex river now— fresh from its springs in Ashdown Forest it flows beside the line, a small stream with no hint of its future greatness.

On its southern bank is Hartfield, our next village, only a little larger than Withyham and with even less to interest and detain us. Castle Field, north of the village, probably marks the site of the hunting lodge of the Barons of Pevensey, and further north still are the ruins of Bolebrook, once the home of the Dalyngruges who built Bodiam Castle. The two capped towers that flank its gateway suggest a castellated mansion of the Sissinghurst type, and as at Sissinghurst, and as we shall soon see at Brambletye, they give an air of strangeness and mystery to an otherwise quietly pastoral landscape. Here we are in the low, flat, sandy country between Ashdown Forest and the Kentish border—a border which becomes the Surrey border further on, where three

88

counties meet in the fields outside East Grinstead, close to the
ruins of Old Surrey Hall.

Brambletye is our chief, if not our only, reason for alighting
at the next station on the line, for Forest Row in these days is,
I fear, a mess. First the railway and then the car have exploited
its situation on the very edge of Ashdown Forest and not much
more than thirty miles from London. The few old cottages in
its climbing street have been cluttered up with unplanned, un-
restricted building. Some of the houses are very handsome, for
we are here on the fringes of what is sometimes called Stockbrokerland, and money has not been spared. But the general effect
is dolefully suburban, especially to those who remember the older,
quieter place. Originally, as we have seen, Forest Row was where
the hunting lords kept their retainers—their huntsmen, their
hounds, their horses. It is right at the Forest's edge, looking towards the beautiful wooded slopes of Hindleap Warren. Such
names as Hindleap, with the Roebuck Inn at the crest of the hill,
and Hartfield in the valley below reveal the nature of the game
that the lords and ladies hunted here in far-off days.

To those days belong also the ruins of Brambletye, in the
fields below the village, on the banks of the infant Medway.
The two crowned turrets of the gatehouse, reminiscent both of
Sissinghurst and Bolebrook, are almost all that survives of the
once ornate and imposing residence of that great Sussex family
the Lewknors. In its green sunny valley Brambletye has now a
pastoral air, and it is restful to sit under its walls and watch the
little stream which shall become so fine a river slide by between
fields of grazing cows and sheep. It must have looked very different in the days of its prime, and early in the last century it was
made the subject of a romantic novel, *Brambletye House* by Horace
Smith, which I have not even attempted to read, though contemporary critics took it seriously as a rival to *Waverley*.

From Brambletye and Forest Row it is only a very few miles
to East Grinstead, but we shall be wise if we do not go there
by the train, but return to Hartfield and there take once more
the road to Kent, with the towers of Bolebrook rising out of
the western fields, and ahead of us some of the loveliest country
in Surrey, Kent and Sussex.

Cowden is in Kent, and was at one time a great and prosperous

89

centre of the iron industry. Its name, according to Furley, signi-
fies "a pastoral site among the dens", though when the historian
wrote to the parson to inquire as to the other "dens" in the
parish, he was told in reply that there was only one and that was
the Parsonage. Iron and slag are still abundant in the neighbourhood, and abundant too are the place-names of the industry—
Hammer Wood, Hammer Pond, Furnace Pond, Spood, and so
on. The site of the village is low, and in June 1703 a disastrous
flood did great damage to the industry by breaking down the
pond bays. Let those who declare our summers are deteriorating
take note of the date.

The village of Hammer Wood is in Sussex, and between it
and Kent lies Holtye Common. This has by now shared the almost
universal fate of commons in the South and become a golf course,
but the adaptation has been discreetly done and has not spoiled
its charms, which, moreover, depend less on its own beauty
than on the beauty that can be seen from it. From Holtye one may
gaze southward over the valley of the Sussex Medway to the
heights of Ashdown; while northward the North Downs rise
above a low wooded countryside which is mainly Surrey but
equally belongs to the Weald. As a girl I spent many happy days
at this meeting-place of three counties, and a favourite excursion
by bicycle or by carriage (for the car, though existing as an object
of terror to horses, had not yet become an inevitable means
of transport) was to Holtye Common and back by the Gated
Road.

This road dipped deep into the valley of the hammer ponds—
a long green sequence that once worked the hammers of Cowden;
but deep as it dipped, there were ancient houses below its level,
for at one happy place it ran along what must have been the top
of the dam. One could look down on a vast tawny hill of roof
or find oneself in a sweet blue fog of wood-smoke from a chimney. Later the road too sank down to the ponds, and entered a
green enclosure between high banks and shadowy woods.
Every now and then a beautiful old house would reveal itself
among apple-trees or farm-steading. It was no hardship to jump
off the bicycle or stop the trap to open (and most carefully shut)
the gates that prevented the stock of all these valley farms from
straying. At the end of the valley, beyond Scarlets Mill, the road

which all this while had been Kent climbed steeply into Surrey,
and brought us home by way of Lady Cross and Wilderwick.

I took the Gated Road again not long ago, and all the gates
were gone. Though the old houses remained they had been
trimmed and dolled up into "gentlemen's residences"—which
of course they originally were. It was the intervening stage of
being sliced into draughty tenements for farm-workers that was
the abuse and the anachronism. The house that was built and lived
in with pride by a rich ironmaster from Cowden may now just
as appropriately be lived in with pride by a rich stockbroker
from London, which in these days is as conveniently placed for
the valley of the hammer ponds as Cowden used to be. Moreover,
the houses have a far better chance of survival than as workers'
homes, so perhaps it is rather simple and unrealistic to regret
such changes.

5

It might be debated whether East Grinstead or Haywards
Heath is the rightful capital of Stockbrokerland. Haywards
Heath has the advantage of being on the main line, but if you
have a car (and what stockbroker has not?) the distance from
London by road to either is about the same. East Grinstead has
the advantage of being near Ashdown Forest, while Haywards
Heath is nearer the Downs. East Grinstead is undoubtedly more
beautiful and interesting as a town, but it is now perhaps rather
too close to the new expansions at Crawley to be relied on to
maintain this superiority for any length of time.

Whatever may be its status in Stockbrokerland, East Grinstead is the capital of north-east Sussex, and for many years was
an assize town, sharing the honour with Lewes, Horsham and
Chichester. The long, unwieldly shape of Sussex—with its
official capital at one end and its cathedral town at the other,
nearly a hundred miles apart—made travel very difficult during
the centuries of bad roads and slow, unwieldly transport. So
for greater convenience the assizes were held in what were,
roughly speaking, the four corners and the various criminals
parcelled out according to the setting of their crimes. The
Judge's House at East Grinstead is lovely to see, and so are
many other old houses in the wide High Street. Here already we

have the slabbed roofs that will become more numerous and more striking the nearer we approach Horsham. A roof of Horsham slate presupposes exceptionally strong construction beneath it, for its weight is enormous, making it quite unsuitable for any form of jerry-building, whether of the present or of the past. Sometimes in days gone by a roof of Horsham slate would, either out of ignorance or vanity, be put on a cottage or small house unable to bear it. These places were called in mockery "Slab Castles", and often the name has survived the house.

East Grinstead once had a theatre, which stood in the High Street and was supplied by visiting companies. A contemporary playbill announces a performance of "Theodosius; or the Force of Love", the lead being played on successive nights by "Mr P. Varanes, who will strive as far as possible to support the character of the fiery Persian Prince, in which he was so much applauded at Hastings, Arundel, Petworth, Midhurst, Lewes, etc." and by "A young gentleman from the University of Oxford, who has never appeared on any stage". The gifted amateur was more popular in the eighteenth century than he is to-day, and this is by no means a solitary instance of his making his début (probably for a consideration) with a seasoned theatrical company. The playbill concludes with the rather pathetic announcement that "the great yard dog that made so much noise on Thursday night during the last act of King Richard the Third, will be sent to a neighbour's over the way".

No doubt it is the cinema which has killed these companies of strolling players who for so long brought entertainment to places very much smaller than East Grinstead. The last I can remember was a family affair which used to visit Rye. It was ruled by a grandmother and the cast was almost entirely made up of her descendants. It stayed in the town for three weeks and every night performed a different play. Though the play itself was never repeated, each day of the week featured a different type—farce one night, tragedy the next, musical comedy the next, and so on. There was a matinée for children on Saturday, while Friday night produced a performance "for adults only". Not one of these plays had I ever seen or heard of before, and I suspect that many of them, like Shakespeare's, were actually written in the theatre. This most engaging survival was brought sadly to an end by Grandmother's death near Lewes shortly before the war.

6

East Grinstead was a great railway centre. I use the past tense because nationalisation threatens to rob it of at least two of the four lines that converge at its two stations. These are on two different levels—the Upper Level and the Lower Level—which in my youth belonged to two different companies, who carefully arranged their time-tables so as to avoid any possible connection. The hope that the train for Forest Row might be two minutes late, and so allow us to catch it from Dormans Land, was never realised.

No doubt East Grinstead will still be left in communication with London and with Lewes, but one cannot deny that in these days Horsham and Tunbridge Wells are both more easily reached by road. We are now on our way back to Lewes, and glide out of the town on a line which may take us there direct by way of Horsted Keynes and Chailey, or else light out across country via Ardingly and bring us in most grandly by the main line.

Our first station, Kingscote, need not detain us, for it is now little more than a suburb of the town we have just left, but the station beyond it brings us to West Hoathly, a charming, secluded village on the western borders of Ashdown Forest. It has no connection whatever with East Hoathly (except that both are pronounced Ho-lye), though it is not so far from it as East Grinstead is from its western namesake. We could have visited East Hoathly when we were on the other side of the Forest at Heathfield, but the village though quiet and pleasant has nothing much to interest us beyond the house once occupied by William Turner, whose now well-known Diary sheds such a depressing light on a small village community in the mid-eighteenth century.

At West Hoathly, too, light is shed on the past, but in a different manner. In the venerable Priest's House opposite the church is a kind of Sussex domestic museum which provides a fascinating opportunity for the reconstruction of the life that is gone. When E. V. Lucas visited the village some fifty years ago this house had been "allowed to forget its honourable age". Since then it has been acquired by the Sussex Archæological Society, which has restored it and furnished it with beautiful objects that were once in daily use by quite humble people.

As I have said earlier, I have no predilection for the Good Old Days, but they certainly contained far less of useful ugliness than the present times, and whether you poked the fire or boiled the kettle or lit a candle or sat down to supper or pulled up the quilt in bed you handled things that were good to look at as well as admirably suited to their function. Nor can one deny that the smock was a more becoming garment than a boiler suit, and when complete with boots and leggings very much more practical than the corduroy trousers tied at the knee which filled the gap between its disappearance and the presentday agricultural uniform of dungarees and wellingtons. Those heavy linen smocks, the last of which I can just remember, were of incredible weight and durability, often passing from father to son, while they displayed the skill of wives and sisters in the beautiful and elaborate needlework which has taken from them its name of "smocking".

At West Hoathly we are back on the heights of Ashdown and once more in the country of the rocks. Names appear like Stonelands and Rockhurst, and on the latter estate is a truly remarkable rock, or rather two of them, one piled on the other, Big-on-Little. They are enormous and rather terrifying, with "bare broad white foreheads" (to quote an eighteenth-century visitor) and giving an impression of insecurity, as if before long inevitably Big must tumble off Little and crush the spectator to smithers. Cobbett, who we know did not like rocks, describes them with a considerable degree of irritation, which also reflects his own puzzlement as to how they ever got into such a position.

"How then *came* this big upon little? What lifted up the big? It balances itself naturally enough, but what tossed it up? I do not like to *pay* a parson for teaching me, while I have *God's own Word* to teach me; but if any parson will tell me *how* big came upon little, I do not know that I shall grudge him a trifle. And if he cannot tell me this; if he say, All that we have to do is to *admire* and *adore*; then I tell him, that I can admire and adore without his *aid* and I will keep my money in my pocket."

Of course Big never was tossed up, but merely revealed in its situation above Little through processes of soil erosion. We are back here on the sandy water-parting of the Weald, where the sand has in many places been washed away from those solid lumps of itself that are the sandstone rocks. We saw them at Uckfield and at Maresfield, and they are also here at West Hoathly and more famously at Tunbridge Wells. I have a vivid memory of these rocks as a very small child, when my father, who always wanted to climb anything that could be climbed, caught his foot in a cranny of one of them and could not pull it out. I clearly recall that my chief emotion as I watched him struggle was the hope that he would never be able to get his foot out, but would remain permanently fixed to the rock. My father was quite the favourite inhabitant of my small world, and I should besides have been frightened to death had I been left to make my way home without him, so what atavist urge impelled me to wish him permanently attached to the scenery is for the psychologist, if not the anthropologist, to determine.

7

Our next station on the way back to Lewes is Horsted Keynes, and before coming to it we pass close to Ardingly, though Ardingly station is on a branch line connecting the line we are on with the main line from Lewes to London. The most conspicuous feature of Ardingly as seen from the railway is the huge red-brick schoolhouse, but hidden away in the church are some interesting brasses of the Wakehurst family, whose Wakehurst Place is not far off. There is also a most remarkable brass of Nicholas Culpeper (relative and namesake of the herbalist) with his wife, ten sons and eight daughters. This part of the country is thickly wooded, for we are on the eastern edge of Worth Forest, which equally with Ashdown is a survival of old Andredsweald, though more closely timbered and with fewer open spaces.

The name of Horsted Keynes is interesting because it is one of the few double place-names in the Weald. These double names, so common in the western counties, are rare throughout Kent and Sussex. At the moment, besides Horsted Keynes, I can think only of Tarring Neville in Sussex and those two beautifully named border villages of the Kentish Weald, Boughton Malherbe and Boughton Monchelsea. The "Keynes" distinguishes Horsted from Little Horsted, a few miles away, and represents the Keynes family whose name is the original de Cahanges minced up by the local tongue. The de Cahanges came here with William the Conqueror, and the knight in armour who, with a lion at his feet, lies on a tomb in the parish church is probably one of them.

A seventeenth-century Rector of Horsted Keynes, the Rev. Giles Moore, has left some past accounts which give food for present thought. He furnished a bed with blankets, bolster, curtains, valance, "coarse 8 qr. coverlett" and "fine large coverlett with birds and bucks" for £7 17s. The main cost was the "fine coverlett", which must have been something very special, if we compare its price of £2 10s. with that of the curtains and valance (and the curtains would have been large enough completely to enclose the bed) at £1 8s. and the two blankets at £1 4s. The whole outfit was bought from "William Clowson, upholsterer and itinerant, who comes about the country with his pack on horseback".

The price of medical attention varied, and was in any case much less than for upholstery. When his maid was ill he paid only fourpence for "opening her veine", while the same operation on himself cost half a crown. But then the maid was bled by a lay practitioner, "the widow Rugglesford", while he was bled professionally by the barber-surgeon. He did not, however, neglect his sick maid, but paid a shilling to "Old Bess for tending on her three days and two nights".

He found it economical to pay a fixed price annually for his barbering, which otherwise cost a shilling a time. In 1658 the sum was sixteen shillings, but in 1671 it had risen to eighteen. There is no suggestion that it also included surgery, but the practical parson deducted one and sixpence for his tithes. He evidently had trouble in extracting tithes from his flock, for he advises his successor: "Never compound with any parishioner till you have first viewed their land and seen what corn they have upon it." But this financial caution did not prevent him being generous on occasion. When Charles II was crowned he gave ten shillings to a young bride married on the same day and sixpence to the fiddlers at her wedding, while "to the collections made at three several sacraments I gave three several sixpences". To his wife he gave no less than fifteen shillings to spend at Lindfield Fair, but the careful woman kept back half a crown, "which she never returned me".

We have been moving rapidly towards Lewes along the western verges of Ashdown Forest and at Sheffield Park station we are back in the valley of the Ouse. The Park itself, which is only a little way off, was at one time closely associated with cricket, which was played not only on one of the best private cricket grounds in the kingdom, but also in the exceptionally hard winter of 1890–91 on the ice of the frozen lake. A frequent visitor to Sheffield Park was Edward Gibbon, a close friend of the first Earl. He lies buried in Fletching church nearby, among the monuments of the Sheffield family. Other and more incongruous companions of the tomb are Sir Walter Dalyngruge (it seems a pity that this fine name should have died out even in its derivatives) and Petrus Denot, a glover who followed Jack Cade and is commemorated by a little brass with gloves on it.

Fletching is only a mile or two from Piltdown, showing how our loop has narrowed as we approach Lewes. The line, however, now leaves the River Ouse, or rather the River Ouse leaves the line, for that persists on its way south with true railway directness, whereas the river turns east before it flows south again with nearly as many windings as the Cuckmere. The surrounding country, however, remains flat and low, for we have left the heights of Ashdown far behind us and are among well-tended parks and park-like woods and water-meadows fed by the Longford Stream.

The twin villages of Newick and Chailey share a station between them, one on the east and the other on the west. There does not seem to be any reason why these two should invariably be linked together, for they are no nearer or more like each other than any other couple of villages; nor has the building "development" from which they both suffer made Siamese twins of them by any connecting ligament. Indeed that is never likely to happen, for no through road runs between them. To travel from Newick to Chailey, you must follow the great west road of Sussex to the cross-roads by the King's Head Inn, and then turn south for a mile and a half along the road from Wych Cross to Lewes. There is a way cross-country, but it is tangled with small lanes and steep with changing heights. Chailey village lies in the valley of the Longford Stream, almost at railway level, while Newick is on comparatively high ground and on the same ridge as Maresfield and Uckfield further east.

West of the cross-roads and high above Chailey is Chailey Common, quite the most beautiful place in the parish. From its heathery expanse, unspoilt and even adorned by the graceful buildings of the Heritage Craft Schools, with their windmill and steepled water-tower, we can look right over meadowy, wooded slopes to the Downs as they rise beyond Lewes—Ditchling Beacon, Plumpton Plain, Blackcap and Mount Harry, stretching in a line towards the west. Chailey village itself is in the foreground, just below us, though we get a better view of it further away on the Haywards Heath road, from which its compact shape and clustered cottages give it the air of a bird's nest full of fledglings. Seen at close quarters neither Newick nor Chailey is very attractive. The churches of both have been much restored, though Chailey's has a pleasing pyramidal spire and in the churchyard two fine old yew trees.

We can now return to the railway and follow the Ouse into Lewes, with one last station at Barcombe just across the river from the Barcombe Mills which was the first station when we set out; or we can descend on Lewes from the heights, like Simon de Montfort's men when from their camp at Fletching they swept down to fight King Harry. Lewes does not properly belong to the Weald. The hill it climbs from the marshes of Iford and The Brooks is a foothill of the Downs, and at every scar the chalk gapes and in every unkempt field the poppies grow. But having found ourselves in Lewes it will be hard to leave it, for the capital of Sussex, in spite of changes, is still very much the lovely, homely place it used to be.

The sunny street and shady byways of Southover in the valley, the old houses clustered round the castle on the hill, the sudden soaring view of Saxon Down from the top of High Street, or the spreading view of Front Hill, Highdole and Newmarket from the churchyard of St Anne's, or indeed the view of Lewes itself from the high turn of the road above Malling, are only a few of its exterior charms; while within it are the private beauties of old churches, old inns, old houses, divided by old alleys with queer, twisted names, and old gardens shady with medlar and mulberry trees.

> "For Lewes town like heaven is,
> And heaven is like Lewes town."

This may be an over-statement and Lewes can certainly be hell on Gunpowder Night, when the sky is red with fire and the blazing barrels bounce down the High Street towards the river—hell too in a smaller way when the races are on and the traffic grinds and jostles through a town the streets of which can neither be widened nor by-passed. But both these activities, especially the first, have the beauty of tradition and are a historic part of the life of the place, so we cannot quite withhold our blessing from them. Nor even if unable to see Lewes as the heavenly Jerusalem can we deny that in one respect at least it resembles its earthly counterpart—The hills stand about it.

CHAPTER V

TO HORSHAM BY THE ADUR AND BACK
BY THE ARUN

I

WE have now left East Sussex. The boundary between east and west runs from the Surrey border by way of Crawley, Cowfold, Twineham and Edburton, and then through the Downs to Portslade. This is only a rough indication, but on the map its course is as firmly marked as the boundaries between Sussex and Surrey and Kent. For it is a legal frontier, established for the same reason as the Yorkshire Ridings—to facilitate the administration of a most unwieldy county.

The scene itself has changed yet once again. Just as there was a difference between the countryside west of Dallington and that neighbouring the Kentish border, so now we are in another landscape from the country round Ashdown Forest. For one thing the Downs have been creeping steadily northward, narrowing the Weald till it becomes scarcely more than a strip at the Hampshire border. It also appears a tamer country because of their contrasting height; the sea of woods and meadows has lost its waves, and the patchwork its colour—here the corn is rarer, and below the pasturing flocks on the green hill are the flocks in the green water-meadows of the Arun and the Adur.

This is the Sussex of the Sussex-lovers as distinct from the lovers of the Weald; and it is certainly a very beautiful county of hill and river and meadow. The flinty, chalky villages, with their flinty, chalky names—Didling, Cocking, Wool Lavington, Barlavington, Pyecombe, Fulking, Poynings— belong to the hill and to the hill too we must regretfully cede delicious Amberley and its Wild Brooks. To us belong the higher reaches of the Adur and the Arun, and the country north of the western Rother, from which the Downs are no more than a view and where the Hurst names still speak of Andredsweald.

There is another change, which concerns me only. When we began our railway tour we were travelling through country which I can claim to know not only proverbially but literally as the palm of my hand; indeed if I were forced to draw a map of either I think I should find the first the easier of the two. The country of the Kent and Sussex borders I have known all my life, and the country immediately west of it I have known for nearly as long. I was brought up to explore the countryside at some distance from my home. Often when friends have shown me their neighbourhood they have explained that their own acquaintance with it was limited until they had a car. Not so my family, and when showing friends my own surroundings I have provoked the question: "Shall we ever reach anywhere you haven't been to years ago on your bicycle?"

The answer is: No, probably not. For not only did we bicycle for quite long distances—seventy or eighty miles a day, thirty or forty for an afternoon run—but we often extended our radius by travelling by rail to some centre such as Polegate or Newenden or Rye. I also discovered that a bicycle need not be confined even to the byways, but in dry weather would ride easily over turf, and with a little help could be lifted over stiles in the same way as the push-cart of my first country rambles. I never pass Firle Beacon without saluting the earlier self that climbed it with a bicycle and then rode over the back of the Downs to Rodmell in the further valley.

The car enlarged my countryside but not nearly so much as might have been expected, and of course all the intimacy was gone. Where we are travelling now I have been only by car or by rail, and my knowledge is not constant or lifelong but covers a series of visits during a period of fifteen or twenty years. So if my memories have intruded too much in earlier chapters, I shall now offend no more.

2

The train to Horsham starts at Brighton, and clanks for many miles along the devastated coast. At Shoreham it turns northwards up the valley of the Adur, where wide green marshes mark the side of the estuary that once filled all the space between the Downs. Once upon a time Bramber and Steyning were seaports like

Newenden and Smallhythe, and also like those derelicts have
been forsaken by the tides both of the Channel and of trade. A
nineteenth-century visitor found Steyning so quiet that "one
almost expects to see a fine green moss over the inhabitants",
while E. V. Lucas, some fifty years later, writes of its "interesting
placidity". Such words might still be written about Newenden
and Smallhythe in their lovely quiet, but to Bramber and Steyning they no longer apply. A new tide had invaded them—the
tide of motor-traffic. Their position close to the big coastal resorts
has put them back very literally on the map from which they
seemed to have been erased. Unlike the two stranded ports in
Kent they have not diminished but rather increased. Their ancient
charms remain, but deeply embedded not only in new extensions
but in such restorations as enshrine "antiques" and "teas". No
doubt they have their quiet moments which I have never known,
as I have entered them only with the invasion and thankfully
escaped towards the Weald.

We cannot consider ourselves really back in the Weald until
we reach the third station on this line, which is Henfield. Here
we are some miles north of the Downs, and a mile or so from
the river, in retired green country, well parked and wooded and
well provided with roads to take us either north or south, though
places eastward and westward are not to be reached so easily.
It seems taken for granted that you wish to visit either London
or the coast, and only lesser facilities are provided for going
anywhere else.

Henfield has a common on which Borrer, the ornithologist,
once saw as many as fourteen golden orioles on a bush. This
bird is almost unknown in these parts—indeed in this country—
and that fourteen should have been present together is sufficiently
remarkable without the further coincidence of a recording
naturalist.

Other attractions of Henfield besides the Common are the
view from the aforesaid common and the parish church. The view
is one with which we shall grow familiar in this new type of
country—a stretch of flat or gently sloping woods and fields
seamed with water-meadows and ending in the great southern
barrier of the Downs. The church, though much restored, is
Early English, with a fine Perpendicular tower. Perpendicular

too is the handsome screen between the tower and the nave, and it is encouraging to note that this is modern and compares favourably with the ancient screen that shuts off the organ loft. There is a thirteenth-century font, and we shall find two brasses and also the tomb of little Meneleb Raynsford, "God's darling", who died in 1627 at the age of nine.

Meneleb is a comparatively mild specimen of the Old Testament names that at this period were bestowed on luckless infants in baptism. We associate these names with Puritan domination and the Commonwealth, but by then they were the names of adults and must have been given much earlier. Thankful and Accepted Frewen were both christened before the Civil War; so too must have been Perform-Thy-Vows Seers of Maresfield, who was married in 1632, while the baptism of Replenished Prior (a girl) took place at Heathfield in 1600. From a seventeenth-century Sussex jury list, quoted by Lower, come such horrific names as Weep-Not Billing, Fly-Fornication Richardson, Kill-Sin Pemble, Stand-Fast-on-High Stringer and others like them. But it is probable that at least some of these names were assumed in later life rather than given at the font, for the Civil War and the Commonwealth would have brought them even more into fashion and at the same time discredited all the Charleses and Jameses of the district.

A few miles north of Henfield at Lashmars Hall, the Adur receives its most important tributary, the Wyndham Brook, and only a short way further on is Partridge Green, the next station on our line. Partridge Green itself consists of little more than an inn and a few houses, but it is the nearest station to Shermanbury, where the parish church is remarkable for having been rebuilt in the middle of the eighteenth century, a century which we have learned to associate more with the falling down of churches than with their reconstruction. It has not, unfortunately, many characteristics of its unusual period, for it was "restored" in 1885. In far-off days, when Shermanbury was Salmonesberie, the original church contained a piscina which, with some old glass, has marvellously survived both its transformations. Between the church and Partidge Green is an old moated house, Shermanbury Grange, which besides the charms inseparable from its kind has an interesting Perpendicular gateway.

The river and the train go on their way together to West Grinstead. They are of course really going in opposite directions, for the river moves sluggishly southward to the coast while the train moves only a little less sluggishly northward to Horsham and the Surrey border. At West Grinstead station we have overshot the village by two miles and lost the river, which has gone to feed itself from the overflow of the lake at Knepp Castle. I suggest that we follow the river, not so much to see Knepp Castle—which is only a fragment of a fragment, though once it was the stronghold of William de Braose and banqueted King John—as to visit Shipley just beyond it. Shipley must be visited not only for the sake of its lovely group of farm, church and windmill but because a member of that group is the home of Mr Hilaire Belloc.

Sussex can claim to have inspired two great men who were very unlike each other—Hilaire Belloc and Rudyard Kipling. Mr Kipling's inspiration was the Weald, out of which he created *Puck of Pook's Hill* and *Rewards and Fairies*, while Mr Belloc's *Four Men* is a—or rather *the*—classic of the South Downs. As a Downsman he does not strictly belong to us, but perhaps we may claim him because he has made his home in a village from which the Downs are no more than a distant view. Geographically if not literally he is ours.

Another writer connected with Shipley is the poet Wilfred Scawen Blunt, who lived for a time at Newbuildings a few miles away. Newbuildings is in direct contrast to King's Land, Mr Belloc's home, for whereas the latter has a low red frontage that in years gone by enclosed a shop window, and a great spreading, sprawling roof, Newbuildings is, unusually for these parts, a tall, compact stone house, grey except for its lovely weathering which has put a bloom of rose and saffron over its walls and those of the columbarium beside it. Also unlike King's Land is its situation, for it is surrounded by woods, and in a ride of the great wood behind the house is the tomb where the poet lies buried.

His funeral was most unusual, for he was buried with both Christian and Mohammedan rites. He had spent a great part of his life in the East, and at one time had embraced Mohammedanism. As a Mohammedan he chose his grave in the wood and ordered the Koran to be read at his burial. But shortly before

The South Downs from North Common

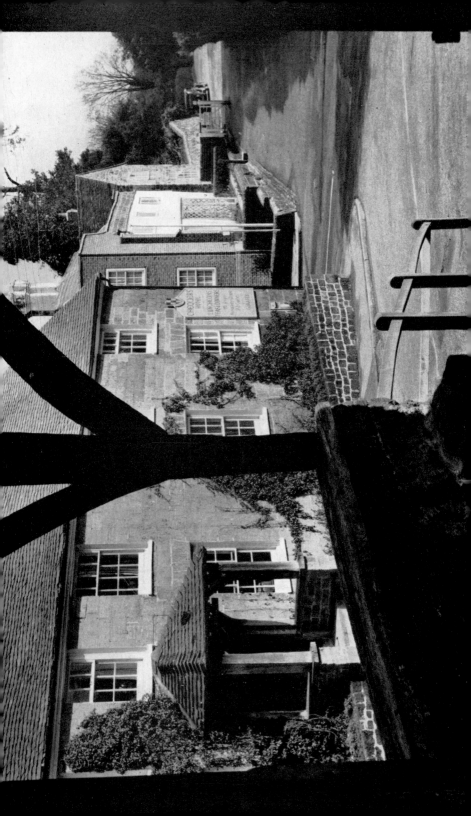

he died he was received into the Catholic Church, and presumably forgot to alter his will, so that his executors were embarrassed to find themselves still legally committed to the reading of the Koran. However, the matter was soon settled. The lonely grave was consecrated and the dead man buried with Catholic rites. Then his solicitor stepped forward and read the required passages from the Koran. So both the Church and the Law were satisfied.

Wilfred Blunt was not only a poet but a lover and breeder of Arab horses. In his latter years he would drive out to visit the family at King's Land, drawn through the lanes in a sort of carriage-bed by two magnificent Arabs. It seems an ideal way of travel for the elderly, or even for the lazy—to lie there in bed at the level of the primrose banks and glide through their scent and freshness to the house of friends.

The name of Hilaire Belloc inevitably conjures up that of his great friend G. K. Chesterton, who was a frequent visitor at King's Land, though he has not, as far as I know, ever written about Sussex. I feel convinced, however, that he received at least one local inspiration. Only a few miles from Shipley on the road to West Chiltington is a signpost one arm of which points to: Roundabout and Smock Alley.

There's a fine couple of names! . . . and as one considers the first can one fail to find echoes of the "Roundabout that makes the world go round"? Chesterton almost certainly saw that signpost when he was visiting King's Land; but I doubt if he ever went down the lane to see what was at the end of it. It would have been taking too big a risk.

Roundabout and Smock Alley . . . such places are best left to poetry and imagination. Even in this little backwater of the Weald, where away from more advertised beauties there is less spoliation than in other parts, one could never expect to find a Smock Alley that lived up to its name. While as for Roundabout—

> " . . . Peace and righteousness (St John)
>   In Roundabout have kissed."

Those words belong to no village on earth, so if we expect

to find anything like them we had better keep our illusions by keeping away; even though

> "All the roads they bound about
> To find the road to Roundabout
> That makes the world go round."

3

West Grinstead, to which we must now return, has an interesting and attractive church, with a shingle spire rising out of its middle and a beautiful old wooden porch. The original building was Norman, but little now remains of it; the rest—nave, pillars, arches, lancets—is Early English, with some old glass in the west window. A more unusual survival is the hinged panel in the chancel roof, which concealed the lever that before the Reformation used to lift the canopy of the hanging pyx. Fragments of painting on the walls recall the days of ecclesiastical gaiety. But even to-day West Grinstead church is more cheerful than most.

In the Burrell chantry are the tombs and memorials of the Burrell family, who for many years lived at West Grinstead Park. Before them the property belonged to the Carylls, and it was as a visitor to this family, Papists like himself, that Pope sat under a tree in the grounds and wrote *The Rape of the Lock*.

> "This verse to Caryll, Muse, is due—"

For the idea of the poem had indeed been given him by John Caryll, and the hero was the latter's cousin, Lord Petre.

There are memorials of the Carylls in West Grinstead church and others of the Halshams and the Powletts, including the unsuccessful grave of Captain Powlett. I call it unsuccessful because it seems unable to retain him. According to a local legend he haunts St Leonards Forest, several miles away. He is, of course, headless, but he cannot legitimately come into the Headless Horseman class, because he has no horse, relying for transport on those of passing travellers. As dusk creeps between the tree-trunks and fills the brakey hollows below the lane, he leaps up behind you on your saddle and encircles you with his ghostly arms. Whether he extends this habit to the bicycle and the motor-car, I cannot say, but if he still depends on horsemen the poor ghost must in these days find death very difficult.

We do not need to stop at either of the next two stations on our line. Southwater has not much to offer in the way either of history or scenery, and Christ's Hospital is just Christ's Hospital, a comparatively recent arrival in these parts, with red-brick walls that out-glare even those of Ardingly. Only a few miles further on we reach the turning-point of our journey at Horsham. Here we are in the capital of West Sussex, which like East Grinstead was also at one time an assize town and now, still like East Grinstead, is the important centre of unimportant railways, the knot of five strings linking it with Brighton, Littlehampton, London, Guildford and Tunbridge Wells. It is not far from the Surrey border and some Surrey country more retired and un-spoilt than that near East Grinstead; for here we have the Surrey commons—Ewhurst, Ockley, Capel and others too remote to attract the wealthy commutor.

Horsham itself is what might be called a good mixed town, not nearly so lovely as Lewes, but offering a good selection of ancient and modern, residential and commercial. Perhaps it is too much of a mixture, for except in the Causeway one can seldom view an ancient building without some ugly intru-sion in the way of shop-front or villa. The Causeway, how-ever, is very nearly perfect—old houses, shady trees, good slabs of Horsham stone under our feet and ahead of us a fine old church.

The best of the church is the outside, whether seen from the Causeway or from the river behind it. It has a tall shingle spire and a magnificent roof of tiles and Horsham slate. It is a big church too, though most of its enlargements are of comparatively recent date, and very little of the original Norman church remains. The various chantries have vanished under the heavy hand of nineteenth-century restorers, but the Shelley chapel survives and in it there is a slab commemorating Horsham's most illustrious son, Percy Bysshe Shelley.

The Shelleys are an old Horsham family, and the poet was born at Field Place, two miles outside the town. His maternal grandfather was at one time Vicar of Horsham, while a later Vicar gave him his first lessons; but he was too much of a rebel to find his inspirations near home. In his poetry Sussex is ignored entirely, and he seems to have turned in disgust from his early memories and associations. This no doubt was due to a child-hood made unhappy by a most unpleasant father, whose memory stood up in his life as a sort of Aunt Sally, to be potted with missiles from such various angles as atheism and the Irish Catholic Convention. Authority was typified in the paternal image and as such blindly assailed.

Another rebel associated with Horsham is the less distinguished son of an innkeeper named Savage, who at one time nearly stepped into history with his impersonation of the recently beheaded Duke of Monmouth. The tenaciousness of rural loyalties is shown by the fact that in spite of his public execution it was difficult to convince country people that the Duke was dead, and more than one impostor with a persuasive tongue in a handsome face was able to collect a following. None of these "rebellions" went much further than the village green, and the justices of Horsham, more merciful than those in the West, were content to treat Savage as a swindler rather than a traitor and sent him to gaol.

Not so merciful was the sentence passed some fifty years later on Ann Whale, a woman who had poisoned her husband. Death at the stake has been so commonly associated with religious martyrdom that we forget that it was also the sentence for other crimes besides heresy, and in 1752 the unfortunate woman was ordered to be "drawn upon a hurdle to the place of execution and there to be burned with fire till she be dead'. In its actual carrying out, however, the sentence was less cruel, for she was strangled five minutes before the lighting of the fire. How far this mitigation was legal, or the effect of growing humanity in the public conscience, I do not know. "The whole ceremony", says a contemporary pamphlet, "was carried on with the greatest decorum and decency, and there was the biggest concourse of people ever known on a like occasion."

The prison at Horsham seems to have been rather a free-and-easy affair under the care of the gaoler and his wife, with liquor a'plenty and festive evenings for the prisoners in what we should now call "association", though the scene must have been very different from what that term conveys to-day. In 1822 a Report of the Society for the Improvement of Prison Discipline states that "there is no employment whatever in the prison". Even the whitewashing of the walls which was then in progress was done by outside labour. The report continues: "There is room enough to erect a treadmill, but the Gaoler says he seldom should have enough prisoners to work it." It is curious to think that the futile, exhausting treadmill was, with the barrack-like stone buildings erected throughout the country, a Victorian notion of Prison Reform.

The gaol, small as it was, had a regular chaplain who seems to have been most assiduous in performing his duties, for he read prayers in the chapel every day and preached on Thursdays. Moreover "he frequently comes into the yard and converses with the prisoners". There is no account of the provision made for Sundays, and one wonders whether the prisoners still attended the parish church, as an old letter shows them doing in 1749:

"There was another sight at Church not so agreeable, it might rather be called a spectacle. The six smugglers that are to be executed in a few days: they come to Church every time there is a service, their melancholy looks (for they seem to behave very suitably to their condition) and the clanking of their chains make it so disagreeable I wonder the people can bear it. For they stand in the middle Isle where it is almost impossible to avoid looking at them."

To change to a more cheerful aspect of Horsham life, the town used to be a great cricketing centre. Nowadays more village cricket seems to be played in Kent than in Sussex; but in the early days of the game Sussex was a pioneer country and gave several famous cricketers to the world, notably Richard Newland who instructed Nyren, "the father of English cricket", Noah Mann, whose heart was "hooked for life" by the permission to call himself Horace after a cricketing baronet, Borrer of Ditchling, Voice of Handcross and many more who would travel vast distances to play in a good match. To Sussex also belongs Reynell Cotton, the cricketing poet, who wrote what E. V.

Lucas, an authority on the subject, considered "the best song in praise of cricket:

"The wickets are pitch'd now, and measur'd the ground,
Then they form a large ring, and stand gazing around,
Since Ajax fought Hector in sight of all Troy,
No contest was seen with such fear and such joy."

Cotton was born in Rudgwick, a village a few miles west of Horsham, which although it is one of the few Weald villages in which I have never set foot, has a special place in my memory. For it was the home of my nurse, and every year on her holiday she would send from it a hamper containing a fowl full of eggs (a delicacy which has long disappeared from the English table but was well liked by our forefathers), pots of blackberry jelly and jam, and a quantity of little yellow heart-shaped biscuits, of which my tongue can still recall the buttery, sugary taste.

4

Between Horsham and its fellow assize town in East Sussex rolls a succession of forests—St Leonards, Tilgate, Balcombe and Worth, all forming part of the great forest ridge of the Weald and ultimately linking up with Ashdown. There are, however, some remarkable differences between these western survivals of Andredsweald and the highlands of the east. In their case Silva Anderida was never Silva Regalis, and they remained virgin lands until the days of the iron industry, when all four provided fuel for the local furnaces. The fact that they are still woodland must be attributed to later plantings, for as early as the seventeenth century the furnaces had nearly eaten them all up. They are to-day more thickly wooded than Ashdown, and there is a greater variety of timber. At Balcombe, for instance, we find glades of beech, a tree all too rare in the eastern parts of the Weald.

None of these forests has high places to compare with the King's Standing of Ashdown, but from Beacon Hill at the back of St Leonards Forest there is at least one notable view. From it the ground slopes steeply to the hammer ponds in the valley whence springs the Adur, and the eye travels across nearly thirty miles of Sussex to the Downs.

"We came to that place where the wood upon the left ends sharply upon that height and suddenly beneath one's feet the whole County lies revealed." Mr Belloc's Four Men had walked from Pease Pottage to the place where long ago St Leonard had set up his hermitage, and thence they saw "the Weald in a tumbled garden". Yet it is not the Weald they had come to view, but

"Wolstonbury above Newtimber and Highden and Rackham beyond . . . and far away westward I see under Duncton the Garden of Eden, I think, to which we are bound. And sitting crowned in the middle place I see Chanctonbury, which I think a dying man remembers so fixed against the South, if he is a man from Ashurst or from Thakeham, or from the pinewoods by the rock, whenever by some evil-fortune a Sussex man dies far away from home."

At the Swan Inn the Four Men had drunk ale "as St Leonard himself used to do, round about nine or ten of the clock on an Autumn morning". But the Saint must have made his own brew, for in his day the forest cannot have known the civilisation of an inn. Nor had it, like Ashdown, submitted to the comparative civilisation of the hunting horn, while at this far west-end of the Weald even the civilisation of the swineherd yet lingered on the verges. We are far from the "dens", and though here and there were other reclamations—clearings and steadings—that survive in such names as Coolhurst, Nuthurst, Slinfold, Cowfold —the dense mysterious woodland remained sealed until the day of the furnaces and forges.

So it is hardly surprising that such a forest should be peopled by strange beings, not only ghosts like Captain Powlett, but dragons and monsters. That one of these actually walked in Tilgate we cannot deny, for there is its mighty footprint for all to see, though the forest that it knew was not the forest we know to-day, but a typical swamp sprouting with the gigantic ancestors of what we now call marestails. But no survivor of its race could have lingered on into the seventeenth century, and we must look for some other explanation of the well-attested "strange and monstrous serpent or dragon" which was seen there by "John Steele, Christopher Holder, and a Widow Woman dwelling neere Faygate", as well as "divers others, as the carrier of Horsham, who lieth at the White Horse in Southwarke, and who can certifie the truth of all that has been here related".

The narrative, which can be read in the Harleian Miscellany, gives a circumstantial description of what might in these days be called a Sussex rival to the Loch Ness Monster. There are the same careful statements by reliable witnesses, there is the same inability to produce either convincing proof or reasonable explanation. In the year 1614 St Leonards Forest must have been at least partly tamed by the iron industry, yet it was still considered "a vast and unfrequented place, heathie, vaultie, full of unwholesome shades and overgrown hollows". The serpent had been often seen at Faygate and within half a mile of Horsham, and

"there is always in his tracke or path left a glutinous and slimie matter (as by a small similitude we may perceive in a snail's) which is very corrupt and offensive to the scent. . . . This serpent (or dragon as some call it) is reputed to be nine feete, or rather more, in length, and shaped almost in the form of an axeltree of a cart; a quantitie of thickness in the middest, and somewhat smaller at both endes. The former part, which he shootes forth as a necke, is supposed to be an elle long; with a white ring, as it were, of scales about it. The scales along his backe seem to be blackish, and so much as is discovered under his bellie, appeareth to be red; for I speak of no nearer description than of a reasonable ocular distance. . . . He is of countenance very proud, and at the sight of hearing of men or cattel, will raise his neck upright and seem to listen and looke about, with great arrogancy. There are likewise on either side of him discovered two great bunches so big as a large foote-ball, and (as some thinke) will in time grow to wings; but God, I hope, will (to defend the poor people in this neighbourhood) that he shall be destroyed before he grow so fledge."

This narrative has been quoted by more than one Sussex chronicler, but as far as I know no one has tried to explain it or to discover what it was that John Steele, Christopher Holder and the Widow Woman really saw. I cannot resist making the attempt, for the story is typical of many others which one can neither accept nor reject entirely. I refuse to dismiss the whole thing as moonshine or the aftermath of an alehouse evening. It has obviously been written with a great attempt at accuracy, and the author is careful not to vouch for the absolute correctness of observations necessarily made at "a reasonable ocular distance". There is also an absence of sensation for sensation's sake, as in another part of the account he is anxious to point out that the creature did not devour either men or dogs, "for his food is thought to be for the most part in a conie-warren which he much frequents, and it is to be found much scanted and impaired in the increase it had woont to afford".

The fact that the observers were simple country people does not provide an argument against their accuracy, but rather a point in their favour, for in such matters as observation and memory, to say nothing of eyesight, the simple countryman is almost always superior to the townsman, even if the latter be a man of education. We must remember, too, that there would be no unconscious temptation to misrepresent the facts, such as we find to-day when such phenomena as the Sea Serpent, the Loch Ness Monster and the ghosts of Borley Rectory are by some regarded as outposts of the supernatural and therefore to be defended with intemperate belief against the onslaughts of those who with equal intemperance deny them for the same reason. To the villagers of Horsham and Faygate the serpent of St Leonards Forest was an entirely natural phenomenon, compromising neither science nor religion, and reported only as a matter of interest. Of course the reporters had no knowledge of the laws of evidence. They talk of "a man going to chase it with two mastive dogs . . . and glad to return in hast to preserve his own life", and of "a man and a woman coming that way, who afterwards were found dead, being poisoned and very much swelled, but not prayed upon". However, we have seen earlier that even names and addresses do not guarantee the truth of a story.

My guess is that what these seventeenth-century villagers of St Leonards Forest really saw was a large snake—possibly not so large as the measurements given, but on the other hand those measurements are not beyond nature, in fact well within it. How the snake came to be there we can only guess, but in those days wealthy men, especially those who had travelled in

8*   113

remote parts of the world, would sometimes collect a private menagerie. Bears, monkeys and even giraffes have been known thus to appear in European surroundings, and though a snake seems less probable, it may have been brought over when small and escaped when full-grown. The "heathie, vaultie" shades of St Leonards Forest would have been an acceptable refuge and the rabbit-warren a reliable source of diet. The form like "an axel-tree of a cart" was probably due to a rabbit in process of digestion. I am not sure about the poisoning, as the evidence for that is vague and circumstantial. The anonymous "man and woman coming that way" may have been poisoned from some other source. The "great bunches so big as a large football" are rather baffling. Is it possible that the "serpent" was really a big lizard? Certain observers saw "large feete", but the chronicler rejects these on the *a priori* ground that "serpents have no feete, but glide upon certain ribbes and scales". A huge lizard, such as the Komodo dragon, would have been a terrifying object to encounter in some "unwholesome shade", and the fact that it was harmless would not have been believed for a moment.

We are left with our conjectures, for the chronicle was never resumed, or if it was it has not survived. It would be interesting to know if the dragon ever "grew so fledge", or whether he was destroyed by some local St George with a billhook, or (more likely) succumbed to a less direct attack by means of a poisoned coney. Curiously, but perhaps significantly, St Leonards Forest is the site of a much earlier dragon story, for St Leonard shares St George's reputation as a dragon-slayer, and is stated to have fought the monster all over the forest, where wild lilies of the valley mark every spot where the Saint's blood was shed.

Then again, little more than a mile north of the Sussex western road, though several miles from St Leonards Forest, is a hamlet called Dragon's Green. I have not been able to discover any local legend here, but a neighbouring farm called Slaughterbridge suggests another George-and-Dragon story, while like our seventeenth-century dragon the monster could have found his meals on Coneyhurst Common near by. All this probably offers more rewards to the student of folklore than to the obstinate searcher after facts.

5

The way south from Horsham lies down the valley of the Arun. To reach it the line forks westward below Christ's Hospital and takes us through low, pleasant, if undistinguished country to our first stop at Billingshurst. This is a large village at the junction of the great west road of Sussex with the old Roman road known as Stane Street. Its name is said to be derived from Belinus, the Roman engineer who constructed the stone-paved road through the wild western verges of Andredsweald, and thus linked Regnum with Londinum, Chichester with London. His Hurst marks an important stopping place on the way, and no doubt provided refreshment and protection for the traveller who had crossed not only the Downs but also many dark and dangerous miles of the Undwelt-in-Wood.

It is noteworthy that this road—the only Roman road that crosses Sussex—is carefully planned to go through as little as possible of the Weald, for here the Downs spread northward half across the county. After Billingshurst we are soon at the Surrey border, just short of which is the site for a Roman gate, at which the venturer into Silva Anderida would have been stopped and questioned. Beyond this gate the motorist cannot go to-day—he must turn east or west, to Horsham or to Rudgwick, for Stane Street has disappeared into private grounds. It reappears some miles further on and runs its straight course through Ockley, after which it vanishes again, and continues this trick of appearing and disappearing until it finally reaches Billingsgate, Belinus's gate into London. From Billingshurst to Billingsgate would be a fascinating expedition for those ready to walk so far and not too scrupulous as to trespassing on private property.

At Pulborough, nearly ten miles south of Billingshurst, we are still on the railway, still on the Stane Street and still on the Arun. Yet the scene has changed, for the water-meadows have spread almost into a landscape and their green expanse has been further enlarged by the western Rother, which at this point joins our river. It is evidence for the denseness and impenetrability of old Andredsweald that there should be at both its extremities rivers bearing the same name. The eastern Rother was probably unknown to those living in the valley of its western namesake.

The name derives from an Old English word meaning an open field for cattle, and is appropriate to both rivers, for they are flanked by wide meadows and marshes still used as fatting-grounds.

Pulborough, which stands a little above the valley, used to be an important post on Stane Street, and was occupied by a Roman garrison, probably equipped with a catapult, whose duty was to defend the junction of the two rivers and the road to the coast. Times have changed and anything more peaceful now than Pulborough could hardly be imagined; for it is largely given over to that most peaceful of all sports—fishing. The two rivers wind through soft green meadows in loops that recall the famous windings of the Cuckmere, and as with the Cuckmere a canal has been cut through the marshes to make the way for water-traffic less fantastically frustrating.

Directly south of Pulborough lie the famous angling grounds of Amberley Wild Brooks, and we could if we wished continue on our railway through these paradisial scenes to the anglers' heaven at Amberley. But the railway is like the river, and also has a tributary, which we shall follow westward down the Rother valley, instead of continuing southward with the Arun. For Amberley does not belong to the Weald; it is on the chalk and belongs to the Downs. And if we feel disappointed when we remember that it has been called the loveliest village in Sussex, let us also remember that it has already been over-much written about and also, like its similarly overwritten counterpart at Rye, it contains in its streets nothing lovelier than the view of itself from afar.

Before we leave Pulborough we should visit the church, which is dedicated to Our Lady of the Assumption and has an Early English chancel that deviates from the straight line of the nave. This deviation, which is to be found in other churches, is sometimes thought to have been deliberate and meant to suggest the inclination of Our Lord's head when he died on the cross. We are often tempted to account for hard facts by pretty fancies, and it is more likely that the crookedness is due to early building difficulties, subsidence and so on. Our ancestors were careless about straight lines; in old houses and cottages walls are seldom "true", and often in churches there are enough slants and other irregularities in columns and arches to make the visitor feel uncertain of his eyesight—as, for instance, Brookland church on Romney Marsh, the interior of which when seen from a certain angle seems to be reeling.

One of the greatest beauties of the western Rother is the famous fourteenth-century bridge at Stopham. This lovely bridge of seven arches was built in the reign of Edward II by the Barttelot family, whose monuments are a feature of Stopham church. Another great family, the de Stophams, is said to have risen to aristocracy on the dues of the ford which, in the days before the bridge, was the only way of crossing the river. In those days they bore no name that has come down to us, but were just plain Saxon folk living Atte Forde de Stopham. It was not till they became rich that they discovered in themselves that Norman blood which even now is still venerated by simple hearts and in their day had certain practical and territorial advantages that our times have lost. The ford had gone, but even with the bridge and the Barttelots, the Manor of Stopham was still there to be hooked with a prefix.

Fittleworth station, the first on the western line, is actually nearer Stopham Bridge than the village of its name. Fittleworth is an enchanting place, with many attractive old houses and a picturesque old inn, the Swan. It stands above the Rother valley between two contrasting types of country. To the north are sandy commons, clumped with firs, while to the south water-meadows and angling streams spread towards the Downs. It is all most unlike the valley of the eastern Rother, which is a landscape of empty marshes without, in its seaward reaches, either road or rail. Here the railway follows the river all the way, and there are roads—none leading directly east or west but crawling in all directions over the valley—and woodlands instead of the bare slopes of Oxney and Chapel Bank. Moreover the Downs that range the whole length of the southern horizon make it appear a different countryside entirely. Here the sea never was, though in older days a wider river spread over what are meadows now. Even in these times the river is much wider than its western namesake, and its width, with the trees overshadowing it and the woods sloping down to it, makes it something altogether different from the marshy, reedy stream which once was Limene.

117

6

Petworth, the next station on our line, is a very old place, as old as the "dens". By the time of Domesday it already possessed a church, which we know was a rare distinction, a manor, a mill and pannage for eighty hogs. For we are now approaching the western verge of Andredsweald. The woods are thinning, and river transport is available through a fertile, open valley. An eleventh-century house-agent might without too great a damage to truth have described it as "within easy reach of London", for so it was in the terms of his own day. Stane Street was only a few miles off and could be reached by water, and from Pulborough the road through the forest was open.

Petworth indeed was one of the few real prizes to be found this end of Sussex, and Robert de Montgomerie no doubt considered himself lucky when King William bestowed it on him after the Conquest. Unfortunately he did not keep it long, for he fell out with the Conqueror's grandson, Henry I, and his estates were forfeit. Later on Petworth was bestowed on Josceline de Louvaine and through his wife, Agnes Percy, passed to the Earls of Northumberland. It remained in their hands until 1670, when the eleventh Earl, whose name of Josceline recalls the family's earliest days, died without a son. His daughter inherited the property and must have been considered a covetable heiress, for the poor child was married three times before she was sixteen. Through her Petworth passed to the Dukes of Somerset and thence, through another daughter, to the Wyndhams, the family that owns it now.

Petworth House is imposing and dominating rather than beautiful. It towers above the narrow, winding streets of the little town, and is best seen when leaving it in the direction of Midhurst. Around it spreads a large park which greatly pleased Cobbett who, as we know, liked his scenery neat and civilised, and the house itself contains a fine collection of pictures made by George O'Brien Wyndham, third Earl of Egremont.

"Proud Petworth, poor people;
High church, crooked steeple."

The steeple is no more than pleasantly askew, and I cannot agree with E. V. Lucas that the church is hideous. It is certainly unfortunate in having been restored twice, once in 1827 and again in 1904, but both these were better dates for restoration than the mid-nineteenth century, which is the period when so many churches were massacred to make a Victorian holy day. It stands, closely beset, in the midst of the town and like everything else is dwarfed by Petworth House, which with its towering walls crowned—as if their height were not sufficiently exclusive—with iron spikes, certainly still appears proud, even if it has ceased actually to be so.

As for the "poor people", the town to-day gives a very different impression, whatever may have been conditions in the past. It looks comfortable and contented and it has the rare advantage of being like the psalmist's Jerusalem, *in se compacta tota*. Mr Walter Wilkinson in his *Sussex Peepshow* calls it "a calm, compact little town with domesticity in its streets", and adds that he will always treasure his passage through Petworth "because in these days of ribbon development it is not always possible to enter the sharp confines of a compact town on a hill and walk out at the other end through a clean division of town and country". Certainly the roads both in and out of Petworth have the advantage of being unlined with the latest offerings either of the District Council or of Private Enterprise. Only a solitary cinema, extra-mural as it were, intrudes on the road to Midhurst.

That road now follows the river as well as the railway, and we should continue our journey by it if we wish to enter Midhurst in the very best way through Cowdray Park. The Downs now seem almost upon us, crowding us up against more hills that have appeared in the north, notably Black Down which is nine hundred feet high and marks the almost mountainous western extremity of the central Forest Ridge.

With our memories of Petworth Park—smooth and Augustan—still fresh upon us, we shall appreciate the contrasting beauties of Cowdray Park—riotous and Elizabethan. Even during the war, when large tracts were under the plough, it contrived to look wild and lovely, with its huge trees and rolling hills which at one spot surround a lake. The Downs no longer fill only the south, but also the west, reaching to the giant in the north, so that as we gaze across the Park towards Midhurst we seem to be encircled with hills. Their slopes, too, are all wooded, so that in the last miles of Andredsweald we have once more a strong sense of the forest that once was here.

The contrast with Petworth extends to the house, a graceful Tudor ruin set in the very lowest part of the Park, totally unlike the flat-faced monster that dominates Petworth town. It has not been rebuilt since the great fire that gutted it in 1793, but not long ago the ivy which used to drape it and threatened its final destruction was stripped off, to reveal the turrets, crenellations and great mullioned bay windows of a Tudor castellated house.

Cowdray was built in the reign of Henry VIII and shortly afterwards came into the possession of Sir Anthony Browne, later to be the first Viscount Montagu. He had also been given Battle Abbey at its dissolution, and the legend runs that one of the dispossessed monks had laid upon his family the Curse of Fire and Water. "By fire and water thy line shall perish." This has been called the Curse of Cowdray, but Battle considers it has a superior claim to it on account of its origin. The disasters, however, that Battle adduces as evidence are more geographical than genealogical, since they have involved members of other families living at the Abbey. On the other hand, the line of Cowdray Montagus did literally perish by fire and water. A week after the burning of Cowdray House the last Viscount was drowned in the Rhine, and the two nephews who were his only heirs were also drowned while bathing at Bognor. This inclines us to the belief that the Curse was an afterthought to catastrophe.

Cowdray House, now a lovely, empty shell, was in its day a very lively place. It banqueted no less than two monarchs—one of them "excessively", though we are left in doubt as to whether the word applies to the expenses of the entertainment or its effect upon the stomach of that poor little boy, King Edward VI, who was the occasion of it all. The other royal visitor was Queen Elizabeth the First, who came in 1591. The Montagus were Catholics, a fact which had not prevented them from accepting the spoils of Battle Abbey, nor—this time in common with many other Catholics—helping their country against the Spanish Armada. The second Viscount Montagu, though an old man, rode

Stopham Bridge

to Tilbury and offered his services to the Queen, and no doubt it was as a reward for his loyalty that she visited Cowdray.

It was a reward, we imagine, which many English noblemen would sooner have done without, for Gloriana's entertainment involved exertions which must have strained the resources of even such a household as Viscount Montagu's. In this case her visit seems to have been something in the nature of a masque, requiring not only the usual routine of stewards, chamberlains, gentlemen ushers, waiters, maids and cooks, but actors, such as the gentleman who stood between two wooden dummies made exactly like him, to greet her when she arrived. It is hard to understand the significance of the dummies. Perhaps they were a joke, though we are pretty sure that Elizabeth preferred compliments to jokes. However, she did not suffer from any lack of these, for the speaker assured her that until she came the house shook and tottered, but that one glance from her eyes had steadied it for ever. He then declared her to be the Miracle of Time, Nature's Glory and the World's Wonder, while the Montagu family stood round "as it were weeping in the bosom", and exclaiming "Oh, happy time! Oh, joyful day!"

Later on another gentleman disguised as a pilgrim addressed her as "Fairest of All Creatures"—she was now fifty-eight and her teeth were black—and hoped that the world would come to an end with her life. There was yet another gentleman dressed as an angler who came to meet her as she arrived at a "goodly fish pond" and proclaimed that her "virtue made envy blush and stand amazed". When not receiving these subtle flatteries from gentlemen in various disguises—one was a "wild man" clothed in ivy—she indulged in hunting, if the sport can be extended to include the view from a turret of sixteen bucks being pulled down by greyhounds on the lawn.

It is worth noting that this fabulous visit to a Catholic household took place in the midst of the post-Armada period, when not only priests but private people who "harboured" them were being hunted and hanged in other parts of the country. But in those days a great house could always protect itself as long as its loyalty to the sovereign remained unquestioned, and as I have suggested the Montagus were rather unusual Catholics. Their odd approach to religion culminated in the fifth Viscount,

Petworth House

who finding himself one Sunday late for Mass, shot the priest dead at the altar. But this was going too far even in penal days, and Viscount Montagu had to lie hid for fifteen years, profiting from his family's past services to the Church by having at hand a "priest's hole", in which he concealed himself by day, coming out only at night, to start with his white-clad lady the convenient legend that Cowdray Park was haunted.

7

Midhurst is not the last station on the little single-track line that would if we persevered take us right out of Sussex into Hampshire. But it is such a lovely old town that we might well be tempted to stay on here at one of the old inns and explore our few remaining villages by road. One of the delights of Midhurst is its nearness to Cowdray Park, and it would indeed be pleasant, after having explored by day Trotton, Easebourne, Rogate, Fernhurst and Lurgashall, to stroll of an evening across the water-meadows, and in the star-chased twilight of the great trees to meet Cowdray's ghosts—not only the sacercidal nobleman and his loyal spouse, but the little King who was really only a pawn, or the great Gloriana herself if she were not too busy haunting somewhere else, while out of any brake might rise a beruffed Elizabethan Angler, or a Pilgrim, or a Wild Man clad in ivy, all with no other topic but our charms.

Midhurst is not, of course, the quiet place that it was. Times have changed since E. V. Lucas wrote: "Midhurst being on no great highway is nearly always quiet. Nothing ever hurries there. The people live their own lives, passing along their few narrow streets and the one broad one, under the projecting eaves of timbered houses, unreacking of London and the world." In sad fact to-day, especially if to-day be Saturday or Sunday or any other sort of holiday, London and the world are passing steadily along the one broad street. For from the point of view of those who dislike noise and traffic the town is awkwardly placed, being on the great west road of Sussex now about to enter Hampshire, also on the road from London to Chichester. The western road has indeed been created by the car, for it is a linking up of many roads, some of which used to be well below main road standards, all of which have been widened and paved and merged into a system that would bring us at last to England's furthest sunset.

While staying at Midhurst we shall be tempted to climb Black Down if only for the view, which spreads Surrey before us as well as Sussex, the North Downs as well as the South. Here at the edge of its great central water-parting we have what is perhaps the best general view of the Weald. We see the whole western contents of the bowl which once was upside-down, but now holds between its raised sides so much civilised beauty of fields and woods and little villages, all of which have emerged out of what not so long ago was a dark ocean of trees.

On the north-east slope of Black Down we shall find the imposing Victorian house which once was Tennyson's—evidently he preferred the Surrey to the Sussex view. It was built by the poet himself in 1868, and he lived here until his death, but like Shelley—though it must have been for very different reasons— seems to have found no inspiration in his surroundings. Another literary association of this part of Sussex is Thomas Otway, the poet and playwright, whose father was curate of Trotton, a few miles outside Midhurst. Here he was born in 1652, but he died miserably in London only thirty-three years later. His plays, though at one time they had a great vogue and made the fame of more than one tragic actress, have had no share in the revival of Restoration drama which has taken Congreve and Wycherley off the shelf. The reason may be that they were mainly tragedies, and tragedy always seems to "date" more easily than comedy. Witness the continued popularity of Sheridan in contrast to the eclipse of his contemporary, Home, whose *Douglas* was in the eighteenth century considered equal, if not superior, to anything of Shakespeare's.

Trotton church, where the Rev. Humphrey Otway once ministered, and where a plaque commemorates his son, has the negative distinction of possessing no chancel arch. It has, however, four unusual and rather beautiful "geometrical" windows, two north and two south of the nave, and all alike—two trefoil lights with quatrefoils over. There is a brass to Lady Margaret Camoys, said to be the second oldest one to a woman in this country, where women were expected to share their husband's last bed— as does the Lady Elizabeth Camoys the fine altar-tomb of Thomas

Camoys, hero of Agincourt. When he married her she was the widow of Harry Hotspur and Shakespeare's "gentle Kate" (though her name was Elizabeth), who was told by her spouse that she swore "like a comfit-maker's wife . . .

> And giv'st such sarcenet surety for thy oaths,
> As if thou never walk'dst farther than Finsbury."

If we, for our part, walk further over Trotton Common we shall see another beautiful view and come finally to Rogate, the last village in Sussex, though not the last village in the Weald, which technically ends at a line drawn between the three Hampshire villages of Lysswood, Fairfield and Clamfield. But this fragment does not concern us, and after taking an admiring look at the tall spire of Rogate church (the interior is not so admirable, having been spoilt by over-zealous restoration) and the cottages that group so picturesquely round it, we may return to Midhurst; though it would be worth our while to go just another mile or two to the Hampshire border, where an old moated farmhouse keeps watch over the boundary and preserves the few arches that remain of Dureford Abbey in its garden wall.

We have now come a hundred and twenty miles from where we started, but we have travelled very much further than a hundred and twenty miles on the little single-track railways which have taken us up and down, across and along the Weald. We have visited a great many villages, few of a size to be called a town, and we have seen the country change from the hop-gardens of the Kent and Sussex borders, through the rolling park-like meadows of mid-Sussex and the heathery heights of the Forest Ridge, to this extreme western region among the hills. We have followed the course of many rivers, we have entered many churches, visited many houses, met many people and listened to many tales. Among so many trees we might well have lost the wood, had not that wood in its ghostly survival— in legend, in folklore, in place-names, in patches of wildness— never ceased to remind us that it was here before them all.

Part Two

Life of the Weald

CHAPTER I

THE WEALD AND HISTORY

I

THE part that the Weald has played in English history is out of all proportion to its size. Indeed English history, properly so called, may be said to have started in the Weald. At first it seems paradoxical that a dense, uninhabited forest should be the womb of history, yet further reflection shows us that at least as a symbol it is appropriate; for such a forest, such a Wild, would be the chaos from which order proceeds, the nebula out of which the stars are born. Not that the denseness and loneliness of Andredsweald are in themselves pregnant. It was its geographical situation which gave it such an important part to play, for it spread to the coast nearest to the Continent, the coast which Cæsar could see from Gaul, while cross-Channel traffic brought him illusory accounts of the riches behind it. Certainly it was the easiest coast for a landing, whether the site he chose were Hythe or Deal or Pevensey or Appledore. The predilections of historians vary, and with them varies the site of the battle in which the Romans finally defeated the Britons.

If Cæsar landed at Hythe or even in Appledore Bay, this battle was probably fought on the banks of the Stour, between Ashford and Canterbury; if he landed in Sussex it was near where Robertsbridge is now, and the river was the eastern Rother. The weight of evidence seems to lie on the Kentish side, in which case Cæsar, having landed at Hythe (more generally favoured by the historians than Deal or Appledore), avoided the great forest, and leaving it to his left marched along its verges to where the Stour flows through a gap in the North Downs. Canterbury was even in those days the capital of Kent, and it was natural that the British should fall back on it from the coast. The Romans marched by night, and the dawn showed them their enemy massed on the high ground above the river.

Though it was a case of seasoned, highly-trained troops being opposed by comparatively uncivilised tribes, the armies were not too unequally matched. The men of Cantium were not only well equipped with modern weapons, but they had, according to Cæsar, a bold and original method of fighting.

"First they drive their chariots on all sides and throw their darts, insomuch that by the very terror of the horses and noise of the wheels they often break the ranks of the enemy. When they have forced their way into the midst of the cavalry they leap from their chariots and fight on foot. Meantime the drivers retire a little from the combat, and place themselves in such a manner as to favour the retreat of their countrymen should they be overpowered by the enemy. Thus in action they perform the part both of nimble horsemen and steady infantry; and by continual exercise and use have arrived at that expertness that in the most steep and difficult places they can stop their horses upon full stretch, turn them which way they please, run along the pole, rest on the harness, and throw themselves back in their chariots with incredible dexterity."

The Romans never attempted to disguise their admiration of a brave and resourceful enemy, but Kentish skill and courage could not maintain the battle against the trained and disciplined legions' long experience of warfare, and in spite of their valour the British were defeated. It was then that the primal forest played its part by becoming the refuge of their flying troops.

To the other side victory was disappointing, for as Cicero wrote to Atticus: "There is not in all the island so much as a scruple of silver nor any booty but in slaves." Cæsar appointed an annual tribute, but left no officers to collect it before embarking his men once more for Gaul. He is not thought to have penetrated further into the country than Essex and Hertfordshire. The whole thing was a disappointment, even though he did not return entirely without loot, for that winter in Rome he offered in the temple of Benus a corselet set with British pearls.

The Roman occupation of Britain seems to have taken place gradually and to have varied in intensity from a state in which the inhabitants lived virtually under their own kings to a rigorous domination which reinforced its terrors by the use of elephants. Actual warfare, however, was confined to the northern parts of the island, where resistance was maintained for many years. In the south and south-east peaceful conditions prevailed, as bear witness the numerous traces of Roman villas, though doubtless such settlement may also be put down to the climate, which was a little less unlike Rome's than that of the north.

A medieval chronicler, Richard of Cirencester, in his treatise *On the Ancient State of Britain*, gives an account of Roman days in the Weald which may or may not be reliable:

"Cantium, situate in the extremity of Britannia Prima, was inhabited by the Cantii, and contains the cities of Durobrobis [Rochester] and Cantiopolis [Canterbury], which was the metropolis, Dubræ [Dover], Lemanus [situated on the Limen or Rother and probably Newenden] and Regulbuim [Reculver], garrisoned by the Romans; also their primary station Rhutupus [Richborough], which was colonised and became the metropolis, and where a haven was formed capable of containing the Roman fleet which commanded the North Sea. This city was of such celebrity that it gave the name of Rhutupine to the neighbouring shores. It was the station of the second Augustan legion, under the Count of the Saxon coast, a person of high distinction.

"The kingdom of Cantium is watered by many rivers. The principal are the Madus [Medway], Sturius [Stour], Dubris [a brook at Dover] and Lemanus [Rother], which last separated the Cantii from the Bibroci. . . . The vast forest called Anderidan stretches from Cantium a hundred and fifty miles, through the countries of the Bibroci and the Sgontiaci, to the confines of Hedui. The Bibroci were situate next to the Cantii, and as some imagine were subject to them."

Kent has always been inclined to look down on Sussex, and here we seem indeed to find a proof of superiority. But unfortunately from this point of view the chronicler is uncertain of his facts and the historians are uncertain of the chronicler. There is, however, no question that the denseness of Anderida Silva kept Sussex for a long time in a more backward state than the sister

9 129

kingdom. In Kent the Romans appear in certain places and to some degree to have penetrated into the Weald, and their paved roads linked the coast towns with important centres inland; but in Sussex they attempted no traverse of the wilderness until its width had shrunk to a few miles in the extreme west. On the coast were cities and luxurious villas but inland the unoccupied Wild. This to a certain extent is also true of Kent, but Kent is a great deal more than the Weald, whereas in those days the only part of Sussex which was not downland was impenetrable forest. The Bibroci are not likely to have been numerous, nor was their habitation between the coast and Anderida extensive. Their fortifications, farms and settlements still remain in the shapes of the hills, where white walls have crumbled and been grassed over, leaving only turfy ridges among the otherwise unbroken swell of curves.

The Bibroci, who survived under the Romans, were destroyed or driven out by the Saxons, who poured into the country on the withdrawal of the occupying troops. This particular corner has always been vulnerable to invasion, as many more than Cæsar knew . . .

"Old Andredsweald at length doth take her time to tell
The changes of the world, that since her youth befell,
When yet upon her soil scarce human foot had trode;
A place where only then the Sylvans made abode:
Where fearless of the hunt the Hart securely stood,
And every where walked free, a Burgher of the Wood;
Until those Danish Routs, whom hunger starved at home,
Like wolves pursuing prey, about the world did roam:
And stemming the rude stream dividing us from France,
Into the spacious mouth of Rother fell by chance."*

It is to be noted that the occupation of France has been considered from 55 B.C. to A.D. 1940 an essential preliminary to the invasion of Britain. In the year 898 Hasten, the Danish leader, was at Boulogne, having ravaged France and Italy, and collecting a fleet of no less than two hundred and fifty vessels he set sail for Kent, making a landing at the mouth of the Rother.

* Drayton's *Polyolbion*, Canto XVIII.

"This port," somewhat inexactly states the Anglo-Saxon Chronicle, "is in the eastern part of Kent, at the east end or the great wood which we call Andred; the wood is in length from east to west one hundred and twenty miles, or longer, and thirty broad; the river of which we before spoke flows out of the Weald. On this river they towed up their ships as far as the Weald, four miles from the outward harbour, and there stormed a fortress; within the fortress a few churls were stationed and it was in part only constructed. Then soon after that Hasten with eighty ships landed at the mouth of the Thames, and wrought himself a fortress at Middleton; and the other army did the like at Appuldre."

By this time Kent was a civilised Christian country, on which the Danes wrought hideous destruction, laying waste towns, villages, churches and monasteries from Appledore to Great Chart. The Saxon forces were led by King Alfred, whose invincible ally was "the great wood we call Andred". Its thickets enabled him to conceal his troops between the two Danish armies and thus prevent their joining. For four years the war lingered undecisively until its futility compelled the•Danish commander to withdraw to France, leaving two of his sons as hostages. Thus Alfred and Andredsweald won the day and the Danes came no more into Kent.

From the defeat of the Danes until the date that every schoolboy knows the Weald enjoyed unbroken peace. During those years, having ceased to be the refuge and ambush of men of war it became instead the feeding-ground of swine. Among its thickets the Sylvans no longer went fearless of the hunt, and human settlement deprived the hart of his citizenship. The population, however, was still mainly outside the wood. Ancient maps show us an Andredsweald closely surrounded by border villages but containing within itself only a few inhabited places. In the Kentish Wild we find only Hadlow, Tudely, Benenden, Newenden, Tiffenden and Palster yet in existence, while further west the settlements are fewer still.

The Normans came. But it is not generally known that before they landed at Pevensey—or probably at many places along the coast between Pevensey and Old Winchelsea—a division of the Norman fleet, with a part of the army, attempted a landing in Romney harbour, having learned from Cæsar that "the common landing place from Gaul" is Kent. It seems strange that this circumstance should be so little known among Kentish men, for the men of Romney repelled the invaders and William started his Sussex campaign with a bloody nose given him in Kent.

The Battle of Hastings, perhaps the most famous battle in English history, was fought upon the verges of the Weald, on the ridge that strikes westward from the back of Hastings and finally joins the great water-parting at Ashdown Forest. The Normans had sacked Hastings and erected a temporary castle there before marching along the ridge to meet Harold, who was advancing from "Andred"—which may have been either Ashdown Forest or its neighbour Waterdown.

William was not an invader in the same category as Cæsar and Hasten. He had not landed on British shores in quest of loot, but because he believed himself to have the right to the English crown, which Harold had usurped. He would, however, if possible have settled the matter peaceably, and before meeting his enemy in battle he offered him the choice of abdication, of single combat, or an appeal to the Pope. He offered further to give up Northumbria to Harold and Kent to his brother Gurth.

But Harold rejected all these offers. He had just defeated in Northumberland the Norse giant, Harold Hadrada, and thought no doubt that he would equally demolish the Norman upstart in Sussex. Indeed at one time it looked as if the Battle of Hastings might end in a Saxon victory. The Kentish men were posted in the first rank and their archers did deadly work. That the Normans suffered heavy losses is proved by their name for the battlefield. At the present day the Town of Battle is divided into two parts, the Upper Lake and the Lower Lake, after Senlac, the Lake of Blood. Also south-east of Battle Abbey, close to the Catsfield road, is a field which still bears the name of Mal Fosse— the ditch where so many Normans were buried, after dying convinced that they had lost the day. If Harold had not been slain it is more than likely they would have been right. But Harold's death from an arrow through his eye demoralised the Saxon forces. He appears to have had no adequate second-in-command, and soon after he fell his army fled.

Senlac, the Lake of Blood—two lakes of blood, the upper and the lower . . . what a name for a tussle between a few hundred horsemen and bowmen *—scarcely more than a skirmish of outposts according to our present notion of armies. Yet that skirmish changed our history far more drastically than the battles of the Marne and the Somme with all their millions. It is also notable that William, unlike most modern conquerors, seems to have viewed his victory with feelings of compunction. It was as an act of reparation rather than of thanksgiving that he built and endowed Battle Abbey—"an expiatory offering for the slaughter which had taken place" . . . the slaughter of a few hundred men.

His guilty feelings, however, did not stop him from ravaging the surrounding country, especially the estates of Harold, Earl Godwin and the Countess Goda, which he laid waste so utterly that in the Domesday Book, compiled twenty years later, this part of the Weald appears as "vastatum fuit".

Shortly after his victory in Sussex it became necessary for him to return into Kent for three reasons—first to punish the wicked men of Romney for repelling his first invasion, secondly to secure the coast and his communications with Normandy, and thirdly to find a decent road to London. In Sussex there were no decent roads, but in Kent a well-paved Roman road was at hand to take William to the capital. He set out, having obtained reinforcements from Normandy, and met with very little opposition within the county, doubtless because the flower of its fighting manhood had perished at Senlac. Dover had surrendered on demand, which had not saved the town from pillage, and William's advance on London was more like a royal progress than a warrior's march.

Between Gravesend and Dartford an incident occurred which Furley in his *Weald of Kent* dismisses as "belief among the credulous". Thomas Sprot, a monk of Canterbury in the reign of Edward I, records that:

"William saw himself gradually enveloped by what bore the appearance of a moving forest; that on a sudden the branches,

* This is Camden's derivation. A more modern idea is that the name derives from a sandy stream skirting the town.

which had been taken for trees, fell to the ground, and in their fall disclosed a host of archers with their bows ready bent, and their arrows directed against the invaders; that Stigand, Archbishop of Canterbury, and Egelnoth, Abbot of St Augustine's, advancing from the crowd, demanded for the men of Kent the confirmation of their ancient laws and immunities; and that the demand was readily granted by the fears of the astonished Norman."

This story may indeed be fabulous, since Lingard states that it was unknown to the more ancient writers, but that belief in it involves credulity is an idea belonging to Furley's generation rather than to one which has known the camouflages of two world wars and lately read accounts of an identical manœuvre being used by the troops in Korea. In any case, fact or fiction, the tale is interesting, as it may have provided Shakespeare with the wood which marched from Birnam to Dunsinane:

> "Let every soldier hew him down a bough
> And bear't before him: thereby shall we shadow
> The numbers of our host, and make discovery
> Err in report of us."

As described in poetry the operation seems so simple and practical that we find it hard to believe that it was not often practised as one of the earliest forms of camouflage, and that even if Thomas Sprot invented it he was straining nobody's credulity by doing so.

One thing is certain and that is that during his journey from Dover to London William made some important concessions to Kent in the matter of the free tenure of land, also allowing the county to retain many laws and usages which in others he abolished. The charter granting the Manor of Wye to Battle Abbey gives a list of prerogatives such as had in the past been conferred by Saxon kings—the freedom from "all Geld and Scot and Hidage and Danegeld, and from the work of bridges and castles and inclosures of parks, and from armies and all aids and pleas and plaints and shires and hundred courts, with Sac and Soc and Thol and Theam and Infangen-thef, and War and Wardpenny, and Lastages and Hamsoken and Forstal and

Bloodwite and Childwite". It is not perhaps surprising that certain Norman charters openly confess that they do not know the meaning of the words they use.

3

So far as history of the Weald has followed Catherine Morland's idea of all history as expressed by her in Jane Austen's *Northanger Abbey*: "The quarrels of popes and kings, with wars and pestilences in every page; the men all so good-for-nothing and hardly any women at all—it is very tiresome." It may be the fault of the chroniclers that history seems largely to have been made by wars. Or it may be the fault of the present chronicler, who has relegated to other chapters the more peaceful changes made by industry and religion. Nevertheless it is a fact that in the first thousand years or so of the life of the Weald most social and political changes were the direct results of wars and invasion. In later centuries causes other than military came into play; also the happy circumstance that the Norman Conquest was the last triumph of the invader robbed later conflicts of their disruptive powers. Wars might be longer and larger and grimmer, but they did not destroy the integrity of the land to the same extent as had first the Romans, then the Saxons and finally the Normans when they swept from the land they had conquered and occupied the legislative and social structures that were there before them.

The Romans had introduced their laws and system of government, the Saxons had established theirs, and now there was to be another complete change, for in spite of their concessions in Kent the Normans set up everywhere the feudal system. This already prevailed over most of Europe and an unripe form of it had penetrated certain Saxon customs, though as a system it cannot be said to have existed in England until Harold's overthrow.

According to it the King became the feudal lord (Lord Paramount) of all the land in the kingdom. Hitherto certain territories, such as most of Andredsweald, had been "Nanesmansland" without a legal owner. But now all the land in the kingdom belonged to the King. Under the King a piece of land, or fief, could be held by a baron or an ecclesiastic, who in return swore fealty and was obliged to perform certain services, mostly of a military nature. Then in his turn the holder would grant smaller portions of his fief to sub-tenants for the same consideration, and these in their turn might subdivide their sub-fiefs, and so on and so on until was reached the inarticulate mass of the people, the villeins, who owned nothing, but toiled as slaves. A highly chastened form of feudalism may still be observed in the Norman island of Sark.

The feudal system meant that the hog-pannages of the Weald were distributed together with the properties of the Saxon landowners among the Conqueror's adherents. Though separated perhaps by miles of forest from the various manors, the "dens" formed a valuable part of the feudal lord's demesne. Such enclosures were no longer a matter of free squatting in Nanes-mansland but were held in fief from the King as Lord Paramount. In this way for the first time the Wild was "preserved" and the foundations laid of those stringent game laws which for so many centuries were to protect the squire's possessions.

The Norman Conquest changed not only the laws of the country but also to some extent the language. French became the language of the Court, the aristocracy and the clerks; though English was still the language of the common people, who had not been driven out as had been the British by the Saxons, taking their language with them into Cornwall and Wales, but remained to put up with the new conditions either in silence or with mutter-ings in their own tongue.

Vestiges of Norman French can be found in the place-names of the Weald, as they also remain in a very different part of England. Beachy Head has nothing to do with beaches but is a corruption of Le Beau Chef, just as in County Durham Petite Mer survives picturesquely as Pity Me. Though the vast majority of Weald place-names are of Saxon origin, there are among them some curious hybrids attesting to the fact that two languages existed together. Blackboys is a combination of the Saxon *blac* or shining with the Norman *bois* or wood. In Herstmonceux and Hurstpierpoint the process is reversed and the Saxon woodname prefixes the name of the Norman owner. Another hybrid is Boughton Malherbe, which is derived from the Saxon *boc-ton*—the town held by book or charter—and the Norman French for evil pasturage. The existence side by side for so many years

136

Cowdray ruins

of these two languages has had the result that in English there are two words for almost everything—one of Saxon and the other of Latin derivation, making our tongue almost the richest in the world. So much we owe to our conquerors.

4

After the Norman Conquest wars, though they did not cease, no longer had such transforming effects on the life of the people. Nor was the Weald the cockpit of those later wars as it had been in the case of the earlier invasions. Sometimes when a house is on fire a corner may escape the flames as the wind sweeps them upwards and over it, so the Wars of the Roses and the Civil War seem to have by-passed this south-eastern corner, except for lesser skirmishes. We have seen how the armies of Simon de Montfort rushed down from Fletching and Chailey to fight the armies of King Harry on his mount, but this is the only decisive major battle to be fought on wealden soil—if indeed we can call Lewes the Weald—between the Battle of Hastings and that last battle which was fought not on the wealden soil but in the wealden air.

This has not prevented the Weald from producing some horrific place-names, such as Slaughter Common near Heathfield and Terrible Down near East Hoathly, both of which are supposed to commemorate murderous affrays, though their dates and the number and nationalities of the contending armies are unknown. In the case of Slaughter Common it has been claimed that the fight was between the Britons under Cædwalla and the Saxons under Eadewine, but unfortunately for the accuracy of this tradition, these foemen actually met at Hatfield Chase near Doncaster. As for Terrible Down, all that even tradition tells us is that the two armies fought up to their knees in blood, or according to an even more lurid version, "till the blood of the slain did the living drown". After this it is rather disappointing to drive past Terrible Down on the main road from Blackboys to Lewes to find a very modest little rough field with a few cows at pasture. But thus the Weald has always healed her scars.

Apart from wars, this part of England is associated with two well-known insurrections, both of which involved a good deal of fighting. The main actions of both Wat Tyler's rebellion and

Jack Cade's took place outside the Weald, for both succeeded in reaching London, where Jack Cade displayed himself in triumph and vengeance and Wat Tyler .was assassinated. But most of their followers were men of the Weald, chiefly the Kent-, ish Weald in the case of Tyler, though Cade had numerous supporters also in Sussex.

The origins of both rebellions were social grievances, of which those urging Wat Tyler were the more genuine. In spite of the Conqueror's concessions, villenage still existed in Kent, and the lowest ranks of the feudal system were in a state bordering on slavery. On the other hand, taxation was heavy, and the more prosperous classes resented the competition of the Flemish weavers whom Edward III had introduced into the county.

There is some uncertainty as to the leaders of this rebellion. They are supposed to have been three—Wat Tyler, Jack Straw and John Ball. But theirs is a shifting identity. Some historians think that Wat Tyler called himself Jack Straw as a sort of generic name for the oppressed peasantry, while others hold that it was an alias of John Ball, the Franciscan friar who in the Market Place at Maidstone preached a new order in which all were equals without vassal or lord. It was his armed rescue from Maidstone gaol that started the rebellion, which might have achieved at least some of its objects had not the slaying of Wat Tyler brought it to an untimely end within a month of its starting.

Conditions, however, must have improved during the next eighty years, for in the causes alleged for Jack Cade's rebellion in 1450 there is no mention of villenage. Jack Cade—"a young man of goodly stature and pregnant wit"—was a very different type of man from Wat Tyler; indeed he was little more than an Irish adventurer throwing himself into somebody else's "private fight", in this case a dispute which had arisen between the Commons of Kent and the King. Kentish sailors had murdered the Duke of Suffolk, the Queen's favourite, and terrible rumours ran through the county as to the punishment that was to be meted out—nothing less than the restoration of Andredsweald. All the thriving villages and cloth-towns, all the furnaces and the forges, the churches and the manors were to be laid waste, and Kent—the whole of Kent, not only the Weald—was to be turned into a forest. The fact that such a rumour could be believed by anyone casts a baleful light on the times and the powers and dispositions of royalty. But it was certainly believed, and in conjunction with the usual grievances due to tax-collectors was enough to provide Cade with a large armed following, whom he led in the spirit of a soldier of fortune, achieving at the start an important success. At Sevenoaks, on the borders of the Weald, he defeated the royalists sent to oppose his reaching London, and a few days later he triumphantly entered the city, "armed in a brigandinæ and wearing a pair of gilt spurs and a gilt salade and a gown of blue velvet". The ignominious sequel to this glory we have already seen.

The sixteenth, seventeenth and eighteenth centuries were years of comparative peace for this corner of England. Once more the flames roared inland, leaving the coastal areas to that prosperity which comes from somebody else's war. The coast itself, of course, had always been liable to sudden attacks and harryings by the French, but the Weald had never felt much sympathy for the Cinque Ports and certainly was not above profiting from their misfortunes. The Wealden ironmasters were war-profiteers whose cannon and cannon-balls brought death to many of their countrymen in other parts of England, but very few of their "pieces" can have been discharged within earshot of those who made them.

Cæsar had proclaimed that the proper landing-place from Gaul is Kent—and the name of Kent can be stretched to include that part of Sussex within the natural as distinct from the artificial borders of the country. Certainly it was with this idea in view that at the turn of the eighteenth and nineteenth centuries this part of England was fortified against Bonaparte. Martello towers mounting heavy guns were erected at intervals all along the south-east coast, and a military road and a military canal, both of which still survive as delicious byways of land and water, were constructed between Pett in Sussex and Hythe in Kent. No doubt these works brought added prosperity to the districts inland. Iron-smelting was practically at an end, owing to the increasing use of coal as industrial fuel, but there were some important local gunpowder works, which survive in the record of a fatal "explosure" at Brede and the name of Powdermill Wood near Battle.

When next invasion was threatened the national enemy had changed from France to Germany and fears and fortifications shifted together from Kent to East Anglia. The first world war, as far as the Weald was concerned, resembled the Black Death in that its slaughter here was neither greater nor less than in other parts. As in other parts the little village war-memorials arose with the lists of local names, the Fuggles, the Boormans, the Huggetts, the Goodsells, the Cloutes, who had died far away from their homes. In one respect only the war seemed closer here than elsewhere. Throughout all its later stages, as the great battles moved westward, there was a continuous mutter and thudding to be heard. In some places it was louder than others; on the high ground near Tenterden it seemed impossible that those guns could be in another country, while down on the marsh there were pockets of silence. Mostly it was a constant pulse upon the air, something less heard then felt.

Air attacks, whether by airship or airplane, were on another route and did not greatly affect the Weald, though a Zeppelin once dropped seven harmless bombs near the old Military Canal at Pett. But in the second world war, though the foe had not changed, his position had. Hitler, like Cæsar, had possessed himself of Gaul, therefore his proper landing-place once more was Kent.

The invasion never happened, but the possession by the Germans of the French airfields made the Weald particularly vulnerable to a form of warfare Cæsar never knew. From the spring of 1940 to the autumn of 1944 almost every conceivable form of projectile was dropped on the peaceful fields of Kent and Sussex. The Battle of Britain, had it gone on much longer, would surely have altered the skeletal structure of Weldishmen, since each man carried his face at a right angle to his neck, as he watched the minnows of the sky attack the whales. Less of an entertainment were the wounded whales when they fell into fields and gardens or went hedge-hopping out of the country; or those single wasp-like planes that buzzed over to drop bombs at random or machine-gun what they misguidedly took for military objectives. Most serious "incidents" were caused by stray planes visiting small towns which had been considered outside the battle area—East Grinstead, where some hundreds of casualties followed a bomb dropped on a crowded cinema, and Petworth, where most of the boyhood of the town was killed or maimed by a bomb which fell on the school.

The last and worst bombardment of the Weald was by fly-bombs in the summer of 1944; though these did remarkably little damage in comparison with what they would have done if allowed to reach their destination. The rural districts of Ashford and Battle were the worst hit, but the prevalent emotion of the inhabitants was pride in the number brought down in their midst. They complained only of the airy references on the radio to "open country", as if the Kent and Sussex countryside, crowded with small farms and villages, were still the empty forest that was Andredsweald.

For this part of England, actual warfare ended in the autumn of that year, as only three rockets were sufficiently out of their course to fall on it. Very soon afterwards the scars were healed; the grass covered the bomb-holes as it had covered the forts of the Britons, broken trees sprouted and clothed themselves anew, ruined houses were restored or pulled down. Only those who know the district well will remember those non-human casualties —the lath-and-plaster cottages that stripped of their weather-tiling stood by the wayside like empty bird-cages, the frame of stout ships' timbers that remained when all the rest of the old farmhouse was gone, the gap-roofed barn with its hovering smell of fire, the skeletal oasts and those which drooped their white heads on their shoulders like dying birds . . . all these have vanished now, and in their place their substitutes now stand, raw, hideous, functional, the final horrors of war.

CHAPTER II

THE WEALD AND INDUSTRY

I

IT is difficult to find in the Weald a view that does not include some form of building. There are often wide stretches of woodland, but the countryside as a whole is rutted with many small lanes beside which old houses and cottages lie like pippins in the orchard grass. The main roads are strung with little hamlets and "towns", some no more than a house or two, others nearly as large as villages; while the farms, being mixed and small, repeat the bright colours of their steading many times in the square mile. Most of this building is a characteristic part of the beauty of the countryside. A Kent or a Sussex landscape of woods and fields only would not be typical and would lack an important aspect of the homely loveliness which marks the Weald. But strangers often ask why this part of rural England is so crowded with small houses. They accept the large ones, the big estates, but this multitude of small dwellings, most of which proclaim they have been here for centuries, requires some explanation.

The reason is, of course, that for many hundreds of years the Weald was the industrial area, the Black Country of England. The idea suggests a picture which must be at once forgotten— the valley of the Yorkshire Swale, with its smoking, grimy towns, its dreary mining villages, its coke-ovens, its foundries, its factories, its stunted, blighted trees. Apart from the fact that everything in the Weald was on a smaller scale and as it were home-made, between the Yorkshire Swale and the Sussex Ouse yawns the vast difference between coal and wood.

The smoke that rose from the Wealden bloomeries and furnaces was the soft blue wood-smoke that fills the air with one of the sweetest scents we know. The power that worked the hammers and the bellows of the forges and the wheels of the fulling-mills trickled through the flag-reeds of little meadow streams or lay spread in the lovely mirrors of the hammer ponds. Even the cinder-hills and the slag heaps and the spoods or cinder lanes proclaimed the sweetness and usefulness of charcoal and wood-ash as compared with the choking grime of coal-dust.

More than anywhere else the difference is shown in the forests above and below the ground. The furnaces and forges worked embowered in their own fuel; the oaks which would one day smelt the iron cast a welcome shade over the workers in the bell-pits and at the anvils. A coal-mine destroys the landscape as effectively as the works it feeds, but the glades of dwindling Andredsweald were yellow with primroses and blue with bluebells till the trees fell.

In another industry one might compare a modern clothing factory with an ancient cloth-hall—the cliffs of brick or stone, the geometrical lines of windows, the roofs that are mere lids of slate, with the many colours, many gables, crooked windows, high chimneys and deep roofs that combined in what was no more than a larger edition of the homes of the workers. Only at night would the two districts—so far apart in time and space— be remotely alike. For at night, just as the glare of the blast-furnaces and coke-ovens streams out into the northern darkness, while their foundries roar, so the furnaces of Kent and Sussex licked out the stars with their flames and thumped the stillness with their hammers.

But, as I have said, in the South it was all on a very much smaller scale. The biggest industrial town was Cranbrook, and the majority of the workers lived in conditions that could only be described as rural. Nor did the furnace or the fulling-mill dispossess the farm. Jack Fuller called the Sussex iron foundries "little tinkers' shops", and even those little shops were scattered over a wide area not only of land but of time. In Mr Donald Maxwell's *Unknown Sussex* there is an impressive design: "The Black Country of the Middle Ages"—a coloured map of the Weald in which all the furnaces are marked by tongues of fire. But the number of these amounts to no more than a few score, and they did not all blow at the same time. The Middle Ages in this map must be taken to cover five centuries, from the thirteenth to the eighteenth, with a few Roman furnaces thrown in for good measure, so these few score are spread out over half a millennium, during which only a limited number would have been blowing simultaneously. The life of a furnace was limited by the surrounding fuel, as it was uneconomic to bring wood or charcoal from afar—when Heathfield blew, Chiddingly was extinct, Westfield was dead before Crowhurst was born and so on. The peak centuries were the sixteenth and seventeenth. Before that the enterprise was limited to a few landowners and later by dwindling supplies of forest trees. So at no time was there the crowd of works and workers we find in the north. In no circumstances could it be so, as each furnace must be isolated in the acres of its fuel. As for the cloth trade, though more compact, it was confined to a small district where it has left us some of the homeliest and loveliest domestic architecture in the country. Of the furnaces only place-names and clinkers on the surrounding tracks remain.

2

Except for farming, the iron industry is the oldest and most continuous in the Weald. Nobody knows when iron was first smelted in the world's history, but tradition puts down the discovery to the accidental burning of a wood in Greece. The earliest inhabitants of Kent and Sussex, the British, are said to have known nothing of it. but this is made doubtful by the contrary fact that certain tribes wore iron as a decoration and even used it as currency.

The Romans instituted the earliest iron works in the Weald. Cæsar mentioned iron as existing "in maritimus partibus", which must mean the coastal districts of Kent and Sussex, and in the third century it was one of Britain's principal exports. Much of it at that time came from Gloucestershire but there were also furnaces in the South-east. Cinder heaps with the coins of Nero and Vespasian have been discovered in certain parts of the Weald, and there are known to have been Roman furnaces at Westfield, Sedlescombe and Beauport. These were all "in maritimus partibus", and would have involved only a slight penetration of Anderida Silva, while the furnace at Chiddingly could have been reached through the valley of the Cuck-mere. There is, however, a strong tradition in favour of a Roman furnace at Buxted, which would then have been in the deeps of the forest, and not so very long ago urns of black earthenware and some fragments of Roman building were found at Frittenden, which during the whole of the Roman occupation was unre-claimed woodland.

The Roman method of smelting was inadequate and poor, for they used no water-power but drove their furnaces with a foot-blast only. As a result the iron was never entirely extracted from the "sows" or ironstone lumps containing it, so much being left that in later times it was often found more profitable to return the Roman "offal" to the furnace than dig for fresh ore. The seventeenth-century historian Andrew Yarrenton tells us that

"the iron is made at this day of cinders, being the rough and offal thrown by in the Roman's time, they then having only foot-blasts to melt the ironstone; but now by the force of a great wheel that drives a pair of bellows twenty feet long, all that iron is extracted out of the cinders which could not be forced from it by the Roman foot-blast."

The iron ore was dug out of the scowles or bell-pits, that is, pits widening towards the base, and was found mainly in the blue Wadhurst clay, though it also sometimes occurred in the yellow Weald clay, at a depth of twenty feet or less. The ironstone was (and is still) scattered throughout the clay in lumps varying in size from an orange to a human head. These were the "sows" that contained up to forty per cent of iron.

The process of smelting started in the blast-furnace, where the iron was melted out of the stone. The "great wheel" that drove the bellows was turned by water-power like a mill-wheel, and the same power worked the hammer in the first forge or bloomery, where the melted iron was shaped into ingots or blooms. The bloomery cinders and blast-furnace slag, being indestructible, were used for road-making and may still be found in unfrequented lanes. The cinders are blue-black in colour and roundish in shape, while the slag is coloured in bands of blue and black and green. Compare the e with the black grit of a coal cinder-track, and you have another illustration of the difference between coal and wood, especially when, as it often happens, they still contain metal, in which case they glitter like glass upon the surface of the lane.

3

There were many more iron-works in Sussex than in Kent,* the reason being no doubt that the part of Kent where iron was to be found was the part already given to the cloth trade. But there were furnaces at Biddenden, Tenterden, Goudhurst and other towns in the coggers' district, and the Kentish furnaces, notably those at Lamberhurst and Cowden, had a higher reputation for good metal and good work than those in Sussex. It is of Sussex that Camden writes when he describes the industry in Queen Elizabeth's reign:

"It is full of iron mines, for the casting of which there are furnaces up and down the country, and abundance of wood is yearly spent; many streams are drawn into one channel, and a great deal of meadow ground is turned into ponds and pools for the driving of mills by the flashes which, beating with hammers upon the iron, fill the neighbourhood round about, night and day, with continued noise. But the iron wrought here is not everywhere of the same goodness, yet generally more brittle than the Spanish, whether it be from nature, or tincture and temper; nevertheless, the proprietors of the mines, by casting of cannon and other things, make them turn to good account. But whether the nation is in anyway advantaged by them, is a doubt which the next age will be better able to resolve."

That, I fear, is a doubt which even the present age has not resolved; but most certainly it was the invention of "ordnance" in the reign of King Henry VIII that gave the iron trade its boom years.

"Master Huggett and his man John
They did make the first cannon."

Unfortunately when the cold light of history is turned upon this rhyme we find Man John in much the same position as the lady whose name was Smith but on her tombstone was called

* The exact figures in 1573-4 were thirty-two furnaces and forty forges in Sussex as against eight furnaces and six forges in Kent.

Jones "to make it rhyme with cherry-stones". Ralphe Hogge's assistant was in sober fact a Frenchman called Peter Baude, one of the many Frenchmen who came to England at this time, partly as Huguenot refugees, partly to teach the improved French method of metal-founding. Another of them was Robert Douce, who worked at the furnace of Pannyngridge near Salehurst, and after one of whose descendants was named the property of Petit Douce, now called Doucegrove, above Beckley Furnace. The "ou" is pronounced "ow" and Robert Douce himself was naturalised under the name of Dowse. Dowses and Douches are still to be found in the country around old Pannyngridge.

The first cannon was a primitive affair—a cylinder of iron bars laid side by side like the staves of a barrel and fastened to a sledge. Another even more precarious variety was formed of rolled iron plates or even of jacked leather bound with broad circles of iron. One might well consider that the firing of these "pieces" was more dangerous to those who discharged them than to those who received the charge. Indeed, though many disapproved of the new weapon, "partly because subjecting valour to chance, partly because guns give no quarter (which the sword often doth)", it was found on the whole to have reduced rather than increased the slaughter of the battlefield. "Since their invention, Victory hath not stood so long a neuter, and hath been determined with the loss of fewer lives."

Alas! that extenuating circumstance did not remain for long. Bigger and better cannon, while they reduced the casualties among those who fired them, were very much more deadly to their foes. The crude cylinder of iron and leather gave place to guns cast in one piece. There was an enormous variety of shapes and sizes, starting with the robinet, weighing only two hundred pounds and measuring only two inches at the mouth, and grading upwards to the great basilisk, weighing nine thousand pounds, with a mouth of eight inches and three-quarters. In between were the ascending ranks of falconet, falcon, minion, sacre, demy-culverin, culverin, demy-cannon and cannon. Balls were cast to the measure of these assorted engines, varying from the dainty little ball the size of a pommander which for many years I found a most efficient paper-weight, to the great ball almost too heavy to lift which I still use as a door-stop and which must have been made to the measure of the basilisk's mouth. These balls were found in the fields close to my home, where iron still is everywhere, in the soil and in the water and in the hard core of the farm lane. The countryside is still as full of it as when Beckley Furnace roared and thumped in the valley below. It is only the fuel that has gone.

The problem of fuel arose early. In the reign of Henry VIII a statute was passed which ordered that in the felling of under-wood of twenty-four years' growth and under there should be left in every acre "twelve standels or stores of oak". Nor was any wood larger than two acres allowed to be grubbed up for tillage.

In Elizabeth's reign another Act forbade the felling of timber "to make coals for buring iron". But as both these Acts specially excepted "places known to be within the Wilds of Kent, Surrey, or Sussex", the pillage of the woods went on.

"The daughters of the Wead
(That in their heavy breasts had long their griefs concealed),
Foreseeing their decay each hour so fast come on,
Under the axe's stroke, fetched many a grievous groan,
When as the anvil's weight, and hammer's dreadful sound.
Even rent the hollow woods and shook the queachy
      ground. . . .
'Could we,' say they, 'suppose that any would us cherish
Which suffer every day the holiest things to perish?
Or to our daily wants to minister supply?
These iron times breed none that mind posterity.
'Tis but in vain to tell what we before have been,
Or changes of the world that we in time have seen;
When, now devising how to spend our wealth with waste,
We to the savage swine let fall our larding mast,
But now, alas! ourselves we have not to sustain,
Nor can our tops suffice to shield our roots from rain.
Jove's oak, the warlike ash, veined elm, the softer beech,
Short hazel, maple plain, light asp, the bending wych,
Tough holly and smooth birch, must altogether burn;
What should the builder serve, supplies the forger's turn,
When under public good, base private gain takes hold,
And we, poor woful woods, to ruin lastly sold.' "

Thus old Michael Drayton in his *Polyolbion* expressed what must have been the feelings of the more sensitive and intelligent of his contemporaries. There is something painful and heart-stirring in the felling of even a single tree—the last crack of the axe which is so much sharper than those earlier ones dulled by the living wood, and then that terrible crashing, rustling fall. . . . A more practical if less poetic protest came from the Admiralty, which pointed out the paradox of using so much wood to cast naval guns that there was a real danger of none being left to build the ships.

In the end, however, it was not so much the exhaustion of the woods that closed the iron-works of the Weald as the much greater cheapness of pit-coal as fuel, so that it was no longer economic to carry on the industry in a region where coal was not. The last furnace to blow was that at Ashburnham, which did not close down till 1828.

Cannon were not, of course, the only products of the forges. Iron, like nuclear fission, had its peaceful uses. One of these was tombstones. Iron tombstones are fairly common in Sussex churches and that in Burwash parish church I have already pointed out as probably the oldest sepulchral slab in Britain. But the most common survivals of the Wealden iron-works are fire-backs and fire-irons, while most schoolchildren know that the railing of St Paul's were cast at Lamberhurst. There are not in the Weald those iron field-railings that are so common in the iron-producing districts of the North; but some beautiful specimens of wrought-iron gates survive, and the reader may be pleased to know that these are still most excellently made in certain Sussex forges. A Sussex forge also made the altar rails, church cross, candle-stands and hanging sanctuary lamp of a recently built church, in welcome change from the ecclesiastical rule of brass. But, of course, the iron no longer comes from local pits—the bloomery (if that lovely name is ever used in the North) and the furnace are elsewhere. Sussex provides only the forge and the craftsman's skill.

4

Before we leave the Wealden iron-industry, I should like the reader to visit a small hamlet which was once a thriving and important iron-works. Beckley Furnace is just within the parish of Brede, at the bottom of Furnace Lane, in the valley of the River Tillingham. I first saw it as a schoolgirl, on an Easter Eve when the apple-blossom was out and the lambs were at pasture in the hammer field, and as I stood there by the bridge in the quiet and sunshine, among the hidden flower-scents, I could have imagined myself in paradise. The little weather-boarded cottages seemed without inhabitants, nobody stirred except the lambs in the field and they made the only sound.

Beckley Furnace has changed very little since that day. To the stranger's eye it is just a number of small cottages clustered together in a hole without the amenities of church or shop or pub. A slightly larger house stands back behind a farmyard and close to a narrow stream which crosses the road under a bridge. If the stranger is on foot and looks down over the bridge into the stream he will notice that both the water and the soil of the banks are tinged with red.

If he were to become more enterprising and turn aside down the path that runs along the back of Furnace House he would find what appears to be the remains of a mill, with a dam and a great wheel, both now lost in the stillness and growth of the wood. Coming out on open ground he would walk along the top of a bank between a full flowing brook and a large, flat meadow. Then in half a mile the valley narrows to within a few yards of the river's edge and he would find himself walking beside the Tillingham, in a pocket of sunshine and silence between sloping woods, with the old timbered face of Conster Manor beaming at him from the south.

A stranger walking the same way two hundred years earlier would have had a very different excursion. Instead of silent cottages and an empty lane he would have found a number of busy workers, digging in the scowles and carting the ironstone to the furnace, while the air would have been full of the roar of flames, the thump of hammers and the constant splash of the furnace wheel as the waters turned it. The wide flat meadow would have been a great lake, spreading most of the way to Conster, while the bank dividing it from the Old Cow brook would be no green turf but a great rampart of cinders. Cinders and slag would have been everywhere on the tracks, over which horses and wagons dragged the felled oaks, while from Wagmary Wood came the crack of axes and the crash of falling trees. As dirty and noisy a hole as could be imagined by anyone who had not seen a similar undertaking at work in the North. But our stranger has not yet known the worst—the ear-splitting roar with which a sacre at test spits its ball across the valley into Forge Field. No doubt he then remembers that Beckley is one of the few furnaces with a reputation for making *great* guns.

It is uncertain when this furnace first began to blow. There are evidences of workings here at a very early date, and some historians think that the Roman bloomeries extended up the valley of the Tillingham as far as Chitcombe, where clinkers and pottery have been found. This part of the Weald could well have been considered in those days "in partibus maritimus", for the great estuary which had made an isle of Oxney would have brought the sea-traffic as near as Udimore, while the oaks of Anderida Silva would also have been close at hand for fuel.

The later history of Beckley Furnace is obscure until the Commonwealth, when it is known to have been at work and, in common with the furnaces at Brede and Horsmonden, to have supplied guns to the Parliamentary forces during the Civil War. It then formed part of the estate of Peter Farnden, a famous iron-master of Sedlescombe. His daughter married Samuel Gott, and the Gott family owned the furnace until the year 1770, when, owing to the rising costs of labour and of charcoal as compared with pit-coal, it closed down.

It had nearly closed several years earlier, when an exceptionally fierce drought dried up the streams around it, so that the great wheel which worked the bellows had to be turned by human treading. The late Mr Edmund Austen, to whose invaluable record of Brede parish I owe some of my facts and all my figures, adds his footnote to this information: "Did the knowledge of this influence Sir George Gray, when Home Secretary, to institute tread mills in Houses of Correction?" Certainly the treading of the mill-wheel at Beckley would not have been the demoralising and degrading labour it afterwards proved in prisons. The men would have known that on their work depended their reputation and their livelihood two powerful incentives altogether lacking in its penal use. That was in 1744, and thanks to the workers the furnace survived its ordeal and continued to blow for nearly another 35 years.

Not only guns were made at Beckley, but fire-backs, fire-irons and brand-irons, while towards their close the works acquired a reputation for the making of brass skillets. When they finally shut down it was understood that they might reopen in time of war, but war and the threat of invasion brought no revival to Beckley, though the furnace at Brede, which had also closed, was rebuilt and restarted as a gunpowder-mill. If Beckley had done the same it is doubtful if we should still have this peaceful survival in the Tillingham valley. For the Brede powder-works blew up not once, nor twice, but thrice, destroying the buildings and killing several of the workers—men with the old Brede names like Gutsell and Sinden, whose heads and limbs were scattered over neighbouring woods. Their memory lives in the dogwood and spindleberry in which this district is rich and which were originally planted to make the kind of charcoal thought to be best for manufacturing gunpowder. What more lovely memorial than a flaming spindle-tree could the hedgerows offer these men who laid down their lives on the home-front against Bonaparte?

5

The iron industry was co-extensive with the Weald. The broadcloth industry, on the other hand, though it made nearly as many fortunes, was limited to the district around Cranbrook, Goudhurst and Headcorn. Weaving, of course, had been practised throughout the country for many hundreds of years. The Romans made cloth during their occupation, so did the Saxons and the Normans, but the cloth they made was coarse and very plain, being woven in natural shades only. The people of wealth and fashion who wanted to wear fine, gaily coloured clothes had to import them from abroad, where they were made from exported English wool.

This anomaly, which is always cropping up in our history, impressed King Edward III. According to Dr Thomas Fuller's *Church History*, "The king began to grow sensible of the great gain the Netherlands got by English wool, in memory whereof

Old Cloth Hall, Biddenden

the Duke of Burgundy instituted the order of the Golden Fleece, wherein indeed the fleece was ours, the gold theirs."

Returning from Scotland after the battle of Halidon Hill, the King invited the Flemish weavers to come "into our kingdom of England for the purpose of working wools there and otherwise exercising their mystery". His agents visited the Low Countries and the first to accept the invitation was John Kemp, no doubt the ancestors of all the Kemps in the Weald, who to-day can be counted in their scores. He came with all his goods and chattels, his looms, his servants and apprentices, receiving a safe conduct from the King for their journey and the promise of his support till their "mystery" was established.

Nor did that promise fail either him or the many who followed him to this country. The imported weavers were well looked after and given every assistance in setting up their looms. Moreover they were protected by laws which forbade both the export of English wool and the import of foreign cloth. Other restrictions were more arbitrary, and there was a tendency for them to multiply in a way that seems to prove that bureaucracy can exist without the Civil Service. In every wool town "Aulnagers" (an aulne is an ell) were appointed, whose duty it was to examine the cloth and fix seals upon it. The manufacturer was also restricted to one mill and two apprentices, and no workman who had not served an apprenticeship of seven years could be employed by him. He was, moreover, forbidden to carry on two branches of the same trade so as to be able to finish his fabrics at home. Finally it was made a penal offence to buy or sell wool under anticipatory contracts, and all the wool manufactured in the Weald must be disposed of at the "King's Staple" or market, which for the Weald of Kent was Canterbury, "in honour of St Thomas".

These orders and restrictions were highly vexatious, especially the last one which involved the transport of valuable goods on unmade roads for long distances through forests where thieves might and indeed did often lurk. But in spite of them the trade flourished and the traders grew rich. The cloth trade was not of course confined to Kent, nor were all the foreign weavers settled there. Sussex and five other counties were fixed on for cloth in general, Essex for serges and Norfolk for woollens. But Kent

Lamberhurst

was the established home of the first settlers and the centre for making broadcloth, and Kentish broadcloth became famous not only through the county but throughout the Continent. Unlike the earlier kinds it was made in a variety of colours, though even those were restricted to a number chosen by this most despotic King, of whom it might be written as of Lady Catherine de Bourgh that nothing was too small for his great notice. The colours favoured by the royal choice do not seem particularly attractive—"russet, gynger, brown-blewe, rattes-colour and green-medly" are some of them.

At first there was opposition to the foreign weavers, but as their "mystery" became known to the people in general, it abated, and many of the native inhabitants of Cranbrook, Goud-hurst, Hawkhurst and other cloth towns engaged in the trade. The secret of the superior cloth made by the foreigners lay in the use of fulling-mills, where the material was cleansed of grease and given a smooth surface. These mills, like the bellows of the iron furnaces, were driven by water-wheels, and the numerous rivers and streams of this part of the Weald were everywhere dammed for water-power. There is said to have been a hundred and thirty acres of water in Cranbrook alone, yielding enough power for a dozen mills. These were not unlike the cornmills, save that instead of the millstones and hoppers were the giant wooden hammers that beat the cloth with a noise which could be heard all over the parish. What with the clang of the hammers in the forges and the thump of the hammers in the mills the Good Old Dayes must have been far from quiet.

One of the great advantages that the clothiers of the Weald had over those in other parts of England was the abundance of fuller's earth. This is a kind of clay and marl containing nitre, which the hammers beat into the cloth till it was clean and dry. Another useful product of the district was the teazle for refining the wool—a process which the Romans had carried out with hedgehogs. The teazle flower certainly appears a more conveni-ent tool, and it was not long before it became the emblem of the Clothworkers' Company.

The industry continued in the Weald for over four hundred years, coming to an end in the eighteenth century, which also saw the end of the iron-works. The reason was partly the same—

the greater cheapness of pit-coal as compared with charcoal—but the Scottish Act of Union with England also had something to do with it. It removed certain trade restrictions which had formerly hampered the Scots, whose country now become a serious rival of Kent in the manufacture of broadcloth. There was also the invention of an early form of machinery which handicapped the less mechanically minded South. In Kent all the looms were worked entirely by hand, and a spinning-wheel called the "Saxon" was used for making woollen yarn. But now in up-to-date factories several spindles were arranged so as to be worked by one and the same action of the spinner, and the spinners of the Weald did not take readily to new inventions. Gradually the manufacture of broadcloth declined in Kent and increased not only in Scotland but in Yorkshire and Lancashire. By the end of the eighteenth century there was not a single clothier left in the Weald.

6

We have paid a visit to an ancient iron-works and it would be just as interesting to visit a former cloth-hall. There are many, very many, of these in the country round Cranbrook, but we must not confuse them with the weavers' homes, of which there are many more. A "hall-house" is not the same as a cloth-hall, for at the time these houses were built they were all "halls" in the sense that the high, barn-like centre was used as the living-place, where before chimneys were invented the fire burned on a central hearth and smoked the rafters. Leading out of it was the "solar", where solitude could be enjoyed by those who wished for it, also some primitive and crowded sleeping accommodation. But the main life of the house centred in the hall, and it was there that the first looms were set up, for the first foreign weavers in Kent were like the first weavers in Yorkshire and Lancashire and worked their looms in their houses. It was not till later that factories or cloth-halls were built to accommodate a number of looms and a multitude of workers.

The invention of chimneys and another type of hearth decentralised the house, and for greater warmth and more accommodation the "hall" was ceiled over and another set of rooms created above it. This was in many cases done centuries ago, and the ancient floor of ships' timbers often seems nearly as old as the rest of the building. Other hall-houses have been divided up more recently, while in these days there is a reverse movement in favour of taking out the partitions and opening the hall to the beauty and the draughts of its original construction.

Except in such a "restored" house there would be little to remind us of the clothiers. Angley and Wilsley and Coursehorne, standing in their lovely gardens, are like Beckley Furnace in its quiet valley. We find it hard to recapture the days that are gone, when here as at Beckley the waters spread and the hammers thumped, though to the ends of peace rather than of war. Even the special Flemish style of building, with its gable-ends and elaborate timber-work, has ceased to be distinctive in a district where there is so much of it and that much has been so much copied.

Though these houses are thickest round Cranbrook they are scattered all over the Kentish Weald, and not only they but the churches of Cranbrook, Goudhurst, Headcorn, Hawkhurst and the other cloth-towns, with the schools at Cranbrook and Sutton Vallence, bear witness to the wealth and generosity of the master-weavers. Since the decline of the trade many of these buildings have also declined—we have seen the sad effects of indifference and neglect on more than one parish church in this part of the Weald. Houses, too, in days when beauty and antiquity had not the commercial value that they have now, were abandoned by the kind of occupier that had built them and sliced into workers' dwellings or (indeed, and) allowed to decay. It is only when fashions in houses changed that they were repaired and restored to owners of a similar type to those who had brought them into being. I like to think (or at least it is pleasant to fancy) that in the abiding brotherhood of their craft, master-clothiers of the Weald look down from Paradise and bless the master-clothiers of Leeds and Halifax and Bradford who (as so many successful Northerners do) have come south in search of warmth and sunshine in their declining years, and in a legacy of health are enjoying the wealth which those old craftsmen left behind them.

7

There were industries in the Weald besides iron and cloth; indeed this small corner of England was in the past a microcosm of that Northern and Midland area which to-day produces not only iron and cloth and coal but pottery and glass. As the furnaces of Lamberhurst compare with those of Sheffield and the looms of Cranbrook with those of Halifax, so the potteries of Brede, Rye and the Dicker can be mentioned in the same (though bated) breath as those of the Five Towns.

The making of pottery is as old as civilisation, and the soil of the Weald, abounding in clay, has always been particularly suited to its manufacture. But pottery as an industry, as supplying the domestic needs of more than a single community, is of comparatively recent date. As an industry it has existed at only a limited and changing number of centres. Potteries, like brickfields, spring up and disappear so quickly that it is difficult to keep track of them at all.

Perhaps the best known Wealden pottery comes from the Dicker, between Hailsham and Lewes, which is associated with an interesting type of black ware. In my young days there was also a pottery at Rye, which made jugs and bowls and other objects in brown and green, heavily glazed, and trailed over with life-size and most natural-looking hops. It also manufactured lustre ware, and what was to me then far more beautiful—vases and jugs made up of brightly coloured broken shards embedded in a kind of cement which was then covered with gold leaf. The great drawback to these was that they could not hold water and their production ceased. But they were things of dream-like beauty in the eyes of a child. Since the last war the pottery at Rye has been restarted, but has not yet made any of those articles that were so characteristic of it once.

I have in my possession various samples of Rye and Dicker ware, also a specimen from a pottery which flourished for a time at Rolvenden. But I have nothing from my nearest kilns at Brede —nearest in space, that is to say, for in time they have been closed since 1892, though their names survive in Potman's Field and Pottery Lane. These names belong to two distinct undertakings, the first to a very ancient pottery which existed in the south-western corner of Broadlands Wood. Various shards found here have been identified by experts as probably belonging to the fourteenth or fifteenth centuries. The Pottery Lane Works were started much later, probably about 1750. By that time potteries had ceased to be purely local and this one supplied a comparatively wide area, though its products were mainly simple objects for everyday use, such as crocks and pans. Even its "mantel ornaments" had their (rather unexpected) uses. A pottery bird, for instance, had a whistle in its tail, so that when built into a chimney the wind blowing through the pipe would frighten evil spirits away. A pottery pig on the other hand made a useful drinking-vessel. The body would hold up to a quart of beer, while the removable head made a convenient mug; so that to boast that you had drunk a hogshead of beer was one of the many ways of pulling the leg of some simple foreigner from the shires.

As the Wealden clay encourages the manufacture of pottery, so the Wealden sands are useful in the manufacture of glass. They have been used for glass-making at Hastings for more than a hundred years, also at Ashurstwood on the borders of Ashdown Forest. But it is sand for glass-making rather than glass-ware itself that the Weald produces now. The Lower Greensand of the Folkestone Beds, the Tunbridge Wells sand and the Ashdown Forest sand are all good glass-making material. Before 1914 it was cheaper to import sand from France, Holland and Germany than to pay the cost of its transport by rail from the Weald to London, but the first world war forced the manufacturers to use supplies nearer home. The chief sources of supply now are the Tunbridge Wells and Ashdown Forest districts. But glass-sand throughout the Weald is a resource which has hardly been tapped. There are deposits at Fairlight, Brede, Crowhurst, Burwash and Battle in this corner of Sussex alone.

In this corner too are the gypsum mines near Mountfield. These owe their existence to a meeting of the British Association at Brighton in 1878, when a committee was formed for a very different enterprise—the sinking of a bore-hole with the object of reaching the Palæozoic rocks in the Heathfield–Battle area. The committee chose for this operation Lime Kiln Wood, near Mountfield, where two borings were put down. Far from reaching any Palæozoic rocks, the first of these bores reached only— though 1,017 feet deep—the upper part of what is known as Kimmeridge Clay. The second boring was equally unsatisfactory from the Palæozoic angle, but the two of them led to the discovery of gypsiferous beds fifty to sixty feet thick and producing the best-quality material.

The Gypsum mines (or Egyptian mines as they are called locally) have been working ever since, and it is thought that there is very much more of this important mineral in the area known archæologically as the "Heathfield–Battle fold". A more recent boring in Petley Wood passed forty-seven feet of gypsiferous beds at 764 feet from the surface.

As an industry the mines themselves are admirably discreet; indeed they appear on the surface as rural as a hop-garden, while the homes of the mine-workers have long been a part of the landscape. Even should they and their contemporary undertaking for the digging of glass-sand enormously increase they are not likely ever again to make a Black Country of the Weald or bring back the nights when our ancestors could not sleep for noise.

8

Farming perhaps should not be described as an industry. To do so provokes those who believe that a farm should exist to satisfy the needs of a family, disposing only of its surpluses in the local market. Such no doubt was farming in days long gone by, in days when wants were uncomplicated and populations small. But to-day, when the bulk of the people lives away from the land and could return to it only at the price of its destruction, farming must take on more and more of an industrial aspect, supplying markets at a distance, and supplying them on a scale that forbids the farmer to subsist entirely on his own produce. Moreover, from almost the earliest times farmers have employed hired workers, thus introducing the problems of capital and labour into agriculture and commercialising its undertakings. It is true that in the past farm-workers were more like junior members of the family than hired employees, living—at least when unmarried—in the farmhouse and eating with the farmer and his children. But even in those days the relations of employer and employed were or could easily become those of the Haves and Have-Nots, and farm labourers as a whole were worse off than the workers engaged in the iron and clothing trades, as is shown by the oft-proclaimed difficulty of farmers in the

Weald of finding adequate labour when these industries flourished. We have already seen that smuggling was a formidable rival to the plough.

There is little doubt that the prosperity of this part of England from the fourteenth to the eighteenth centuries was due to other sources of wealth than agriculture. However, agriculture must have had its share of the spoils, for the farms were then the shops of the community and supplied the markets where a thriving population spent its money. Then, just as the local tradesmen are the first to feel any financial slump, so when one by one the looms came to a standstill and the furnaces shut down, the industry that had preceded and had survived them found itself badly shrunken.

The days before the repeal of the Corn Laws were bad old days all over England, but after their repeal the farms of the Weald revived in what was now a purely agricultural area. The former Black Country had become a land of small mixed farms, most of which belonged to large estates and were cultivated by tenant farmers. The boom-years of the nineteenth century, to which a sort of communal memory looks back as to an earthly paradise, was not the age of the yeomen. That came some sixty or seventy years later with the selling-up of the big estates after Lloyd George's Land Act, when many of the farmers bought their farms.

Alas, poor yeoman! After only a very few years in the tangles of mortgages and Queen Anne's Bounty, the farms were for sale again at prices which reflect defeat or even despair. Much good agricultural land went to the builders, as small syndicates descended like vultures on dying farms, tearing off their edges in "plots" and leaving the rest to rot in a plague of docks and thistles that would infect the whole neighbourhood, while the farmhouse, stripped of its weathering and proclaimed Ye Olde by a mass of rotting beams, became a trap for guileless Londoners.

It required a total war to restore the farms to prosperity, by means which removed the last rags of their primitive status. Harassed by bureaucrats, controlled by boards, littered with licences, riddled with restrictions, even the smallest farm to-day is as much an industrial undertaking as any factory. The farmworker is still almost the worst-paid worker in the country, in spite of the fact that his wages have risen to a point where the farmer hesitates to employ him. It is rare now to see more than one hand on a farm which used to employ a score, and that rich number of perquisites by means of which a labourer who tilled his own garden could manage to live almost without money have been translated into hard cash and short commons.

Nevertheless it is true that a man may now make a decent living out of farming, and the countryside of the Weald to-day has a far more prosperous appearance than it had twenty years ago. The war has proved mixed farming to be the best and most profitable kind. The specialised poultry farms that crowded the district after the first world war withered one by one for lack of imported foodstuffs. It is now plain that a man must grow food for his cattle and not depend on the hazards of the sea, while the farmyard hen once more leads her little brood round the dunghill and scratches under the stack.

9

Farmers of the Weald, however, have always been inclined to specialise. After all, it was the specialised hog-farm which brought us our civilisation. Without the swine there could be no mixed farming in what once was Andredsweald. After the hogs, the hops. Their cultivation is still the specialised industry of the Kentish Weald and the part of Sussex adjoining it. They have been grown in these parts since the beginning of the six- teenth century, when they were introduced by Henry VIII, who then promptly suppressed them, it is thought as the result of pressure from the herbalists who saw their trade in wormwood, cinnamon, cloves and horehound depreciate in favour of the "wicked weedes" now grown for flavouring beer.

The hops were also unpopular for theological reasons, being considered a Protestant plant because their introduction coincided with the rise of Protestantism in the Low Countries of their origin and the dissolution of the monasteries in this. That being so it is worthy of remark that their cultivation was restored under Queen Mary, whose counsellors must have viewed the situation from the secular rather than the ecclesiastical angle. From that date they took their place with corn and roots among the normal crops of an ordinary Kentish farm. Their growth was encouraged by the Sheriff of Kent, Reginald Scot, who in 1574 published a book entitled *A Perfect Platforme of a Hop Garden*; but though more regularly and generally grown in Kent than in Sussex it was not till comparatively lately that they became a specialised industry.

Till then the hop garden primarily supplied the wants of the farm it belonged to, and the beer was mostly brewed at home. There was a long time to go before the brewery attained the co-operative status of the mill. The small oast-houses with only one kiln which may be seen in so many farms are purely domestic affairs, like the cellar wine-press of a French peasant family. Later on the oasts increased in size and number and supplied the local brewery. To-day all oast-houses work primarily for the brewers who have moreover built their own legions of them in districts specially favourable to hop-growing, such as the valleys of the Medway and the Rother, where the black traditionally shaped kilns of Messrs Whitbread, standing in rows like elegant widows each side of the main house, contrast most favourably with the hideous corrugated-iron factories Messrs Guinness have set up at Bodiam and Udiam.

We may deplore the passing of the domestic oast-house and the industrialisation of the hop-garden. But we must keep two things in mind. First, that the hops are grown to flavour the ale of a population eight times as large as that they used to supply; second, that their cultivation is a difficult enterprise, requiring much labour and often involving the farmer in heavy losses. Even in these days of the Hop Marketing Board, farmers are constantly selling their "quotas"—and sad to say, it is often to farms in a distant part of England, Worcester or Hereford, the only other counties where hops are grown. In the last twenty years hops have vanished entirely from the upper reaches of the Tillingham Valley, and probably, had it been left to independent farming, the Rother Valley would be empty too.

Without a doubt they are the most chancy, vulnerable things that ever came out of the ground. Every kind of blight descends upon them and every type of weather seems equally bad for them. Even if they survive as far as the oast-house they may perish on the drying-floor, and yet again when that last danger is passed and in their great pockets they travel up to London, they may rot in warehouse. In days when labour was cheap and plentiful such a hit-or-miss form of cultivation was less hazardous to the economics of the farm. But mounting costs have run ahead of improved methods of growing, tying and drying, and even with the Hop Marketing Board at his back the small farmer with only one or two farmhands is shy of a crop less likely to bring him profit than loss. The hops indeed are most flourishing where they are most specialised and industrialised.

Cobbett tried to invent an "imperishable" hop-pole after seeing the work involved each year in cutting, stripping and setting up new poles in every garden and the trouble caused by such of these that rotted in the damp soil before the end of the season. The problem was partly solved by creosote, but the modern industrial hop-garden contains no hop-poles of the old-fashioned sort, only supports for the wire cage from which descends the cat's-cradle that still requires the skill of the tiers—the men on stilts who reach the wires and attach the strings which the women tie a few feet above the ground. Hop-tying is a rural craft which is practised only for a few weeks in the year, but throughout the entire process the industrialist has every now and then to stand aside for the craftsman.

In the factory oast-house that Messrs Guinness have erected at Bodiam all the old driers are still at work. The fuel is oil, the processes are mechanical, but without the expert knowledge of Mus' Mepham, Mus' Sinden and their brethren the best results are impossible. I shall never forget the look I once saw on an old, experienced face, faintly lit with a smile of mingled contempt and toleration for such goings-on, especially as the goings-on seemed unable to go on without him who had watched the fires and regulated the draughts at Lordship oast every September for thirty years. But all he said was: "The scrubbetts still work by hand."

I understand that in certain of these factory-oasts even the scrubbetts have been mechanised, and already a final piece of mechanisation is being attempted in a hop-picking machine. This moves slowly towards perfection, as so short a time of the year is available for test and experiment. I have been told that the chief difficulty is to create a machine which will pick the blossoms while leaving the foliage. But I do not think that if and when success is attained its invention will be the popular catastrophe that some imagine. By that time it may not be easy to find hop-pickers.

There are two kinds of hop-picking. The first, which is characteristic of the Sussex hop-country, belongs to the small undertakings that employ local pickers only. For their benefit the schools are closed in September instead of in August; indeed twenty years ago the whole district seemed to close down—domestic help was unobtainable, shops were understaffed and life stood still while every available woman and child and not a few of the men gathered round the bins to earn the only good money of the year. On their work in the hop-gardens depended their winter comfort of warm clothes—a whole family could be clothed by three weeks' picking at twopence a bushel.

Since then the improvement in wages, both agricultural and domestic, has reduced this source of supply, and some of the farms that prided themselves on their exclusiveness have been forced to engage pickers from outside. Help of this kind involves all sorts of restrictions and regulations. The days are gone when the only preparation a farmer need make for the arrival of a hundred people was a cartload of straw on the floor of his largest barn. Huts must be provided and adequate methods of sanitation. There are, of course, always the "cart people", who come into the district to pick fruit and remain over the harvest and hop-picking. These gentry are now more acceptable than they used to be, for the reason that they are able to fend for themselves. But local opinion has always been strictly against them, with a tendency to accuse them of more crimes than they actually commit.

"Pickers from London" were until a few years ago regarded as a Kentish luxury, but now the industrialised undertakings of the Rother Valley also import them, and I am told that "the hop-pickers' express" will still run on the line between Roberts-bridge and Bodiam when all other passenger traffic has ceased. Here we have moved many years from the straw in the old barn. Rows of neat hopper-huts that with only a small stretch of accuracy might be called "chalets", a shop and a health centre with a trained nurse in attendance, would have rejoiced the heart of my father who in his days as a country doctor protested in vain against the accommodation offered the invading hordes and threatened every year an epidemic which always let him down by failing to start.

A hopping holiday at Bodiam has at least some of the amenities of a holiday camp, but it is just that camp which now threatens to check the supply of workers. In former days a hopping holiday was the only sort the East London workers could afford, and was moreover, as with the local people, a part of their winter providence. Now with improved wages and holidays with pay, it is only the select number who really enjoy hop-picking and prefer the real country to a holiday camp that continue to come amongst us. So it is possible that by the time the hop-picking machine is perfected its introduction will be a boon to the employers and cause very little grief to the employed.

10

"Surrey," said Mrs Elton to Jane Austen's Emma, "Surrey is the garden of England."

"Yes," answers Emma, "but we must not rest our claims on that distinction. Many counties, I believe, are called the garden of England as well as Surrey."

To which Mrs Elton's reply is:

"No, I fancy not. I never heard any county but Surrey called so."

Had she never heard of Kent? This is the county which by tradition and common consent has enjoyed the title for years before Mrs Elton or her creator were born. The garden is not a flower-garden. If we are in search of wild flowers, we shall find more in the West, in Dorset, Somerset and Devon, though the primroses and bluebells of the Weald are an unforgettable part of spring. But Kent has always stood for the garden type of cultivation as opposed to the purely agricultural, for crops of hops and fruit that grow not in "fields" but in "gardens".

The reason for this goes back to days when tithes were claimed from fields and not from gardens, which made it economic to describe as a garden the acres one had planted with the pretty new fruit called a cherry that the foreign weavers brought over with them from the Continent. The evasion was not so successful in the case of hops, as one of the trials and injustices of hop-growing has been the tithe on its acreage.

Kent was famous for its fruit farms as far back as the days of Lambarde. Of Tenham he writes:

"Here we have not only the most dainty pieces of all our shire but such a singularity as the whole British Island is not able to pattern. . . . This Tenham, with thirty other parishes extending from Rainham to Blean Wood, be the Cherry Garden and Apple Orchard of Kent. But as this at Tenham is the parent of all the rest, and from whom they have drawn the good juice of all their pleasant fruit, so is it also the most large, delightsome and beautiful of them. . . . Here our honest Papist, Richard Harrys (fruiterer to King Henry VIII), planted by his great cost and rare industry the sweet cherry, the temperate pippen, and the golden renate . . . he (I say) about the year of our Lord Christ 1533 obtained 105 acres of good ground in Tenham, then called the Brennet, which he divided into ten parcels, and with great care, good choice, and no small labour and cost, brought plants from beyond the seas, and furnished this ground with them, so beautifully, as they not only stand in most right line, but seem to be of one sort, shape and fashion, as if they had been drawn through one mould, or wrought by one and the same pattern."

Who could want a more vivid description of a thriving Kentish cherry garden or apple orchard as it still is to-day? And it is doubtful if even to-day a grower could do better than his seventeenth-century predecessor who according to Thomas Fuller sold the fruit of a thirty-acre orchard for a thousand pounds—"there being a failure in the neighbouring orchards". The district of Tenham does not, of course, form part of the actual Weald where the soil is not so well adapted to fruit-growing. Nevertheless the specialised fruit farm is everywhere in the Kentish Weald, and has even spread across the border to adjoining parts of Sussex, where orchards are taking the place of the disappearing hops. But cherries are no longer the chief crop grown in these parts, which is and probably always will be, apples.

It is this concentration of "garden crops" which makes the eastern parts of the Weald so lovely in spring, when the orchards are abloom in acres of pink and white, and from the high lands around Goudhurst, Pembury and Lenham one looks down on as it were a sea-wave that has caught the sunset. In autumn the scarlet and russet apples among the green make another sort of beauty, while green and gold drip from the aisles of the hop-gardens with a scent almost as intoxicating sweet as the scent of those same hops drying in the oast.

Another "garden" beauty lies in the chestnut plantations. These, of course, are not really gardens, but their ordered planting contrasts with the wildness of the woods that were here before them, and of them as of old Lambarde's cherry-garden it might be said that they stand in most right line and seem to be of one sort, shape and fashion. They often occupy the sites of the old woods that were cut down long ago to feed the furnaces, but few of them are more than a hundred years old. For them the highest season of their beauty is the winter, when their boughs are bare and the woodman moves among them with the single weapon that cuts, cleaves, strips and shapes the wood, while the blue smoke of the fires that burn his "rubbidge" rises slowly to mingle with the mist and smudge it over the tops of the trees.

The woods are sold "standing" for cutting every twelve years or so, and provide the district (and remoter parts) with fencing, which is a growing need now that that good old hedger who prided himself on the hedge he "laid along" without introducing a single extra stick has given place to those who hack and chop and fill the gaps as best they can with spiles. Every single scrap of a chestnut clump or "tott" has its uses. The poles are split for fencing, though some still go entire to the hops, the bark and ply-wood make the Sussex trug-basket, the branches are useful in "binding" the clay of the clearing tracks or even for making primitive defences against the sea at Winchelsea Beach or Camber Sands. The small stuff goes for pea-sticks and kindling, while the woodman takes home the "chucks" for his fire.

These plantations extend considerably further west than the hop-gardens and commercial orchards—indeed they are to be found in all parts of the Sussex Weald, but they are still thickest on the Kent and Sussex borders. Mr Hilaire Belloc's "Weald in a tumbled garden" is more a matter of the small, mixed farms, such as form the general pattern of the whole under those decorative "dainty pieces" of fruit and hops.

CHAPTER III

THE WEALD AND RELIGION

I

THE religious history of the Weald dates from the very earliest days of its human habitation. Many centuries before the shadow of another Tree was to fall on it from Canterbury, its oaks were sacred to the Druids, while the Saxon invaders found in its ashes the World Tree, Yggdrasil. These trees are still the most common in the Weald. Though no longer a part of worship they spring up in our hedges, crowd our woods, burn in our fires—memorials of past glories and sanctities, now cheerfully dispossessed of their divinity to supply our human needs.

The fact that Gaul and Britain practised the same religion has been considered by some as proof of the existence of an isthmus connecting the two counties. No doubt there was this connection in the remote past, but whether it co-existed with human life is conjectural. All we know is that the people on both sides of the Channel had the same Druidical religion and that Britain was the chief seat of its learning, whither students from Gaul flocked for instruction, though the "Rome" of this *Ecclesia* was as remote from Gaul as Anglesey.

Here the Arch-Druid lived in pomp and seclusion, ruling over a hierarchy of priestly ranks, whose office passed from father to son, though their Patriarch himself was elected. The Druids were a theocracy, for they controlled not only the religious but the secular life of the country, educating the young and administering the civil and criminal laws. For their colleges and seminaries they used the forests, instructing their students in the depths of woods, the groves of which were also their temples.

Their worship was closely bound up with the oak. This has been considered a sacred tree by many other religions, but the Druids went further in proclaiming it the most sacred object in

nature. Everything about it was holy, the leaves, the wood, the flowers, but especially the mistletoe, that strange white florescence springing mysteriously, according to no laws, from no known seed. Andredsweald (though it would be centuries before it was called by that name) was then a holy place, where the Holiest grew in his ten thousands. On the sixth day of the moon, which was the beginning of their months and years, a Druid clothed in white (according to Jung, the archetypal colour of redemption) ascended the tree and with a golden knife cut the all-healing plant, which fell in its whiteness on a white woollen cloth below. Beside it two white oxen were sacrificed. The Weald was a temple almost as soon as it was a forest and long before it was a farm.

But for worship and instruction the Druids required a whole circle of oaks. It had to be wide enough to be open to the sky, even though the trees stood densely round it, and this raises the question as to whether the stone circles with which we are familiar were not originally substitutes for tree circles in places where no oaks grew. Certainly no stone circles have survived within the Weald, which provided the oak so lavishly. The monoliths of Stonehenge, Stenness and other places may have been stylised oak-trees, and it is perhaps a strange thought that the Gothic, which for most of us in this country stands for a specifically Christian architecture, springs from such a stylisation, and is in fact a departure from Christian tradition, according to which the House of God is evolved directly from the house of man. Enter a Gothic cathedral—Salisbury, Winchester, Rheims, Chartres, Cologne—and you enter a forest of stone. The soaring trunks of the columns spread their boughs overhead in foliated arches, the narrow glades of the aisles give vistas through darkness to slants of light; there are no broad views, only the mystery that belongs to Andredsweald. It is significant that this type of architecture is found most abundantly in those northern countries where Druidic worship once prevailed, as if a forest pattern of trees had been stamped on the minds of succeeding generations.

The actual beliefs of the Druids we can only guess at, for theirs was essentially an esoteric and occult religion. Nothing whatever was allowed to be committed to writing, even their numerous hymns, some of which were so long that they took twenty years to learn. From the little that we know it appears that their teachings followed the same pattern as those of many other early religions. According to Furley, who quotes from d'Aubigny's *Faiths of the World*, they believed that:

"Man was placed in the circle of courses, good and evil being set before him for his selection, and upon his making choice of the former, death transmitted him from the earth into the circle of felicity. If, however, he became vicious, death returned him into the circle of courses, wherein he was made to do penance in the body of an animal, and then permitted to resume his human form. The length and repetition of this probation was determined by the vice or virtue of the individual but after a certain number of transmigrations his offences were supposed to be expiated, his passions subdued, and his spirit dismissed to the circle of felicity."

Very different from the religion of the oak was the religion of the ash. The Saxon invaders brought with them a barbarous system already in its decline to persecute and virtually exterminate the Christianity which at the end of the Roman occupation was flourishing in many parts of Britain. The religion of the ash was a religion of war and violence rather than of worship and poetry, and the gods of Asgaard were gods of combat and slaughter, whose favourites among men were those who fell in battle. Scandinavian polytheism still lingers in our days of the week, where sun and moon, Woden and Thor and Freya find their commemorations. All classes from the king downwards believed in magic and a principle of evil whose name was Loke. Even the principle of good, Woden the All-Father, cared nothing for human virtues and the pure joys of life but demanded human sacrifices. The world was Yggdrasil, the gigantic ash, with a rainbow in its branches and a serpent at its roots. At a given time it would be burned by avenging gods, who later on would meet their own doom not in fire but in darkness. This was the faith the embers of which Augustine was to find when he came to Kent.

2

There is a legend that the ash provided the wood of the Cross, and in consequence the tree fails and dies after thirty-three years.

It is certainly short-lived in comparison with the oak which stands for centuries, but the legend more probably arose out of the purple blossoms of the ash, which, at the end of its leafless hanging twigs, look like drops of blood. These exquisite flowers are at their most beautiful budding round about Good Friday and Easter, and the Vexilla Regis, that great hymn of the Cross, is sung at the time when all the ash trees in the wood are adorning themselves with purple as they come into bloom.

" Arbor decora et fulgida
Ornata Regis purpura. . . ."

Thus Yggdrasil is baptised, but when St Augustine came to Kent the World Ash was barely a memory. The religion of the Anglo-Saxons had dwindled to mere superstition, such as made King Ethelbert receive the missionaries out of doors, where magic was considered less potent than in a house. The story of the evangelisation of Britain from Rome under Pope Gregory the Great is too well known to be repeated. What is not so well known is that the country was not so much converted to Christianity by Augustine and his monks as re-converted. Before the end of the Roman occupation England was at least in part a Christian country, and the Saxon invaders overthrew not the altars of the Druids but the altars of Christ.

The time of Christianity's first arrival on these shores is uncertain, but it was very early. Even if we discount the legends of St Paul and St Joseph of Arimathea in the West, there is evidence for its introduction in the first century. Pomponia Græcina, wife of the first governor, Aulus Plautius, is said to have been a Christian, also Claudia Rufina, wife of Aulus Pudens (mentioned by St Paul in his letter to Timothy), who was the daughter either of Caractacus or of Cogidubnus, King of Regnum. These were, however, no more than Christian ladies resident in a pagan country. The credit of introducing Christianity to Britain as a missionary force is given by St Bede to a British chief, Lucius, who applied to Pope Eleutherus for missionaries to instruct his subjects in the Christian religion. But whatever its origins, it is a fact that much of Britain was Christian when the barbarians came.

The invaders stamped it out entirely. It is doubtful if it lurked even to the extent it was found lurking in Japan, where mission-aries returning some hundreds of years after the Jesuit martyrdoms discovered small surviving communities without church or priest but with a system of Christian life and doctrine still at work among them.

Augustine had little opposition to face from paganism, which was virtually at an end, so that his wine could be poured into an empty bottle. Moreover, Ethelbert's consort, Bertha, was her-self a Christian from France. The king's conversion was followed by that of the majority of his subjects. Kent became the first entirely Christian kingdom in England, and the head of English Christianity took up his residence in Canterbury.

Sussex has a very different story. Instead of the first county to be converted it was the last. Between Canterbury and Chichester spread the whole length of the Undwelt-in-Wood. The faith eventually came by sea to the shores beyond the forest and it came from very much further away than Kent.

St Wilfred was a Yorkshireman who had had plenty of troubles in his northern diocese. When finally dispossessed and cast out he took refuge in Sussex, which he had already visited once before when driven by a storm towards the coast. On that occasion the unfriendly savages had not allowed him to land, but when he arrived the second time he found them less truculent, being in the clutches of a three-years' drought, which had reduced them to such misery that they were committing mass-suicide by whole-sale drownings and jumpings off cliffs. St Wilfred saved the community from extinction by teaching them how to fish, a process of which they were ignorant, having never learned to make nets. He built a monastery and converted the neighbouring chiefs. Paganism was not dead in Sussex as Augustine had found it in Kent, so his task was a much harder one, but he succeeded, and in a surprisingly short time, for Wilfred, apostle of Sussex, was in the county only five years.

In those five years he worked incredible changes, teaching the people the wisdom of two worlds, and establishing not only the Christian Church but a civilised community. The little town of Paganham which the Chief Ceadwalla granted him on his conversion became a seventh-century Utopia, free from tyranny, from the demands of military service, from taxes and from want, living entirely in peace and practising the peaceful arts. No wonder that for a time the most popular Christening name in Sussex was Wilfred.

But it must be remembered that he lived and worked only on the seaboard edges—his cathedral has long been under the sea—and it was not till after his death that the light trickled slowly between the packed tree-trunks of Andredsweald. The swineherds no doubt took their Christianity with them when they accompanied their flocks into the wood, but surprisingly few Sussex vills or settlements were provided with churches when the Domesday survey was made. The churches came later, and partly as a result of that act of contrition which the Conqueror made for the slaughter of Senlac.

Battle Abbey soon was only one among many of the religious foundations in Sussex, though for obvious reasons few of them had houses in the forest itself. Robertsbridge Abbey, six miles from Battle, was deepest in the Wild, though far from isolated, as in those days the Rother was navigable to well above this point. The Robertsbridge monks were Cistercians, and their vocation was the salvation of the land as well as of souls. As in Yorkshire they reclaimed the treeless wolds, so in Sussex they tamed and cultivated the thickets of the Weald.

The twin forces of agriculture and religion worked together for many hundred years. Their humble progress is expressed in the familiar group of church and church farm, as the plough and the cross took possession together. That other great saint of Sussex, St Richard, seems as remote from these parts as his predecessor St Wilfred or his own cathedral city, isolated at the far end of the diocese and still an administrative problem to-day. But we are told that the churches in the Weald increased to such an extent that the Devil decided to drown them by letting in the sea at Devil's Dyke. We know that he was frustrated by an old woman's candle, but we do not know how many churches he hoped to drown. Certainly none of them was as big and fine as some of the churches in the Weald of Kent, for in Sussex at that time there was no industrial boom and when it came people no longer spent their money on churches.

Attempts have been made to prove that the term "Silly Sussex" is derived from the Old English *siligh* or blessed and related to the modern German *selig*—that "Silly Sussex" is in fact "Holy Sussex". But, apart from the claims of alliteration, it would be difficult to prove that Sussex deserves the adjective more than Kent. It is true that on entering the county from Hampshire we are met at Rogate by the imperative of prayer— *Rogate quæ ad pacem sunt Jerusalem*—but no scholar would endorse such a derivation. As for monastic foundations, Battle Abbey did not build more churches or priories in the Weald than the monks of Canterbury built on Romney Marsh, nor is there anything in Sussex to match the famous shrine of St Thomas the Martyr, which attracted pilgrims from all over the world, and in England was not second even to Walsingham. Certainly "silly" springs from the same root as *selig*, but how far had it gone on its way before it was first applied to Sussex?

There is, however, a sense in which it rubs against, even though it does not actually hold, the meaning claimed for it. For a long time "silly" people—the fool, the village idiot—were regarded as being in an especial manner under the divine protection. Even now in certain Eastern countries the mentally deficient are considered privileged—unable to grapple with the affairs of this world because they are better equipped for another. This aspect of silliness is strikingly brought out in Dr A. H. Layard's study of an English "natural", *The Lady of the Hare*. Here he shows how the soothing away by analyses of conflicts in a defective subject's mind resulted in the discovery of unusual gifts and graces. So even in the modern sense of the word it does not seem that Sussex need be ashamed of her silliness, and certainly this sense is easier to accept than the idea that the county, pagan for a hundred years longer than the rest of England and constituting a diocese of which for centuries certain parts were inaccessible to others, ever became a proverb of sanctity to her Christian neighbours.

There is a type of church architecture known as the "Sussex Head". We find it in Udimore and other places where the stub of a tower squats against the roof of the nave, a rustic style entirely lacking in grandeur, impressiveness or even dignity; some might even say it looked silly. But it has its humble appeal and most truly its place in the landscape. If we take the Sussex Head as a symbol for Silly Sussex we get both senses of the word.

3

The Reformation brought the changes we all know. Perhaps that most felt in the Weald was the dissolution of the monasteries, which in these rural parts had a special importance as social and educational centres. It would be idle to pretend that all of them had lived up to the ideals of their founders or even to their own beginnings in the Weald, but their dissolution without any other provision being made for the needs of the people undoubtedly brought great misery, which the Poor Law of nearly a hundred years later did little to relieve. Moreover, the reformers put themselves in the wrong from the start by grabbing monastic property for the Crown, which enriched itself equally with the jewels of St Thomas à Becket's shrine and the lands of Battle Abbey. The inspiration of it all was openly proclaimed as loot, in which, it must be confessed, more than one Catholic had a share. Of course, apart from the King's supremacy, the doctrinal conflict had not yet arisen in this country. The King, as head of the Church, persecuted those he suspected of Genevan heresy, while Cranmer when made Archbishop of Canterbury had to send his wife and children abroad.

The more drastic changes came later. Indeed for the next fifty years the religious story of the Weald is one of sharp swings from side to side. Continental Protestantism, abhorred by Henry VIII, overran the country during the reign of his son, to be driven out again by his elder daughter and then restored by her half-sister. The Weald did not submit without protest to all these upheavals, for we are told that "five hundred Weldish-men" supported Wyatt's rebellion; but this was as much a political as a religious move, and for the most part the inhabitants of Kent and Sussex seem to have kept their feelings (if any) to themselves. There is, however, one curious item in the church-wardens' accounts of Brede parish, near Rye—"Itm payd for drynke when the Imags was taken down." It has been suggested that this drink was given because it was impossible to find anyone to commit such an act of sacrilege when sober.

Through these same accounts we can see the Reformation moving as it moved through three reigns. In the first year of King Edward VI we find that "hognell money", that is, money collected at Christmas by carol-singing and devoted to the buying of wax-candles for the church, was paid in as usual, and there is also an item for "mendyng the sensors". But in that same year the images were taken down and the altar cross removed and hidden in a case. The following year the cross was sold to Robert Oxenbridge of Brede Place, but there does not seem to have been any drastic removal of the church furniture until after a visitation by the King's Commissioners in 1549. On that followed what must have been a general sale of church affects:

Itm of Symond Pryor for a Surplys	4*d*.
Itm of John Alfrod for a holy wat' pote	∠. 8.
Itm of John Tomlyn for a vestment of dornek	10.
Itm of Wyllm Alford for an aube	2. 2.
Itm of Ric barons for an ault clothe	3. 0.

and so on and so on down to—

Itm of Mr Oxenbridge for the old tapers in the Rode loft

Itm of Mr Oxenbrydge for the bolls of the Candyl-styks.

In thus disposing of the goods of a well-equipped church the churchwardens must have made a fair amount of money. Some of it was spent on providing a Whole Bible in English for the Church, according to the King's injunction, which further ordered the Paraphrases of Erasmus upon the Gospels. But these expenses were trivial compared to what they had to pay out in 1553, when under a Catholic Queen they were obliged to find replacements for all the goods they had dispersed.

Itm for pyx	20*d*.
Itm for a holy water stope	6.
Itm to old bacheler for bryngung the holy wattr stocke to church	2*d*.
Itm to Leonard Wood for an hook of yron to hyng ye holy wattr stoke upon	2.
Itm to the said Leonard for nails	2.

Other items were more expensive. Books for the church, including presumably a Missal, cost seventeen and fourpence,

and though John Fyshendaill received only a shilling for providing an ell of canvas "to paynt the Roods on", it cost five times
as much to have the said Roods or crosses painted; while John
Gybbon received no less than eight shillings and fourpence for
"X elves locotain" or coarse linen. I can find no instance of any
of the original property being bought back, and it is probable
that the cross found by workmen at Brede Place in 1826 was the
original "Crose of Sylur and Gylt" which Robert Oxenbrydge
bought from the churchwardens in 1547.

When Queen Elizabeth came to the throne the pendulum
swung again, and Brede church returned to the condition of the
last reign but one. There is, however, no record of any further
sale of church property, and indeed no reference whatsoever to
the change till 1593, when a memorandum appears in the churchwardens' book to record that "John forward minister and parson
of bread, in the parish church of bread" read "the articles whereupon it was agreed by the Archbishops and bishops of both
provinces and the whole clergye in the convocatio holden in
London in the year of our lord god 1562 according to the com-
putatio of the Church of England for the avoyding of the dyver-
sityes of opinions and for the stablishing of consent touching trewe
religion".

It may be wondered why the rector waited thirty years
before reading as he was ordered the Thirty-nine Articles in
his church. The reason no doubt lies partly in the slow movement
of those times, when printing was a comparatively new art, and
small villages like Brede were cut off from the rest of the country
by miles of almost impassable roads, to say nothing of what
remained—and in those days it was much—of the darkness and
dangers of Andredsweald. But it is also true that many Catholics,
including certain parish priests, believed that once again the Old
Religion would come back. The pendulum had swung so often
that they had learned to expect changes. Besides, it was said that
the Queen did not really favour the New Religion. She had been
crowned according to Catholic rites and she would not have
deposed the Marian bishops had they been willing to acknowledge her supremacy. It was even said that she had considered
marrying King Philip of Spain. Moreover, there was always a
chance that the party supporting Mary of Scotland as the rightful

Queen might gain the upper hand, in which case it would be just as well not to have publicly read out a set of articles condemning her religion. Some parish priests of Marian appointment, too loyal to renounce their faith but too timid to proclaim it, even said Mass privately and then later on led the people in what they called the Christmas charade of Mattins and Evensong.

This state of uncertainty was brought to an end by the execution of Mary Queen of Scots and the defeat of the Spanish Armada. Philip of Spain had counted on finding a fifth column of Catholics to support him in England, but the English Catholics did not want to see their religion established by the forces of a foreign power and their Queen deposed to make room for some minion of Spanish Philip's or indeed Philip himself. We have seen how Lord Montagu of Cowdray offered his services to the Queen and won in return the doubtful blessing of a visit from her to his papistical home. There were many like him. Henceforth the Catholic faith was linked up with a foreign power and no one expected the pendulum to swing again. Catholicism was driven underground by penal laws, while temporising priests shrugged their shoulders and read the Thirty-nine Articles.

4

But there are other aspects of the Reformation which do not appear in churchwardens' accounts. It must seem strange to those who stand apart from these things or even to those who do not that men have been found willing to die for two opposed and contradictory systems of belief. The number of those who laid down their lives for the New Religion under Queen Mary was almost exactly the same as those who died for the Old Religion under Queen Elizabeth—about three hundred.

Nietzsche has said that "a man need not be willing to die for his opinions, but he should be willing to die for the right to hold and change them". I doubt if any of those six hundred citizens of Britain died for their rights. They died for the reality that they had met in different ways, in different places. Christ sometimes walks in the field, especially if he is driven out of the city by the worldliness and indifference of those that dwell in it. *Invenimus eum in campis silvæ*—I met him in the field of the wood;

so I will die for the field of the wood while other men die for the city.

Most of the martyrs of the Weald were Protestants. The main Catholic persecutions were in London and the North, but the South-east seems to have turned early to the New Religion, probably on account of the constant arrivals of Protestants from France and the Netherlands. These men came over as refugee tradesmen—as weavers and iron-smelters—and brought their beliefs with them. Owing to the weaving trade alone there was a continual to-and-fro between the Cranbrook district and the Continent, and as far back as the reign of Henry VIII, Englishmen living in Flanders had been arraigned for heresy by the King's agent and thrown into prison. Richard Harman, a native of Cranbrook but domiciled as a merchant in Antwerp, went so far as to petition the Emperor for his release. The King's agent, John Hackett, suggested to Cardinal Wolsey that he should be charged with treason and his delivery as a traitor applied for, since to be a Lutheran was to be a traitor—"as soon as they have passed the sea they know neither God nor King".

Wolsey, however, had far too much to reckon with at home to trouble himself with the affairs of obscure heretics abroad, and John Harman was released in 1529, when he had the satisfaction of turning the tables and getting John Hackett locked up.

Cranbrook was later to have martyrs who paid the full cost of their beliefs. We have already met that undesirable local character, Bloody Baker of Milkhouse Street. Part of the horror of the times was the delegation of civil and ecclesiastical administration to local tyrants, who were able thus to work off private spites and enmities. Baker's victims were executed at Maidstone, but it was he who sought them out, pursued them, examined them—sometimes under torture—and condemned them. On July 13th, 1557, five women and two men were burnt alive as heretics, including William Allin, a miller much beloved for his charity and generosity. Bloody Baker was more lucky than he deserved when he died just after Elizabeth's accession.

There were Protestant martyrs, too, at East Grinstead and at Lewes, the two East Sussex assize towns. In 1556 Thomas Dungate, John Forman and Anne Tree were burnt at East Grinstead, while Lewes had ten martyrs. One of these was an

ironmaster named Richard Woodman of Warbleton near Heathfield, betrayed by his rector, who had been a Protestant under
Edward VI but had thought it prudent to return to Catholicism
under Queen Mary. We may marvel that the Vicar of Bray
came so late in history, for the lists of Wealden incumbents
during the Reformation period show a surprising tenacity of
office, or should we call it tolerance?

Lewes has always made a feature of its martyrs. Their memorial
stands high above the town, and no town in England commemorates Gunpowder Treason more zealously. Guy Fawkes' Day has
always been popular with those who enjoy dressing up and
making a noise, but in many places it has degenerated into a
mere carnival procession of decorated carts, whereas in Lewes
all the old traditional customs are faithfully observed. The
blazing barrels still roll down the street, the "Archbishops" and
"Chancellors" of the various municipal wards still stand up and
make their speeches before lighting their bonfires, and Lewes is, I
believe, the only town in England where the Pope is still burnt
in effigy. In spite of this, Catholics go to Lewes on Gunpowder
Night to see the fun, knowing very well that to be a "guy" is
often a compliment in these days. Not so long ago one of our
Sussex bonfire societies, moved entirely by admiration and good-
will, burnt Mr Henry Hall.

5

Queen Mary, with a crudeness that some would call honesty,
burned her subjects openly for their religion. She might, like
Elizabeth, have made a political show of it, for equally with
Elizabeth she had been declared illegitimate and her tenure of
the throne was insecure. But she obstinately proclaimed the religious motive behind her persecutions, adhering to the statute
de heretico comburendo, which her father had revived, and earning
for herself an odium which was not shared by her more astute
but equally ruthless sister.

The Protestant martyrs were a cross-section of the British
people, ranging from high-placed ecclesiastics to tradesmen and
servants. The Catholic martyrs were mainly priests and those who
supported and "harboured" them. The seminaries of Rome,
Rheims and Douai trained and sent into this country priest-
adventurers pledged to give their lives as martyrs for their faith.

There were numerous Catholics still left in England, men and women who had not subscribed to the new religion or in spite of heavy fines attended their parish church. It was to those that the priests came to minister, and from their houses they converted Protestants and recovered the still larger number of those who under fear or duress had lapsed from their allegiance. The majority of these seminary priests were pursued and taken by the Queen's agents and put to a grisly death for high treason, though to the last protesting their loyalty to their queen and to their country. A number of those who harboured them and helped them suffered the same fate. But it was a decentralised and individualistic society, and certain well-known Catholic families were able not only to live comparatively in peace but also to help their co-religionists without being penalised. We have seen how Sir Anthony Brown of Battle and Viscount Montagu of Cowdray rode the storms of the Reformation, and the Carylls of West Grinstead were another family who regularly harboured priests and survived it.

West Grinstead was indeed an island of peace among the tides of persecution, and Mass was said there throughout penal times, first at the Park and later at the house which is now the presbytery. The "Captains", as they were called for security reasons, who landed from some silent craft among the creeks and inlets south of Chichester, would make their way cross-country, through the Sussex Wild, and break their journey in the reasonably safe harbourage of West Grinstead before making their hazardous way to London or to some Catholic centre beyond it. For those who landed in Kent there was a similar refuge at Twyssenden, an old house on the road between Goudhurst and Scotney Castle. This house is one of the few houses in the Weald which contains a genuine priest's hole. Many claim to have them, but I doubt if they are true specimens of this particular type of refuge, which are all constructed more or less on the same plan as designed by the martyr Nicholas Owen. They are more likely to be smugglers' holes, smuggling having been a far more widespread activity in the Weald than harbouring priests.

6

The Reformation had triumphed in England, but the golden age of peace and holiness had not arrived with it. For the Weald especially these were troublous times. We have seen how many of its inhabitants had received their Protestantism direct from the Continent, and to these the Elizabethan compromise between Rome and Geneva was as unsatisfactory as to the Catholics. By the time that Laud became Archbishop of Canterbury, and by the same appointment diocesan Bishop of the Weald of Kent, religion had fallen to a very low ebb. He found many churches in a state that could be described only as one of indecent sluttishness and ruin. No longer did the rich weavers spend their money on the House of God; the people had lost interest and the parsons, most of whom held more than one living, had neither the energy nor the money to perform their part and keep their chancels in repair. In many churches the Communion Table, standing in the nave according to the injunctions of the Book of Common Prayer, had been debased to secular uses, such as acting as hatstand for the congregation; while unauthorised Puritan divines, under the title of lecturers, occupied the pulpit, sometimes preaching "in a very disorderly manner for three hours at a time".

Laud made himself enemies by ordering the churches of the Weald to be repaired and to be decorated with pictures and stained glass, while the Communion Table was moved to the east end of the chancel and protected with rails. He also ordered a surplice and hood to be worn while reading the service. These modest reforms earned him a reputation for trafficking with Rome, and though it is not known that any Weldishmen were present when a furious mob attacked Lambeth Palace, their sympathies would certainly lie with those who did so.

When the Long Parliament assembled in 1640 it received no less than twenty petitions from this part of England. The towns and villages concerned include Tenterden, Goudhurst, Horsmonden, Rolvenden, Yalding and Tunbridge, and the signatories such good Kentish names as Witherenden, Iden, Haffenden and Iggulden. They mostly complain of pluralism, which was an abuse of the times, owing partly to the scarcity of clergy and partly to the poverty of congregations unable singly to support a parson. At Maidstone it was complained that though a town of six thousand inhabitants could well afford to support a rector, the Archbishop received all their tithes and took no care of the parish, putting in a curate who was also rector of Boughton

Malherbe. The rector of Tenterden was also non-resident and forbade his curate to preach and catechise on Sunday afternoons, and moreover had cited ten poor labourers for non-payment of their Easter offering.

The people seem to have been unhappy in their lot, and also to have made their pastors unhappy. How difficult they were as a flock is shown by Laud's own diary of his visitation:

> "At Biddenden I have suspended Richard Warren, the Schoolmaster, for refusing the oath of allegiance, of canonical obedience and to subscribe to the Articles. Besides, this precise man will read nothing but Divinity to his scholars: no not so much as the grammar rules, unles Mars, Bacchus, Apollo, etc., may be blotted out."

"This precise man" is a straw that shows which way the national wind had begun to blow in the matter of scholarship. Half a century earlier Shakespeare had based his plays on stories from the classics or from European and English history. These stories would already be well-known to his audiences, even those who were illiterate—Bottom and his company were "clowns" but no one saw anything incongruous or surprising in their choice of the tragedy of Pyramus and Thisbe for their play—and the spectators' enjoyment would be much like that of the audience of a modern pantomime, whose pleasure does not depend on the plot or on any surprises it may have to offer but on the manner in which is presented a familiar story. When we come from Shakespeare's plays to Milton's *Paradise Lost* we see at once what has happened—Mars, Bacchus, Apollo, etc., have indeed been blotted out and their place taken by Scriptural characters who in their turn are far removed from those that animated the York Cycle and the other mystery plays. Laud belonged to Shakespeare rather than to Milton and did not like to see the gods of classical learning dethroned even from the "grammar rules"; but in the fierce light of Cromwellian puritanism the gods had begun to fade, and by the following century they were gone.

The Archbishop did not suffer from Puritans only. At Sittingbourne he found a number of recusants, "and the Lady Roper is thought to be a great means of the increase of them. I have given strict charge that they be carefully presented according to law." He also invoked the law to deal with the Anabaptists and Separatists round Ashford, who were "very busy, miserably poor, but bold against all church censure, so that without some temporal help from the judges we know not what to do". In spite of this "temporal help", however, he had in the end to acknowledge that the Puritans of the Kentish Weald, "especially in and about the parts round Ashford", were a task beyond his powers.

7

Towards the end of the seventeenth century the "Separatism" of the Weald was greatly encouraged by the immigration of Huguenots from France. When the Edict of Nantes was revoked by King Louis XIV a multitude of French Protestants who had lived at peace for nearly a century, under the protection of their sovereign, were forced to leave the country. Many of them settled in the Channel Islands, but others travelled as far as England and to these the Weald was both geographically and sympathetically a likely refuge. They particularly favoured the districts adjoining Rye; indeed so numerous did they become in that neighbourhood that a part of the town was given the name it still bears of Rye Foreign. The names of the foreign settlers, duly anglicised, still survive in this part of the Weald; Vidler, Guiver, Poile, Comport are all names that originally came from France, as did also the dark hair and eyes and small round faces that are to be found to-day among the fair, blue-eyed, long-faced children of indigenous Sussex families. Words, too, linger that must originally have been learned from a foreign mouth. To be in a mess is to be "in dishable", and after the harvest the hens are put out, not on the stubble but on the "grattans", where they scratch up the corn that the reaping machine has not taken away.

This immigration was bound to affect the religious life of the country. The Huguenots were welcomed because of their misfortunes and their resistance to Rome, but their type of religion was more akin to Nonconformity than to the Established Church, and for the most part they attached themselves to Nonconformist congregations. The penal laws against "separatists" were relaxed or repealed long before those against "recusants",

Preacher's house and oasts, Ewhurst

and soon all over the Weald, in Sussex and in Kent, rose a number of chapels and meeting-houses, which owing to the simplicity and homeliness of their eighteenth-century construction, so different from the garishness and vulgarity of their Victorian successors, are still a part of the beauty of our countryside.

Particularly attractive is the old chapel by the Ypres Tower in Rye. This was badly damaged by a bomb during the last war, but has now been restored to its old picturesque integrity. A tiny chapel—a cottage among the houses of God—is one of the quaint beauties of the hill from Darwell Hole to Woods Corner, near the crest of which stands the Mocksteeple. There is also a chapel in Ewhurst which still bears its original appearance of a private house, thus linking up not only with the early penal days of "separatism" but with the early penal days of Christianity itself. I have already written of the attractions of the Unitarian Chapel in Tenterden and the derelict beauty of Chapel Bank. There is an interesting old chapel, too, at Shovers Green near Wadhurst, which has—most unusually among such buildings—a queer, shut, sinister appearance, due to the huge grim shutters that blind its windows.

In this chapel ministered for a time that unauthorised, unofficial apostle of the Kent and Sussex borders, James Weller, G.M. or Gospel Minister. Here he preached one of his most sensational sermons, one indeed which drove the congregation out into the lane in a state of riot, "hollowing: Horrible! Bominable! Stuff!" The stuff in question was High Calvinism, that most ferocious of all Christian religious systems, which Weller, the meekest of men, by some strange affinity of opposites preached everywhere as his Gospel.

No one could say he did not realise the import of his sinister "good news", for he himself had lived for years with the conviction that he was damned. The story of his life and struggles, both spiritual and material, is told in a curious little book published at Cranbrook in 1845. *The Wonders of Free Grace* gives a vivid, artless picture of religion in the Weald at the beginning of the nineteenth century; so as few of my readers can have met with this obscure record of an obscure Weldishman, it may not come amiss if we let James Weller speak for himself and tell his story in his own rather peculiar language.

185

The Weald near Shover's Green

8

"I was born in the parish of Headcorn, Kent, Dec. 30th, of poor but honest parents. . . ." Then the stereotyped phrases suddenly break into : "At the age of seven or eight I remember to have been the subject of strong convictions of sin . . . notwithstanding I turned to my youthful follies, taking the wicked for my companions, from one of whom who had been taught to commit sin with greediness by an infidel, and who likewise had met with a severe judgment from God in the deformity of his features through drawing the flesh of his eyes down his cheeks, I nearly lost the sight of one of my eyes by a sharp stone which he threw at me."

In spite of this warning, he soon afterwards attacked his sister with a pocket-knife, "the blade of which I had desperately drawn through her hand." His father, not unnaturally shocked at such behaviour, "threatened me with very rigid punishment". The terror into which the little boy was plunged by this threat, even contemplating suicide by drowning himself, sheds some light on the origin of his fears of hell. In his despair he prayed for help, and surely enough deliverance came. When he took out his father's dinner to him in the field he found his crime entirely forgotten in the man's interest in a pair of wild ducks which had sprung up out of the river. "This merciful interposition of the hand of God begat in me very great humility and my heart seemed to melt within me with gratitude."

About this time he had another consoling experience :

"Going a journey with my father about midnight, as I lay upon my back on the loaded van, looking upwards to the starry heavens, I saw, in an instant, a bright shining light in the opening sky, and *one* appeared to me in vision, like unto the Son of Man in full strength, whose countenance was most beautiful to behold, with a crown of pure gold upon his head and a golden reed in his hand; he walked three or four steps upon the wings of the wind, and pointed at a large star or meteor with the reed, which ran along the air and then disappeared: the Person returned and the heavens closed that I saw him no more. At this my mind was filled with solemn awe and reverential fear, yet mixed with delight."

This seer and sinner was less than eleven years old, for he had only "just turned eleven" when his father died and he and his family had to go into the poor-house. Here he had much to endure before being prenticed out by the parish overseers at a farm called Great Moatenden, "where many changes took place in my feelings, and my conscience became so tender, that though there were apples in plenty I dared not take one without asking leave"

In spite of this model behaviour his career as a farmhand was pretty disastrous. He seems to have moved from farm to farm, through a succession of accidents, ill-treatments and bullyings, no doubt a poor worker because underfed, accident prone and a constant temptation to the latent sadism of those around him. Once he ran away, but was forced by poverty to return to his parish for relief. Finally, at Little Boy Court, near Ellcomb,

"a greater sight of the depravity of human nature was to be shown me. The vain tricks of youth grew strong upon me and my heart lusted for vanities. I learnt to sing vain and carnal songs, and tried to persuade myself that religion was but a fit of melancholy, or that there was plenty of time to be serious in a future day. But it was not in my power to obscure the light that shone into my conscience, and often with shamefacedness have my knees been bowed under the manger of the stable, and a cry gone forth to the Lord for mercy."

Weller had been brought up in the doctrine and practice of what he calls the Steeples of the Crown of England—no doubt a confusion of the old Puritan sneer at Steeplehouses with the official position of the Established Church—but at Little Boy Court he was attracted to the Wesleyans, whose early forms of worship seem to have been very different from those of their present-day adherents. "With continual cryings, howlings, groanings, shoutings of 'Amen' etc the place was all confusion." Certainly it was a great change from the ordered, mannerly ways of the Church of England, though very much what Wesley himself had encouraged on his preaching tours. The matter of the services, too, as well as the manner, was all that was most dangerous to a mind like Weller's, for the Wesleyans preached hell and damnation as vigorously as any Calvinist, but being Arminians urged their faithful to save themselves from these by living good lives. Poor Weller struggled with "dead works" and "legal prayers", before in despair he transferred himself to the Old Baptist Chapel at Smarden, where he was frightened into fits by the doctrines of predestination and election. "That true, then my soul was for ever lost, for a feeling testimony of reprobation seemed to pervade me."

Neither Arminianism nor Calvinism, Universal Redemption nor Particular Election seemed to offer him the smallest hope: "The Lord has turned all my comeliness into corruption, destroyed my sandy foundation." Sometimes he sought to save his soul by "carnal works", at others he gave way to dreams of Judgment and everlasting hell, again at others he sought release from his spiritual torment in "public-house company" and "wicked mirth", striving, he says, to stifle conscience with a song. His state was not helped by a conviction circulating in the Weald at this time that the end of the world was near. "O, how I shuddered at the thought of standing before an angry God! Yet this was my only expectation from day to day."

The early part of the book is merely a repetition of these woes and his efforts to escape from them, and it comes as a decided surprise to the reader when in the midst of it all he suddenly gets married. We are told very little about the young woman whom he took for his wife in Frittenden parish church, but her lot could not have been easy, for though "for a few weeks after marriage my place was regularly filled again at church and all forms duly attended to, trying to keep conscience at ease . . . a consciousness often pervaded my soul that something more was wanting to make me fit to die"—whereupon he rather inconsequently started "getting into company and drinking".

Then his health began to fail, and his terrors increased as he thought death was drawing near. What disease he had we do not know, nor probably did he, but he was constantly passing in and out of hospitals and infirmaries as well as being nursed at home by the poor woman he had chosen. Charitable people befriended him. "The gentlemen of Headcorn hired a cottage for me in Laker's Court and sent my wife and two children up"— nor disease nor debt nor damnation seem to have checked the increase of Weller's family—"allowing us *twelve* shillings a week. . . . On the Lord's Days, went to the Churches and Chapels by turns, but heard nothing for myself, my case never being described at either place."

It could not go on. It was bound to end some time, either in self-destruction (which he often contemplated) or in release. A day came when confined to bed by his sickness,

"meditating on death and eternity, I thought "Tis certainly all over with me, *I am a lost man.*' O, how I tried to pray once more! But words failed me, and I was as one awaiting the execution of his sentence of condemnation and death. I clearly saw the justice of God in my eternal overthrow, and actually bade adieu to the world, closing my bodily eyes with an 'Amen' to my own destruction."

Shall a man be found willing to serve God for naught? Evidently this man was so willing, offering his own soul as Abraham offered Isaac. And as with Abraham the sacrifice was both accepted and remitted, for with this supreme offering of himself the psychological lesions broke, and James Weller's mind escaped from its obsession.

"A sweet glowing flowed into my bosom, and run through the whole of my frame from head to foot; and a brilliant light, like a shining of bright silver, overshadowed my soul: it also appeared to fill the room in which I lay."

On this "the Wedding Day of my poor soul", James Weller was Saved. From henceforth he need no longer fear hell, for he had been shown his election by Sovereign Grace. He was at peace, and though the health of his body did not improve with that of his mind, he found himself entering on his first experience of tranquillity. An immediate effect of the change in him was to send him to his Bible, a book he had hitherto shunned for fear of the judgments it contained. Like many simple people—and others not so simple—he had practised the *Sortes Biblicæ*, and had had an unhappy knack of turning up lurid texts breathing fire and judgment. He was now no longer afraid; nevertheless he "trembled and shook" when, "providentially directed to the 61st Chapter of Isaiah", he came upon the text: "The Spirit of the Lord is upon me; because the Lord hath anointed me to preach good tidings to the meek." At first he cried out, "Not me,

Lord, not me!" But when the Book opened a second time at the same place he realised that he must no longer seek escape, for "the Lord had anointed me to preach the Everlasting Gospel to poor sinners".

His beginnings were cautious, amounting to little more than telling his story to those of his friends who guessed some happy change from his altered countenance. The friends responded in kind—"The hand-basket came daily, with wine, meat and money; and my soul ran out in thankfulness to my dear Lord day and night." Then, in course of time, he was invited to address small gatherings in private houses, and though at first exceedingly nervous at the thought of speaking before strangers he grew confident when he saw the effect of his words upon his hearers. At one house in Ulcomb there were no less than thirty people present, and "it seemed as though a light shone in the room; and . . . the Lord was pleased to help me very much, and owned the testimony by setting the Broad Seal of his pardoning mercy upon the soul of a poor woman present (Mrs W.) who had been in deep waters about three years".

At about this time he seceded from the Baptist Chapel in Maidstone which he had been attending ever since his conversion, and joined the Strict or Particular Baptists, who had renounced the doctrine of Universal Salvation and preached that of Election. "The new connexion treated me with much kindness and . . . it was hinted by some that I should one day become a Minister, as I had gifts in prayer." But when the point was actually reached "concerning my filling the desk on a Lord's Day afternoon . . . this was objected to by two or three of the proprietors of the place on the ground of my being ignorant of grammar".

However, the objectors were overcome, and without apparently any lessons in grammar, Weller occupied the pulpit on Sunday afternoons until later in the year he moved to Smarden. "It being in the season of hop-picking I and my wife engaged a place, where, the chief part of the pickers being Wesleyans, who had heard of my preaching, they entreated me to give them a lecture in the garden." He was, however, determined not to speak out of doors, and it was not until the scene was transferred to a friend's house that he consented to address the Wesleyan hop-pickers on the subject of Free Grace, evidently to their great discomfiture. " 'Ah,' they said, 'he is a Calvinist and we know that Calvinists' doctrine is dreadful and comes from hell.' However, I left this with them to dispute about, and as far as in me lay told out what the Lord told in." He also occupied the pulpit of the Old Baptist Chapel at Smarden, while on Sunday evenings he preached in a house in the churchyard at Headcorn. "But my preaching here gave offence to the Clergyman and soon we had notice to quit."

This led to his overcoming his reluctance to preaching out of doors, for on the next Sunday evening, finding the house shut against him, he delivered his discourse in the open air. He did this three times before being invited "to a little chapel at Frittenden". He preached, of course, without having had any sort of ordination or religious instruction and it is not surprising that in time some of his hearers began to question his bona-fides and his doctrine. He was accused of being a "Baxterian", a "High Haldenite", a "Beemanite", a "Huntingtonian". These all refer to heresies and schisms peculiar to the Weald, where "Separatism" had become fissiparous. The Huntingtonians here had nothing to do with "the Countess of Huntingdon's Connection", as might first appear, but were the disciples of William Huntington, S.S. (Sinner Saved), who was very nearly a contemporary of Weller's and remarkably like him.

He was born at Cranbrook, the illegitimate son of a farm labourer. His real name was Hunt, but he claimed that the letters of the alphabet belonged to all men and improved his name accordingly. After a youth not unlike Weller's he too went through the experience of conversion and began to preach High Calvinism. Like Weller he had visions and claimed to have been "fed by ravens" during his days of poverty. But most unlike Weller's was his marriage to a Lady Sanderson, widow of the Lord Mayor of London, and his prosperous ministry at Providence Chapel in Cranbrook; though when Weller had read his *Kingdom of Heaven taken by Prayer* "I kissed it and blessed God that ever such a man had lived before me."

Cranbrook was the spiritual home also of the Beemanites, with whose founder our James had some slight acquaintance. It started badly, for "when I got into the Chapel the devil set in upon me in such a way that I verily wished myself out again".

It was the devil who when he saw the man of God go into the pulpit "with his knee-breeches, buckled shoes and grave countenance", put into his heart the dreadful words, "There goes the pope of all." At this his soul trembled within him, "but for my life I could not avoid the thought". However, when it actually came to the preaching, "The whole of the subject was made very savoury to me. . . . I had never heard such a sermon before in my life and can in truth say it was a confirmation to me in the faith of God's elect."

All this time Weller was himself, in spite of criticism, preaching throughout the Weald of Kent. He preached at Maidstone, Headcorn, Frittenden, Smarden and other places, but until now he had never gone further away from home than Cranbrook, so it was something like a shock that he realised the Lord was calling him to preach the Gospel in Sussex. Just as a man of Macedonia had appeared to St Paul crying "Come over to Macedonia and help us", so a man of Sussex, "a Mr H., a Miller, in Ticehurst", appeared, not in a dream but on the road within half a mile of Headcorn. "He had passed but a few rods, when these words were powerfully impressed upon my mind: 'That man has come out of Sussex to invite you to go down there to preach'; at which I immediately said, 'Dear Lord, I am not fit to go into Sussex.' "

However, when he reached his home he found that the stranger—for at the time he had not the smallest idea who he was—had left a note inviting him to preach at Shover's Green, on the road between Ticehurst and Wadhurst. There was no escape from such a manifestation of the Lord's will and poor James "obeyed the call by writing a note to say I could be there, the Lord willing, the first Sunday in May"

After thus committing himself he experienced terrible distress of mind, and finally set out on a Saturday morning for the far land of Sussex, expecting the very worst. "And O! what a journey it was!" Nevertheless, he came safely to the end of it and was hospitably received in a farmhouse near Wadhurst, where however he had little sleep and at four o'clock in the morning "dropped upon my knees by the bed side, mourning, sighing and groaning. . . calling myself a fool for going there in such a sad plight. In agony I threw myself upon the bed, wishing I had never known life."

On the way to the chapel, when he and his host had crossed two little meadows and come to a narrow path between hedges,

"My friend being a few yards before me, I felt inclined to run away and watching him, made a step or two for such purpose; but the thought rushed into my mind in an instant that my pony was at his house; wherefore, with a sigh, I went forward again, saying to myself, 'Well, I must go whether for life or death.'"

We can account for at least some of his terror when we remember that his peculiar beliefs forbade him to make any preparation for his discourse. He could only "tell out what the Lord told in", and there was always a chance that the Lord might tell him nothing, in which case he would stand before them all silent and humiliated. He had not even decided on a portion of Scripture to read, but opened the Chapel Bible entirely at random. There he

"read what first met my eyes, which was the 103rd Psalm, during the reading of which my chains fell off and my soul was set at sweet liberty. I wept in joy at the condescending goodness of the Lord, and blessed and praised him with all my heart; and in simplicity told the people what he had done for my soul."

This really moved his simple country congregation, though from the first there was the usual disapproving element, which later was to gain the upper hand. "I was invited to go down again and continued going once a fortnight for some time." It was not for many months that he was "hollowed publicly in the streets", and by that time he was as well-known on the Sussex side of the border as in Kent. The riotous scenes outside the chapel served only to increase his fame, and he was invited to preach in the chapels at Mayfield, at Burwash, at Peasmarsh, also "to a few people in a thatched cottage at Udimore".

The reader must long have been wondering how all this time Weller earned his daily bread. Preaching to small congregations of agricultural labourers is not likely to have kept from the door that wolf which seems so constantly to have had his forepaws inside it. What did he do for a living as he rode his pony to and fro across the Rother and the Kent Ditch? How did he support

his relentlessly increasing family? The answer to the latter question is: mainly on charity. His book alternates the matter of
his discourses and his spiritual experiences with the "miraculous"
interventions of Providence to save him and his from debt and
starvation. "The promise of the ravens feeding me the Lord
fulfilled to the very letter"—a statement which suggests something more sensational than "the perfect stranger who told me
that he had it forcibly impressed upon his mind to assist me",
and thereupon paid the fourteen shillings he owed the baker.
His life is full of the generosity of others, either "perfect strangers"
or those who found his preaching "savoury".

He had, however, his fits of anxiety and distress, and one
of them occurred as far away from home as Romney Marsh.

> "One morning after preaching on the preceding evening at
> Old Romney, my trying position in temporal things was
> vividly brought before me, and the enemy cast me prostrate
> by it. 'Look at this debt,' said he, 'and look at the other! See
> how your family increases! None but a madman would travel
> the country as you do, at the uncertainty whether your ex-
> penses are paid or not! See man, you have travelled *one hundred
> miles* when you reach home this week, and have received but
> *four shillings and sixpence* for your labour.'"

He regarded such anxieties as of Satanic origin, and indeed they
were unwarranted, for at breakfast that very day a grateful
member of last night's congregation presented him with five
pounds.

It would be to libel him, however, to say that he lived on
charity alone. He made several abortive attempts to earn his
bread. At one time he kept a little shop, at another he had the
temerity—some would say the effrontery—to open a school,
and all his preaching journeys were accompanied by sales of tea,
which he peddled at cottage doors. But he never seems in any
of the chapels where he ministered to have taken a collection.
He evidently had no head for business, and it was entirely the
suggestion of others that he should have his own chapel at
Robertsbridge.

"A friend at Robertsbridge offered to give me a house to
turn into a chapel, with a lease of fifty years, and £10 per annum

towards the support of the cause." This gave him great searchings
of heart, for he was torn, he tells us, between Robertsbridge and
Burwash, where for the last two years or so he had had a more or
less regular ministry. However, the *sortes Biblicæ* yielded "Come
out from amongst them and be ye separate", and at the same time
others of his friends began to offer him money for the construction of "Bethel"—that grim little house of God which stands in
Robertsbridge Main Street, wedged tightly between two cheerful
next-door neighbours. The die was cast—if we may use so carnal
a metaphor—and for the first time since her marriage it looked
as if Mrs James Weller and her children would have a settled
home.

The foundation stone was laid in November 1842, and the
opening took place the following year.

> "Mr W. Cowper, from the Upper Dicker, Hellingly,
> preached morning and afternoon, from 'My doctrine shall
> drop as the rain, my speech shall distil as the dew, as the small
> rain upon the tender herb, and as the showers upon the
> grass . . .' and Mr G. Abrahams (the converted Jew) from
> London, in the evening, from 'For every house is builded by
> some man; but he that built all things is God.' We had a very
> full congregation, and the Ministers were much favoured in
> their own souls; but as for myself, I was sorely tried the whole
> of the day with my own debts and that of the Chapel."

With these characteristic words "the poor worm the author",
who did not long survive his establishment in a settled ministry,
takes leave of his readers. It is possible that by this time mine
may think that they have had more than enough of *The Wonders
of Free Grace*. But its stumbling phrases have told us much that
more learned historians have missed of the life and religion of
the Kent and Sussex borders in those bad old days before the
repeal of the Corn Laws, when labouring men, denied the fruits
of their toil on earth, turned in yearning ignorance to the free gift
of heaven.

CHAPTER IV

WITCHES, GHOSTS AND FAIRIES

I

IN the matter of religion we have seen that the inhabitants of the Weald showed a considerable degree of independence, if not indeed of contrariness, being inclined to all forms of "separatism" from Roman recusancy to the more eccentric variations of Protestant dissent. But in the grosser matter of superstition we find them very much less original and more inclined to follow the common herd, which perhaps is natural in ways of darkness. The accounts of witchcraft and of hauntings in these parts are very like the accounts of witchcraft and hauntings in other parts of England, and when we come to fairies Sussex Pook is the spit brother of Yorkshire Hob.

Other counties, too, have shared the Sussex preoccupation with the devil. Devil's staircases, devil's cauldrons, devil's punch-bowls, devil's elbows abound all over England, and the Prince of Darkness is blamed throughout the realm for the awkward situations of some of its churches. There may be a certain amount of originality in the story of Devil's Dyke, but I'll warrant that the devil has had, if not his nose, then his hoof or his tail in more than one sulphur spring, while Mayfield competes for his tongs with Glastonbury. In the Weald we say it is unwholesome to eat blackberries after Michaelmas, for then the devil spits on them. But they say the same in Cornwall and in Brittany.

Perhaps the devil in the Weald, particularly in Sussex, may have the distinction of being a more simple and homely character than he is elsewhere. We saw when we were at Mayfield that he can be friendly as well as vindictive, and this is possibly due to a confusion in folklore origins between him and the dispossessed gods of the oak and the ash. We know that these lingered in Sussex long after they had disappeared from the rest of the country, and it is easy to believe that the local mind saw their departure less as error giving place to truth than as another instance of the natural process of the old giving place to the young, senile old Woden and tired old Thor giving place to the vigorous young Christ.

While accepting and practising their new faith the Sussex people may nevertheless have pictured the old gods going into hiding in some dense wood or lonely hollow of the Downs. Was not the devil said to keep guard over the golden calf hidden in the depths of Trundle Hill? That legend may have its root in a stripped pagan altar. No doubt the early Christian priests taught their flocks that the old gods were "of the devil", and no doubt the communal mind held memories of cruel rites. But the gods were old now, and feeble, and perhaps a little silly. The people were no longer afraid of them as they lurked in hiding, but made jokes about them and told stories of their discomfiture. In time these jokes and stories would become attached to the spirit of evil with which their Christian beliefs associated the old gods. It is generally believed that the horns, hoofs and tail of the typical Christian devil are derived from the dispossessed god Pan, and it is probable that in spite of the intervening gods of Valhallá, the memory of the Roman god lingered among those who had once been under Roman rule. Pan was a kindly god, and his good nature may account for a similar quality that sometimes appears in the Sussex Satan.

2

Very much less tolerant and amiable than the atmosphere surrounding the devil is that surrounding the witch. In this the Weald conformed to the rest of the country and the rest of Europe, to say nothing of the new American colonies. The belief in witchcraft has existed almost universally from the earliest times, but there is something peculiarly sinister in the outbreak of witch-hunting which occurred in the period immediately following the Renaissance. It is not that witchcraft had never been proscribed and punished before that day, but not till then had there been the same persecution, the same blind orgy of mob hysteria, as if, indeed, a backwash of superstition had followed the waves of enlightenment that broke over Europe at the Revival of Learning. A situation not unlike it appeared in the nineteenth century, when notable advances in science and mechanics were accompanied by the excesses of Spiritualism and the rappings of the Foxe sisters.

Witch-hunting was not confined to any one form of religion. It was the pursuit of Catholic and Protestant alike, for both believed equally in the Powers of Darkness. But the quarry in Catholic countries was altogether more sinister than in those in which the abolition of the Mass had made the blasphemies of Satanism impossible or, rather, meaningless. Satanism involved the Black Mass, a form of sacrilege which offered no temptation to those who frequently saw the sacred liturgy parodied with ribald gestures and comic Latin by "mumpsimus men" at fairs. In England, Scotland, Sweden and Denmark the main attack of witchcraft was on man rather than on God, and its rites were Protestant and non-liturgical. In Scotland the witches mocked the Presbytery with their sabbaths and their covens. Many of them—no doubt under pressure—gave detailed accounts of these assemblies to which they rode through the air, crying "th'out, th'out, th'out and about", and then after listening to the preaching of a tall, dark man, returned shouting "rentum tormentum".

One of the most sinister aspects of the witch trials is the full and detailed confessions of the victims. The witches were not condemned against the evidence. It is only the nature of the evidence and the way it was obtained that were a travesty of justice. Apart from confessions very like those now being made at trials in eastern Europe, the prosecution admitted and indeed often largely depended on "spectral evidence"—that is, the evidence of victims who had seen the accused in dreams or visions acting malevolently towards them.

Most of the witch trials in the Weald, whether in Kent or Sussex, bear a strong resemblance to one another. A person or an animal fell sick and died of an unknown disease—an event very likely to happen in days when so little was known about medicine—after having offended either in person or through the owner some unpopular local character, a circumstance that must have been just as common then as it is now. Prosecutions were many and the prisoner was seldom acquitted, though by no means always condemned to death. For instance, when Joan Usbarne of Hailsham in 1572 "bewitched to death one bull value 40s. of the goods and chattels of John Browne", her sentence at East Grinstead assizes was only one year's imprisonment. The same was meted out at Horsham in 1577 to Alice Casselowe of Mayfield, though the ox she "bewitched to death" was valued at £4, and she had also done the same for two pigs, valued at ten shillings.

When human life was involved the law was more severe:

"At the assizes at East Grinstead Margaret Cooper wife of William Cooper of Kirdford, surgeon, on the 1st of April 1574 bewitched Henry Stoner who languished until the 20th of April, when he died at Kirdford. Another indictment: on the first September 1572 bewitched William Fowler who languished until the 4th of September following, when he died at Kirdford. Another indictment: on the 1st June 1574 bewitched Elizabeth Fowler wife of Thomas Fowler who languished until the 20th June, when she died at Kirdford. Sentence, hanged."

But when in 1591 at the East Grinstead assizes "Agnes Mowser of Fletching, spinster, on the 29th of April bewitched Ann Flemens who languished until the 20th May following, when she died," the sentence was only imprisonment for one year. Perhaps like the legal dog she was allowed one bite, but even so the justices seem to have been remarkably lenient. It is also notable that contrary to a popular notion the sentence is always hanging and not burning. Indeed, throughout the country there is no record of a witch being legally burnt at the stake. Such executions, however, were sometimes carried out by the mob, after the manner of an American lynching. Thomas Hardy once told me that his father had witnessed the burning of a witch at Dorchester. Hardy was born in 1840, so even if he heard the story as a child and his father witnessed the execution as a child, it could not have taken place earlier than the second half of the eighteenth century.

But it is to the credit of English justice that even in those times of panic and mob hysteria the prisoner was sometimes acquitted. In 1648 Thomas Creed and Dorothy Avery of Cranbrook were both acquitted of bewitching ten "setts of oade" worth £60, and Creed was again acquitted four years later when he was tried for bewitching two mares. In the same year, however, four Cranbrook witches, one of whom confessed her guilt, were hanged at Maidstone, and five years later two wretched women, Mary Allan and her daughter of Goudhurst, were hanged for nothing more than owning a black dog. "They did feed and employ an evil and wicked spirit in the likeness of a black dog, with the intent and purpose that they, with the aid and help of the said evil and wicked spirit, certain evil and devilish arts might use against the public peace." We all know the witch's black cat, but it is hard for our modern minds to conceive that human beings like ourselves could sentence to death a poor wretch for possessing and feeding such an animal.

The greater barbarity that we find here may perhaps be due to rumours of Satanism in the Weald. We know that the district round Cranbrook and Goudhurst was in fairly constant communication with the Continent, and a more "total" form of the Black Art may have been imported from France. There is evidence that a man named Tarver practised Satanism in a house near Milkhouse Street. It must have been a diluted version of it, for the true rite requires the offices of a renegade priest. But the idea that terrible doings of an unknown kind were afoot at Branden—which until quite recently, when the atmosphere suddenly changed, had a very evil reputation as a haunted house—would have greatly increased the terror, and therefore the cruelty, of Weldishmen.

3

The confessions of these witches must all be suspect, because of the conditions under which they were made. But even so it seems clear that some of the women believed themselves to have passed through some form of abnormal experience. The confessions at the Scottish witch-trials are elaborately circumstantial in their accounts of the sabbaths, the covens and the Black Man, and it is hard to believe that they are entirely without foundation. A most curious document has survived among the Harleian manuscripts, entitled "The Confession of Certain Persons con-

Oasts near Broadoak

cerning the Spirits at Rye". This is the confession of Susan Swapper, wife of Roger Swapper of that town, who describes in minute detail how in the year 1607

"about midnight, she being sick in bed with her husband, four spirits in the likeness of two men and two women appeared unto her, the one man young without hair on his face and tall named himself Richard, and he was in a white surplice to the ground, and the other man was a short thick man with a long grey beard and named himself Robert, he was in a white satin doublet and hose pinked. One of the women was young and in a white waistcoat and green petticoat, with a veil about her neck and a white kerchief on her head, and the other woman was young and all in white. And one of the women called herself Katherine and the other Margery, and they appeared unto her two or three nights together."

One's first thought is that Susan Swapper was the victim of a joke on the part of her neighbours, but in that case it is strange that neither she nor her husband should have recognised them either on this occasion or on any other. It would seem more likely that she was a victim of her own sickness, but, if so, her hallucinations were shared by her husband, for when on a later visit the spirits tried to pull her out of bed and she cried to him for help "he laid his hand over her to hold her and his arm was so lame for two days that he could not cut his meat".

The spirits continued to plague her until "she asked them in the Name of the Father, etc. 'What will you have me do?' and the woman in the green petticoat said 'I would have you go to young Ann Bennett and call her, and go into the garden with her, and dig and set sage.' "

The plot thickens round "young Ann Bennett", who "thrust a spit into the ground and heard a sound and being sick departed without setting any sage". Whereupon about three nights later the spirits reappeared at Susan's bedside, and one of them asked her "when young Ann Bennett had been with her and she answered yesterday and then he said . . . that there was money hidden in the said Ann's garden among the thyme. And that the field at Weekes Green was ploughed and the crock was broken

201

Looking from Rotherfield towards Mark Cross

and some part thereof was found and the rest left behind." Later on

"The tall man appeared and asked her if she would go with him and she said 'Aye, by God's grace if you tell me whither,' and he said she should go to Weekes Green. . . . And she did learn the way of Ann Bennett and did go thither, and there did see the tall man stand in the street, and he called her to follow him through a rye field into the green field next to it, which she did, and in the middle of the field there was a valley on one side and bank on the other, and he told her in that valley there was a pot, and gold in it, and a chain upon the top of it, and beside the pit under a little stub there was a crock, mettle, with three legs, in which was money. And he bade her sit down upon a bank, which she did, and then she saw a man all in black on the one side of the hedge and a woman in green on the same side going one to meet another. And she thought the ground did move under her as she sat, and then she cried 'Lord have mercy upon me! What shall become of me!' and then the tall man came to her again, and willed her to arise and go home, but she could not arise, and he willed her in the name of God to arise, and then she arose and went home sick to bed and the man vanished away."

As in the account of the Dragon of St Leonards Forest, one seems here to be trembling all the time on the edge of a natural explanation. These remarkably substantial "spirits" are human beings in search of hidden money, to which they believe that Susan Swapper can provide the clue or can obtain it through young Ann Bennett. But if their forms are substantial, their operations are hazy and meaninglessly complicated.

"And after the tall man Richard willed her to go to the said Ann Bennett and demand of her a piece of raw powdered beef, which the said Ann gave unto her and she delivered it to him and he cut it in pieces and laid it in the window, but she knoweth not what became of it. . . . And saith that she hath diverse times given them water and once bread, and the spirits did consume the water, and when they left any water the same was blackish and the tub became freckled with white." And so on "until that day in the morning that Burditt was slain she saw the Spirits Richard and Robert walking upon the bank coming up the Gungarden (in that part the great ordnance lay) and the piece which brake and killed Burditt, being discharged at the departure of Sir Thomas Waller of Rye. And that day Ann Bennett's son was buried she, going by the church, saw the Spirit Richard go into the church, and he went all in white, and the night after Richard said to the rest of the spirits that the preacher's mind was not on his sermon."

These visions are at times so solid that we find it hard to believe they had no existence at all in a three-dimensional world; and quite probably they had, but had become mixed up with poor Susan's hallucinations. I think we might guess that this poor woman, threatened and badgered and perhaps tormented by her examiners, dived into the rag-bag of her broken memory and brought up a wild mixture of dreams and facts. She was probably more than a little "simple", and in such a woman in such a state of terror, the image-making faculty that we all have in our minds, but which for most of us functions only in our dreams, would lack the restraints confining it to dreamland.

But the "spirits" are by no means exclusive to Susan Swapper. Young Ann Bennett told her that she had seen

"eighty or a hundred of them and they were all fairies. And she saith that one spirit in the likeness of a woman great with child appeared unto her and wished she had some apples, and she did afterwards give unto her three apples, whereof she did eat two and the third she cut in four quarters and flung away."

This last circumstance, together with the cutting up of the beef by Robert, would help to convince the examiners of the diabolical nature of the apparitions, for "Scattering" is a sign of witchcraft. Ann Bennett may have realised this, and when she herself was examined, the visions she described were of an edifying, indeed heavenly, nature.

"She [Susan Swapper] told her, this examinant, that one of her spirits willed her to look up into the element, and she did so, and saw six candles, to her judgment. And after that appeared unto her two angels in her chamber, and one of them having a white fan in his hand did let the same fall, and she stooping to take it up, the angel gave her a box on the ear, rebuking her that she being a mortal creature should presume to handle matters appertaining to heavenly creatures. And those two angels had each of them a prophet and those angels would reveal to these prophets and to no other persons the cause of their coming. And that their coming was to cut off the wicked from the earth."

We do not know what happened to young Ann Bennett as the result of this examination, or indeed to Susan Swapper. But the magistrates can hardly have failed to be favourably impressed by such an edifying vision, even if one of the angels—who brings a happy suggestion of William Blake—had boxed the visionary's ears.

4

Strange and disappointing as it may seem to some, the very solid fairies in this sad unfinished story are more correctly in the line of fairy folklore than the ethereal Tinker Bell or gauzy beings of the Christmas pantomime. Students of folklore tell us that the belief in fairies comes from the co-existence of a small, inferior race of Little People with others of larger build and a more advanced civilisation. The situation has existed for a time in most countries. In Scotland the Picts were overcome by the Scots and took refuge in the hills, and the same thing happened when the Saxons drove out the British. The Picts were very small people, if we are to judge by those of their villages which have been unearthed and in which it is impossible for a normal adult to move about unless bent almost double; and though the British were probably larger they were not nearly so large as the big Saxon warriors who dispossessed them. They were small, but they were sturdy and very strong, and so are the fairies of the earliest legends, who would steal out at night from their hiding-places and thresh a whole floor of wheat with their little flails.

It is hard to say why they should be so well disposed towards the people who had driven them out. No doubt the memory of old wrongs had faded, and perhaps they were attracted by the bowls of milk left about for such useful assistants. But their activities were not entirely benevolent. They are said to have stolen children and put their own less attractive infants in their place, thus creating the legend of the Changeling. They are also reputed to have kidnapped adults, which may well be true. All this belongs to the old, old days, when the Little People still existed precariously on the verges of a supplanting civilisation. But certain solitary survivors seem to have lingered in remote parts up to a much more recent date—Aiken Drum, the goblin of the Scottish Border, whose mouth was like "a slit which a horn had ri'en", and the hob I once met in an old-fashioned book of clerical reminiscences, who as late as the nineteenth century would creep into the barn and do the work of four men in a single night.

During the centuries the legend has grown. It was not considered diplomatic or even safe to talk disparagingly of the Little People, and gradually years of polite allusion flattered them into beautiful and powerful beings.

> "How beautiful they are, the lordly ones,
> That dwell in the hills, in the hollow hills."

Certainly the hills were this people's dwelling, but our conception of a dwarf or a gnome or a goblin fits them better than the green armour of a Fairy Prince. We can see the transformation at work in Shakespeare's *Midsummer Night's Dream*, where we find both types of fairy—Oberon and Titania and their prettily named courtiers, and among them Puck, whose antics are those of the hob with a dash of the mischievous nature spirit which his name suggests and which is found in many of the place-names of the Weald.

Here in the Weald the fairies belong definitely to the old utilitarian, pre-gauze type. They had, however, this in common with the pantomime fairies—they could dance. "They was little folks not more than a foot high, and used to be uncommon fond of dancing. They jound hands and formed a circle, and danced upon it till the grass came three times as green there as it was anywhere else. That's how these here rings come upon the hills." This is according to Mas' Fowington's mother in Mark Anthony Lower's *Contribution to Literature*. Fairy rings, however, are also in the Weald called hag-rings or hag-tracks, suggesting the more sinister capers of witches; and indeed in other ways the operations of witches and these rustic fairies are very much alike. Mas' Fowington tells the shocking story of "an ol' brother of my wife's gurt gran'mother" who, surprised that the heap of threshed corn on his barn floor was generally bigger in the morning than he had left it at night, "bein' an out-and-out bold chap, dat didn't fear man nor devil, as de saying is, he made up his mind dat he'd goo over some night to see how it was managed".

After he had waited some time "laid up behind de mow", he saw

"a couple of liddle chaps about eighteen inches high or dere-away come into de barn without uppening the doores. They pull off dere jackets and begun to thresh wud two liddle frails as dey had brung wud em at de hem of a rate. He would a been froughtened if dey had been bigger, but as dey was such tedious liddle fellers, he couldn't hardly help bustin right out a laffin. Howsomever he pushed a hanful of strah into his mouth and so managed to kip quiet a few minutes a lookin at um— thump, thump; thump, thump, as riglar as a clock. At last dey got rather tired and left off to rest derselves, and one an um said in a liddle squeakin voice, as it might a bin a mouse talkin: 'I say Puck, I tweat; do you tweat?' At dat Jeems couldn't contain hisself nohow, but set up a loud haw-haw, and jumpin up from de strah hollered out, 'I'll tweat ye, ye liddle rascals; what bisness a you got in my barn?'"

Those words were his undoing. The fairies ran out, but as they passed him "he felt such a queer pain in de head as if some-body had gi'en him a lamentable hard thump wud a hammer, dat knocked him down as flat as a flounder". At last he contrived to doddle home, but looked so tedious bad that his wife at once sent for the doctor. The doctor was of course no use, and poor old James languished like any victim of witchcraft until at last he died, "Poor man! sorry enough dat he'd ever intafered wud things that didn't consarn him."

A very similar story is told by W. D. Parish in his *Dictionary of the Sussex Dialect*, with such differences as that the fairies were feeding the farmer's horses instead of threshing his wheat, that they did not enter the barn supernaturally but 'crep in at the sink hole", and that they wreaked their vengeance not on the carter who interrupted them but on his horses, that "got so thin and poor he couldn't bear to be seen along wid em". It contains, however, the identically same remark that the fairy makes in the first story: " 'Puck,' says he, 'I twet, do you twet?' And thereupon this here carter he jumps up and says 'Dannel ye,' he says, 'I'll make ye twet afore I've done wud ye!' " It is obviously the same story going about the Weald and probably the rest of England. What foundation, if any, it has in fact it would be useless to speculate.

The Weald, at least the Sussex part of it, is supposed to refer to fairies as Pharisees. This is a confusion due to the common use of a double plural. Even to-day posts and oasts and ghosts will on the local tongue become posteses, oasteses and ghosteses. By the same process fairies would become fairieses, which when pronounced with the broad Sussex "a" sounds very like Pharisees. The word is used in the plural only—a single fairy would not be a Pharisee—but that some confusion as to its origins existed also in the minds of the users is evident from the statement of Lower's Mas' Fowington that he believed in fairies not only because his mother had seen them but because they are mentioned in the Bible. We should remember that he was probably unable to read, so would never have seen the word in print, though we cannot help thinking that some of its scriptural contexts must have puzzled him.

5

Ghosts are always made an interesting part of local superstition, but the ghosts of the Weald seem on the whole to be of a retiring nature and to be known to few outside their parishes. There is, of course, the unpleasant Captain Powlett who leaps on your crupper when you are so rash as to ride through St Leonards Forest after dark, and there are the ghosts of Cowdray, though these have been "explained" in that disappointing fashion which used to spoil Victorian ghost stories, by the nocturnal prowlings of the murderer Viscount and his wife.

W. D. Parish in his *Dictionary* quotes a man who told him he had seen a ghost in Firle Park. It had passed close to him in the shape of an enormous white horse accompanied by a bluish light. One might think, as Parish did, that a white horse cannot have been so rare in those parts as to need a supernatural explanation, but as the man in question was ill for nearly a week after seeing it, there was obviously something wrong, either with him or with the horse.

I have no doubt but that the Weald contains many haunted houses the rumour of which has not reached me, but personally I know of only two and in neither of them have I seen even the smallest shadow of a ghost. I have already mentioned Branden, near Sissinghurst, which was once the home of the infamous Tarver. For many years it had the reputation of being haunted, and people whose word I accept have told me some strange tales of their experiences. Mr Ian Davison, for many years the owner, has described the haunt—a very complicated one—in his book *Where Smugglers Walk*. He himself on more than one occasion "saw" Tarver and experienced those curious alternations of heat and cold that are characteristic of such manifestations. Personally I was aware of nothing more definite than a sinister atmosphere and on one occasion the unexplained terror of a huge dog.

The other haunted house I know, Brede Place, not far from Rye, has also been made the subject of a book. Mrs Clare Sheridan, a daughter of the house, has given an account of her experiences in *My Crowded Sanctuary*, published during the war. The ghosts she knew, and she seems to have been on most intimate terms with them, are amiable and friendly spectres, quite different from those with which local rumour has peopled the house and garden. Brede Place (originally known as Ford Place) is one of the oldest houses in the district. It was built by Sir Thomas Atte Ford towards the end of the fourteenth century on the site of a still earlier building, and not long afterwards passed into the hands of the Oxenbridges, who occupied it for the next 225 years. Sir Goddard Oxenbridge is supposed to be one of the haunters. Legend has most unjustly made him a giant and devourer of infants, who met his end by being sawn in half by the children of East and West Sussex. He is said to haunt the Groaning Bridge over the streamlet just outside the park, where this execution took place. But if he haunts at all—and no one on whose word I can rely has ever seen him—it is more likely that this good and pious man is distressed by the diversion to other uses of the money he left for chantry masses for his soul.

The Oxenbridge family sold the Brede estate in 1619 to Sir Thomas Dyke, and about a hundred years later it was sold again to Sir Edward Frewen, whose family occupied it until a few years ago. Sir Edward already had his family seat at Brickwall, Northiam, and let Brede Place as a farmhouse, from which it deteriorated into a nest of labourers' dwellings. Nothing was done for it in the way of repairs and it became each year more dilapidated, until in the end it was uninhabitable. Such a house would be a godsend to the smugglers of the eighteenth century, and it was no doubt they who put about the legend of its being haunted, in order to scare the neighbours away. In 1826 bricklayers at work there found a hiding-place full of smuggled treasures which, being typical men of Sussex, they immediately closed up again and refused to talk about. Later on, however, the Frewen who then owned the house was allowed to purchase the gold cross which we have seen before in the churchwardens' account of Brede parish. It was then the property of a man called Richardson, who said it had been given him by old Crofts the bricklayer with these words: "I shall never tell you where we opened or what we saw, but I'll give you this, which I found in the place at that time."

Very much later Brede Place was let by the Frewens to the American author Stephen Crane, who in common with many of his literary and famous visitors had some rather frightening experiences which no one could explain. At the beginning of the twentieth century the Frewens came into residence and the place was civilised with bathrooms and electric light. But rumours of a haunt still persisted and continue to persist, though to visit it now is to arouse much the same feelings as those which both disappointed and reassured Catherine Morland when she visited Northanger Abbey.

More characteristic of the legendary Brede Place was my first sight of it many years ago when it stood, gaunt and empty, with black, broken windows, above the tangle of its derelict garden. I was six years old and had been taken to see it by my nurse as a "great treat". Unfortunately on the way we had met an old countryman who had obviously relished the effect on my infant mind of his stories of ghosts and bogeys. I can remember an uneasy picnic meal in a field below the house, my fears of the supernatural jostling with highly realistic memories of the fire I had been taken to see the same morning at Little Knights Farm, where several horses had been burned to death. The life of a Victorian child was not always so sheltered as some imagine.

Chapter V

TONGUE AND TEETH

I

PLACE-NAMES will always be of interest to those who love both their language and their countryside. Opening a place-name is like opening a secret drawer in which some ancient document lies hidden. This, of course, like many ancient documents, may be indecipherable; on the other hand it may tell us much of the past history of some village or farm—who built it, who lived in it afterwards, the part it played in the social economy and so on.

Take Horselunges, for instance. At the first sight the name is meaningless and grotesque, but open it and see. First we find the Hurst prefix, telling us of its wooland origins, linking it with the first hog-pastures of the Weald, with the "dens". Then we find attached to it a manorial term signifying the outskirts of an estate. Early mentions of the place in old deeds and court rolls give it simply as Hurst or Herst. It was not till the middle of the fourteenth century that the termination was added on the occasion of a strip of adjoining land becoming part of it. In an ancient manuscript in the British Museum it may be read that in the year 1318 Agnes, wife of William de Lyngyver, released the land to Philip de Herst. The place now becomes Hurstlyngevre or sometimes Herstingmere, which through the following centuries rustic tongues twist and mumble into Horselinger and Horselunger and finally Horselunges, where it sets and becomes fixed at the time that names are frozen.

It is worthy of note that surnames as we know them now do not yet exist. Both Philip and William are named after their estates and their Christian names are those in common use. But in their signatures (if they are able to write) we may already read the territorial surname, since they must distinguish themselves from many other Philips and Williams, just as Philips and Williams of lower degree must distinguish themselves by their trades. Similarly Robert de la Brok, Simon atte Grove and Laurence atte Well have taken what probably will in future become the surnames of their descendants—generations of Brookses, Groves and Wellses—from their homes beside wood and water. These in their turn owe them their present names of Brook House, Grove Hill and Well Shaw. There is as it were a commerce, an exchange between men and places—a man takes his name from a place, then gives it back for the place to remember him by. Thus Pashley Farm remembers Robert de Passelye and Shornden Wood remembers John de Sarndenne, and Mansers Shaw remembers Manasseh de Herst. Doucegrove remembers a Huguenot Robert Douce, and Eggs Hole remembers a far-off Saxon Egga. Some memories are quite short—that, for instance, of Banister's Town, a hamlet near Rye, which was built in the nineteenth century by a certain "Bowler" Banister and is sometimes called Bowler's Town. Those novelists who in despair of the libel laws give their characters the names of places are doing only what history has done down all the years.

Indeed, so much are the names of people involved in the names of places that some authorities on the subject would give all place-names a personal origin. But this theory is not easy to maintain, because so many derive quite obviously from other sources. Several, for instance, embody conditions of tenure. We have already seen that Boughton Malherbe is named after its book or charter, while Leap Cross, in the same district as Horselunges, probably owes its name to the thirteenth-century custom of *lep*, by which tenants were allowed to pasture their cattle in common on any land within the manor between Michaelmas and Martinmas. Flitteridge Wood near Fletching is supposed to commemorate an ancient dispute (Old English, *geflit*) as to its possession, while Wish Wood derives openly from an East Sussex measure of land.

It is only to be expected that many place-names in the Weald should derive from the iron industry. Everywhere, up and down the county, are the Cinder Hills, Hammer Ponds, Ordnance Fields, Forge Lanes and Furnace Woods, to say nothing of all the compounds of iron—Ironlatch, Iron River and so on. These, being no more than three or four hundred years old, are still clearly descriptive of their origins, but in older names the local tongue has mumbled away the meaning, though we may still recognise in Bucksteep a "steep place overgrown with beeches" and in Peasmarsh the "marshy land where peas were grown". Shadoxhurst was once "the wood of shady oaks", and Rushlake Green the "open place beside the rushy brook", while Playden may have been either "Plega's swine-pasture" or more pleasantly "the pasture of play", that is, "where the swine sport". Hungry Hatch and other hunger-names such as Starvenden were given poor lands in contempt. Heathfield, as we saw earlier, proclaims its barren, heathy origins in Andredsweald, while Maresfield has moved only one letter from the pool or mere that named it. But Mayfield has two interpretations as far apart as "Our Lady's field" or clearing and "the field of the stinking calomile". It should be noted that the only certain fact about place-names is that none of the authorities can agree about them and that the interpretation of almost every one is in dispute.

Generations of rustic use have so altered so many names that their origins are often hard if not impossible to trace. The tendency has been to approximate a difficult name, the meaning of which has been forgotten, to some homely object of common life. This accounts for Eggs Hole and it also accounts for Kitchenhour (former home of the Norman family of de Cecinore), Kitchenham, Glasseye Farm, Poppinghole lane, Pepper-in-Eye, Horseye and all the grotesques. More beautiful distortions are Fairlight of Farlegh and Clearhedge Wood of Clavrigg. Monday Boys has doubtless grown out of a Norman *Mont des bois*, just as Blackboys celebrates the marriage of two tongues in "Shining Wood".

The broad vowels and guttural consonants of the Weald have created a series of names that for charm and quaintness it would be hard to match elsewhere, except perhaps in Essex. We have already encountered many in our wanderings up and down the countryside, and now for good measure here are Scullsgate, Pondtail, Pookreed, Mizzards, Fairhazel, Plawhatch, Limbo, Maidenbower, Hobstevens, Goldstrow, Honeycrock ("honey" is a Weldish joke and stands for mud), Oxteddle's

Bottom, Lambstand, Withyland, Doozes, Buddlewish, Starnash (said to be named after the visit of a sea-swallow or tern), Hareplain, Harebeating, Rats Ramble, Sprattersreed, Isle of Thorns, Summer Lane, Buddle Wish, Light Row, Warninglid, Trubweek and Tweazle Wood.

2

"Lookee, you be purty, my love, lookee, you be purty. You've got dove's eyes adin yer locks; yer hair is lik a flock of goats dat appear from Mount Gilead.

"Yer teeth be lik a flock of ship just shared, dat come up from de ship-wash; every one of em bears tweens, an nare a one among em is barren."

So begins a Sussex version of the Song of Songs, prepared by Mark Antony Lower for Prince Lucien Buonaparte. From it we may gather that the speech of the Weald is much like that of other southern districts. In the west we find a difference, but the counties of Hampshire, Sussex and Kent speak very much alike. It is a slow speech, with broad vowels and slurred consonants. Even to-day Londoners will say they cannot understand it, though by this time an increasing influx of strangers has produced two distinct ways of talking, one for addressing "foreigners" and one for use among your own countrymen.

I am sometimes asked if the folk of the Weald still use the old dialect words, such as those that give such incomparable raciness and character to Parish's *Dictionary of the Sussex Dialect*. The answer is that they still do—sometimes. Many of the old words seem to have dropped out, but others remain, and not with the old people only. A man will still say he is "queered" when he is puzzled and will talk of "spanneling" the floor with his muddy boots. To "terrify" is often used as a synonym of to hurt or to destroy—"the mice have terrified the spinach", laments the gardener, and "this'ull properly terrify you", warns his wife before putting iodine on his cut hand. "Properly", by the way, is a useful adverb denoting the exceeding and superlative in all it qualifies—"I'm properly angry"; "he's properly made up wud dat new place of he's". It is, of course, pronounced "praaperly".

A farmer or other employer may still be called "Mus'",
while his wife is always "Miz'". "Maas", formerly the title of
those employed, if married (otherwise the Christian name only
was used), has now descended to children and animals, with the
exception of the fox, who is always *Mus* Reynolds. On the other
hand, certain words that used to be considered dialect have
passed into official language, such as in the phrase "the land
is in good heart" which constantly appears on auctioneers'
advertisements of farm sales. "Heart" for condition belongs
to the land only; it does not apply to human beings. "How is
your wife, Mr Sinden?"—"She's tur'ble awkward" or "She's
tur'ble ornery" is the reply if the lady is not well. If she is in good
health the language is more conventional—"Nicely, thank you."
"Tur'ble" is as useful a protean as "praaperly", and functions
as both adverb and adjective.

Some of the local words still in use are old words that occupy
an honourable place in the language but are now seldom met with
except in books and in certain instances overseas. "Fall" for
autumn is one of them, and there is something particularly lovely
as well as descriptive in the term "fall of the year". In the Weald
the withered grass is "sere", the shoemaker or cobbler is the
"snob", while "cad" is an inferior who helps you in your work.
There is also the ancient word "morris" used as a verb in much
the same way as "dance". "I looked out of de winder and dere
was Father morrising in de lane" comes from a villager's account
of an old man on the spree. Another way in which the typical
Weldishman still keeps close to an older speech is in his rejection
of the present participle. We have latterly in English grown very
slipshod about this; our phrases slide into it continually. "It's
raining" we say when the Weldishman says "it rains"—or rather,
"that rains", preferring "that" to "it" as a pronoun—"I am
waiting" instead of "I wait"; "my sister is standing there"
instead of the terser "there stands my sister". In this both Shakespeare and King James's Bible are on the Wealden side of speech.

In eastern parts of the Weald both in Kent and Sussex there are
also words of French origin, brought over by the Weavers and
the Huguenot refugees. We have already noticed some of
them—"grattans" for stubbles, "dishable" for disarray. "Valiant"
is another, denoting size and substance rather than courage,

while "boco" still does duty for a large quantity, and a jug may be a "crutch". The word "cater" can be either a verb or a noun—"they went catering around by the fields instead of kipping to the road"; "not this cater of the wood". It is possibly derived from "quartier", which was a land measurement of the Huguenots.

There is a third group of words which I find it hard to place, for they seem to be personal property, for owner's use only, and I cannot help suspecting that some of them are also his private invention. The Weald is the home of onomatopœia. "She judders", says the mechanic to describe an unhealthy noise in a car engine, but when the window rattles, most graphically it "bibbers". Thus I suspected "scrump" of being a home-made word for a small, unsightly apple until I saw it on a greengrocer's label for a cheap lot of windfalls. But I still doubt "sprod", as used to describe the junction of a branch with the trunk of a tree. It is indeed in the dictionary, but there it describes "a second-year salmon"—which is not at all the same thing. We may be thankful that in spite of the radio and so-called education a Weldishman's speech is far from standardised. Though he may not, like Humpty Dumpty, make words mean what he chooses them to mean, he is perfectly capable of inventing words of his own if those in common use fail to suit him.

I have already mentioned the double plural which is responsible for the confusion between fairieses and Pharisees. It is still heard to-day, though not so often as it used to be. But as common as ever is the double negative—"I ain't got no more to say"; "I can't find it nowheres". There is something very graphic and decided about it, and I should be sorry if it left our speech. Still surviving, too, though not so widely, is the substitution of "d" for "th"—dem and dat doing duty for them and that, as has been plain from our quotations. It is possibly due, at least in part, to dental causes, which may also be responsible for that indistinctness which strangers complain of. I do not mean that the teeth of the Weald are worse than in other rural districts, but I have never met elsewhere so many people who, having lost their own, seem content and able to do without any. No doubt in the past expense was the reason—good artificial teeth took a lot of money out of a man's wages and cheap ones generally fitted badly. But I have known the wife of a prosperous farmer firmly refuse to

Walberton Church and village near Old Heathfield

let him provide her with a set of false teeth. She could eat perfectly well without teeth, she said, and so she could. All she wanted was two to crack nuts with, and these she had managed to preserve—has preserved, indeed, until the present day when, deep in her eighties, she still uses them for cracking nuts. "The teeth I crack nuts with" are still the ones that matter most in a Weldishman's mouth, and he would not exchange them for the most gleaming set the National Health Service could provide— or even for a pair of silver nutcrackers.

3

Teeth form a natural bridge between talking and eating, and our survey of the Weald would be incomplete without a glance at the Weldishman's table. It must be owned that here we are not likely to find any famous or appetising local dishes, and visitors from more favoured parts are often surprised and inclined to feel superior. Splits and clotted cream and saffron cakes from the West, Yorkshire pudding and hot tea-cakes from the North, hot-pot from the Midlands, dumplings from East Anglia and cheese from almost everywhere make odious comparisons with the meagre offerings of the Weald.

"But you have such beautiful meadows; why have you so little cream and no cheese at all?" The answer is that our meadows may look beautiful, rich and lush, but the pasture they provide is often inferior, matted with couch grass and weeds, and our local herds are not good milkers. To-day many farmers keep Jerseys, or more economically one Jersey to give richness to the abundant but thin milk of a herd of Friesians; but in the past when gastronomic reputations were made elsewhere we had only our own shorthorns, which sometimes have not enough milk to suckle their calves. Cheese no doubt was made in those times for local consumption, but it was of poor quality and unable to compete with other kinds when improved transport made these available. The Weald is emphatically not a dairy country, and the authorities were wise when they insisted that the numberless arable acres which, because of low prices or for lack of labour, had been allowed to become pasture should be restored to their former tillage.

15   217

Fruit and hops have for the last three or four hundred years been the main agricultural products of the Kentish Weald, and a definite tradition exists of Kentish beer, fruit pies and home-made wines. Until sugar-rationing brought their manufacture to an end during the second world war, home-made wines were to be found on many a poor man's table and brought both Kent and Sussex into successful competition with other parts of the country. By no means to the taste of all, they nevertheless greatly improved the fare of the ordinary field labourer. Plums, apples, gooseberries, in fact anything in the garden, not excepting turnips and potatoes, could be turned into wine with the help of sugar and patience. In those days, too, beer was brewed on most farms, so though the eating of the Weldishman might be poor, his drinking was well provided.

The state of the farm labourer during the period immediately before the repeal of the Corn Laws was a state of abject poverty bordering on starvation. The "hungry forties" were hungry indeed, and the men who worked in the fields must often have looked back longingly on "the pork and cabbage every day" which they had once despised. A piece of stale bread and a mug of water—for who could afford sugar to make wine?—was then the average fare. Mr Edmund Austen in his *Brede, the Story of a Sussex Parish* tells of a local farmhand, William Whatman, whose entire wages went to pay for his family's weekly grist of corn at the mill:

> "He used to relate how he started off in the morning with only a crust of bread for his dinner. At noon he sat on a log beside a beautiful spring of water into which he dipped the crust to soften it, at the same time asking for God's blessing on it. In after years, when in a position to procure a more plentiful supply of food, he said: 'No meals had ever tasted so good as those by the woodland spring.' "

We must remember that what he had eaten was real bread, made from stone-ground corn naturally grown, something very different from the chemical substitute we eat to-day. But it is not from men and conditions such as those that local delicacies spring. Whatman, however, had a knowledge of better things as well as a rather grim sense of humour, for "one Saturday nigh he had a penny left over which he invested in an ounce of caraway seed. He took it home to his wife, and told her to mix it in the dough, and they would *live on biscuit* that week."

So it is not surprising that such local dishes as do exist in the Weald are definitely in the nature of "fillers".

> "My wife made a bag pudden,
> And stuffed it full of plums,
> And in it put two lumps of fat
> As big as my two thumbs."

This would have been a Weldishman's dream of heaven in the days when the corn-stacks sprouted before Repeal. Fat was his great treat, and pig fat the most easily come by, so in Kent and East Sussex we still have "lardy johns", a sweet biscuit made with lard and sugar and sometimes enriched with currants.

Recently the Hastings School of Cookery prepared a regional dinner for a London competition. Most of the courses would have appeared only on the Squire's table, but I give them here to show that a meal can be made out of the local dishes of even this gastronomically unprovided corner of England. It began with Southdown mutton broth, which of course belongs to Sussex rather than to the Weald, as does the broiled Hastings gurnet which follows. But Ashdown Forest pie, made of partridges and mushrooms, is a true Wealden dish, depending on local produce only, and it is the same with huckle-my-buff, a British version of zabaglione, made with ale instead of marsala.

A favourite dish in the Weald at the present day is rabbit—the poor man's chicken, and sometimes the rich man's too, to judge by anatomical vestiges in expensive restaurants. When baked and served with bread sauce and sausages it is not unlike roast fowl, and this accommodating animal may also serve as veal if properly thumped into steaks and fried in batter. Beans and bacon are another much favoured dish, but for many years before the war pig-keeping was on the decline, and the war made a district which started its civilisation with hogs almost forget the taste of pork. The Weldishman does not like what he calls "trouble", and a pig, despite appearances, is not an easy animal to rear, nor are turkeys, which are rarely seen in these parts, otherwise much given to poultry-keeping.

EPILOGUE

So we leave the supper-table with its homely dishes and stand for a moment on the high place outside the house, to watch the evening fall over the country that spreads between us and the far-off Downs. "The glaucous country like a hilly sea" . . . "a tumbled garden" . . . "the dim, blue goodness of the Weald"—these lines are with us as we watch the fields fade into the growing dusk. When at last even the gold of the corn has been swallowed, the fancy takes us that the ancient forest is back again, filling the chalk bowl of the Weald with darkness. Old people say that the sea comes back at nights to those river marshes that once were estuaries, and even as we watch, the mist has once again islanded Oxney and made a cape of Udimore. Mist for the sea and darkness for the forest . . . thus the old country is created again out of night.

If we could put the machine of time into reverse or draw the film of local history backwards through the projector we might see by daylight in slow motion what is now so swiftly made for us out of shadows. Standing on this same spot, still looking south, our eyes move over the hillside beyond the stream, and suddenly the roofs in Furnace Lane are gone. They were not here fifty years ago; instead of them the hop-gardens are filling the Tillingham Valley from end to end and spreading up the hillside till they reach the corn. New oast-cowls appear as oast after oast, since made over to storehouse or dwelling, comes back into use, and if only we can call a past September out of time the air will turn our hearts over with the sweetest smell on earth.

In the fields we can hear the voices of the workers. The rumble and rattle of the tractor has ceased and the ploughman is back with his quiet horses, soothing and feeding the ground instead of tearing it—the ploughman, the cowman, the teamer, the looker, the hedgers and ditchers, a dozen men or more on every farm. Never have we seen so many farmhands at work together, talking and shouting to each other across the fields, and even singing—singing though they are hungry. Hungry children sit bird-scaring for sixpence a week, while their fathers work from twilight to twilight for a shilling a day. The good old days are not so good—not those in the first years of the Good Queen's reign.

Things were better during the war, even though we lay awake at night for fear that Bony might come. The new Military Canal gleams in the moonlight like a bright sword, and the camp beside it, with the lights streaming from smart new officers' quarters, and the sound of marching feet on the new military road all give us confidence. High prices have put the Squire and the farmer in a good humour and their people share the benefits. Indeed now our life is not so bad, with its natural ways and natural food and substantial clothing and caudle cups and all the fun of the fair.

Once again the scene is changing as we slip back from the few prosperous years of agriculture into industry. The farms are still among the fields, but they are fewer, and the good houses that we see are the houses of the ironmasters, while the rows of cottages like caterpillars under their long, humping roofs are for the men who work in the bloomeries and forges. Conster is still in the Tillingham Valley, but the valley itself has changed. A line of great ponds stretches down it from Beckley Furnace, and from beyond them comes the thump of a hammer—thump, thump, thump, the air is thick with the thumping of hammers and the smoke of burning wood. At night the sky is painted red with the fire of many forges, and across the stillness comes the thump of hammers far away, as bloomeries work at Ashburnham, at Sedlescombe, at Brede, at Brightling, at Dallington and Mountfield and Burwash and Robertsbridge and Buxted, and even from across the Kentish border where furnaces at Hawkhurst and Goudhurst and Tenterden are busy arming the country for the French wars . . . for the Civil War . . . for the Spanish war . . . as history and armaments recede to the abortion of Master Huggett and his man John.

Thump, thump, thump . . . we might be in Middlesbrough or Sheffield; thump, thump, thump . . . or in Leeds or Bradford. For these are the hammers of the fulling-mills, beating the cloth which the foreigners have made and which is bringing prosperity to the villagers and townships across the border, where the weavers have settled and built their houses and their cloth-halls. There are still some furnaces at work, but they are fewer, and between them spread the miles of forest land they will finally devour. The woods are all around us now, closing in on us, closing in on the townships, on Cranbrook, shrunk to a mere village beside the River Crane, on Goudhurst, on Tenterden, while Battle is little more than Battle Abbey and the Cistercians guard the bridge at Salehurst.

The farms are now only on the outskirts of the villages, islands of tillage washed by a sea of trees. The roads between them are mere rutted tracks, and few travel by them unless of necessity. William marches along the forest ridge behind Hastings to meet Harold on his way from Andred. The Anglo-Saxon barbarians have landed on the Kentish coast and are driving the Britons westward. A bloody battle rages on Terrible Down.

But we may still occasionally find a bloomery at work, though there is no longer a thump of hammers or sigh of bellows, for the days of water-power are over and the fires are fanned by a foot-blast only. We are back in the Roman occupation and may watch a legion march along the straight paved road that Belinus has made between Londinium and Regnum. The church spires are all gone, and soon the villages will have gone too. Not one is left in all Anderida Silva. There is a great wooden city and a castle at Newenden—at Anderida . . . but now that too is gone and the wood is everywhere.

We stand among the thickets and our view of the Downs is lost beyond the crowding trees. In the darkness of the oak and the ash our hearts are comforted when the swineherd passes by in charge of his master's hogs. They rootle in the rich mast . . . then they too seem to change. There are still hogs around us, crashing about in the wood; but these are no domestic swine— they are fierce, wild tuskers, now with the deer the only burghers of this Nanemansland. From the far verges come the chants of the Druids, but soon even they are silent, and nothing remains but that which men living five hundred years later will know as Andredsweald, the dense, deep, dark, Undwelt-in-Wood.

BIBLIOGRAPHY

Sussex Archæological Collections.

Sussex Notes and Queries.

The Place-Names of Sussex, by A. Mawer and F. M. Stenson (Cambridge University Press).

Highways and Byways in Sussex, by E. V. Lucas (Macmillan).

Sussex, by Esther Meynell (Robert Hale).

Unknown Sussex, by Donald Maxwell (John Lane).

Notes on Sussex Churches, by Frederick Harrison (Cambridge, Hove).

The Sussex Bedside Anthology (The Arundel Press).

Sussex Folk and Sussex Ways, by John Coker Egerton (Methuen).

Brede, the Story of a Sussex Parish, by Edmund Austen (Adams, Rye).

Udimore Past and Present, by Leonard Hodson (Robertsbridge).

Kentish Fire, by F. C. Clark (Adams, Rye).

Chimes of Cranbrook, by Ian Davison (Cranbrook, The Eagle Printing Works).

The Works of the Late James Weller, ed. by Robert Waters (Waters, Cranbrook).

Kent, by Richard Church (Robert Hale).

History of the Weald of Kent, by Robert Furley (Igglesden, Ashford).

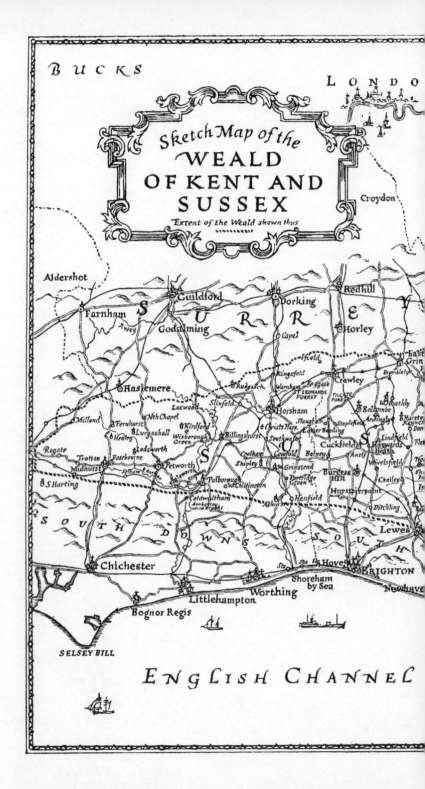

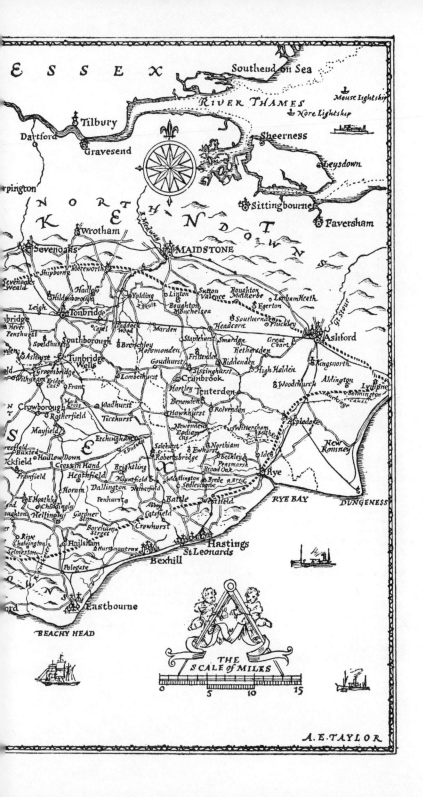

INDEX